Islamophobia and Acts of Violence

INTERPERSONAL VIOLENCE SERIES

SERIES EDITORS

Claire Renzetti, PhD
Jeffrey L. Edleson, PhD

Islamophobia and Acts of Violence

The Targeting and Victimization

of American Muslims

EDITED BY CAROLYN TURPIN-PETROSINO

OXFORD
UNIVERSITY PRESS

OXFORD
UNIVERSITY PRESS

Oxford University Press is a department of the University of Oxford. It furthers
the University's objective of excellence in research, scholarship, and education
by publishing worldwide. Oxford is a registered trade mark of Oxford University
Press in the UK and certain other countries.

Published in the United States of America by Oxford University Press
198 Madison Avenue, New York, NY 10016, United States of America.

Library of Congress Cataloging-in-Publication Data
Names: Turpin-Petrosino, Carolyn, editor.
Title: Islamophobia and acts of violence : the targeting and victimization
of American Muslims / Carolyn Turpin-Petrosino.
Description: New York, NY : Oxford University Press, [2022] |
Series: Interpersonal violence series | Includes bibliographical references and index.
Identifiers: LCCN 2021050732 (print) | LCCN 2021050733 (ebook) |
ISBN 9780190922313 (hardback) | ISBN 9780190922337 (epub) |
ISBN 9780190922344
Subjects: LCSH: Islamophobia—United States. |
Muslims—Violence against—United States. | Racism—United States.
Classification: LCC E184.M88 I64 2022 (print) | LCC E184.M88 (ebook) |
DDC 305.6/970973--dc23/eng/20211108
LC record available at https://lccn.loc.gov/2021050732
LC ebook record available at https://lccn.loc.gov/2021050733

DOI: 10.1093/oso/9780190922313.001.0001

9 8 7 6 5 4 3 2 1

Printed by Integrated Books International, United States of America

CONTENTS

Preface vii

Contributors xiii

Islamophobia, the irrational disdain for Muslims, Muslim culture, and the Islamic faith, is a metastasizing social ill that continues to function just under the radar of much of the public. Nevertheless, it is an existential problem, especially for Muslims, despite the passage of time of nearly 20 years since the September 11th tragedy. This event ushered in heightened Islamophobic attitudes, increased policing of Muslim American communities, and a rise in anti-Muslim-motivated hate crime. U.S. Muslims' victimization occurs as spontaneous acts of harassment or threats of violence as well as deliberate, planned attacks that sometimes involve the use of weapons of mass destruction.

Anti-Muslim sentiment appears to have a longer trajectory across the European Union than in the United States (Intelligence Report, 2008). This is likely due to the European Union's long-standing trend toward globalized immigration patterns and concomitant xenophobia resulting from these developments. Some explain that there are clear distinctions in the experiences of Muslims in the European Union compared to those in the United States (Oprea, 2017; Strabac & Listhaug, 2008). That discussion, however, is not the purpose of this volume since a rigorous comparative analysis of expressed Islamophobia in the European Union and the United States is beyond the scope of this writing. Here the primary focus is on the manifestation of Islamophobia and its related acts in the United States, proper. Even with centering on the U.S. experience alone, there are wide-ranging perspectives in the literature on this issue.

We narrow the lens to two central themes in this volume: first, the acculturation of anti-Muslim portrayals, which lay the foundation for
the mainstreaming of Islamophobic attitudes; and second, the virulent
product of acculturation, which is the targeting of the Muslim community
for discriminatory treatment and or violent victimization. The etiology of
Islamophobia includes aspects of Orientalism, racism, xenophobia, and
religious bias. It is a multifaceted social problem further complicated by
its inherent intersectionality. For example, the victimization of a Muslim
may be prompted by religious bigotry and the perception of "foreign-
ness/xenophobia," or it could be triggered by "religious bias, xenophobia,
and racism," as all three biases could simultaneously drive the acts of a
perpetrator.

The authors of this volume collectively bring an interdisciplinary lens
to the complex subjects of Islamophobia and anti-Muslim hate crimes.
The following frameworks were enlisted in the examinations to follow,
including feminist theory, theology, sociology, criminology, and communication science. The variability of foci invites the reader to appreciate a
sample of the vantage points in the burgeoning scholarship surrounding
Islamophobia and anti-Muslim hate crime. The first two chapters of this
work provide broad overviews of Islamophobia and how such attitudes
become normalized and part of mainstream culture in the United States.
Subsequent chapters are far more granular and give more specific treatment to manifestations of the victimization of the Muslim community.
The volume ends with a concluding chapter that raises several critical
questions regarding the state of Islamophobia and anti-Muslim hate crime
in the United States. What follows next is a summary of the central ideas
shaping the content of the eight included chapters.

Chapter 1, "The Nature and Scope of Islamophobia and Anti-Muslim
Hate Crime in Contemporary America," serves as a primer providing an
abridged introduction to this vast topic. In addition to discussing the distinction between Islamophobia and anti-Muslim-motivated hate crime,
Turpin-Petrosino also considers the history of Orientalism, the politicization of anti-Muslim bigotry, and its effect on public policy as well as
the Muslim community's perception of safety and security. Concluding

observations note the growing efficacy of the Muslim community to empower its members through increased awareness of legal protections and employable strategies while simultaneously observing caution in the pursuit of everyday activities.

Chapter 2, "The Structure, Impact, and Power of the American Islamophobia Network," provides a detailed description of how some organizations that reflect Islamophobic bias utilize economic and political influence to promote antagonistic policies toward the Muslim community. Arain and Barzegar introduce the reader to a representation of structural Islamophobia, referred to as the Islamophobic Network. Presented as an expose, the authors lay out the functionalism of a network dedicated to suppressing Muslim freedom and culture in the United States largely by inciting fear and furthering ignorance.

Randy Blazak brings into sharp focus the harmful effects of anti-Muslim victimization and the subsequent psychological trauma that ensues. In Chapter 3, "Ripples of Hate: Measuring How Hate Crimes Hurt More," Blazak's research illustrates how "waves of harm" can result, even across communities less proximal to the victims or the location of brutal hate crimes. Using the Portland, Oregon, commuter train murders in 2017, which were triggered by Islamophobic ideation, he documents the nature of the resulting trauma experienced by Muslims and non-Muslims alike, noting the unique impacts of those more directly connected to the targeted victims. Much of Blazak's discussion serves to underscore the reality and extent of community impacts regarding hate crime trauma, reiterating the recognition of its compounding and long-term harmful effects.

In their analysis of terrorist plots aimed at the Muslim community, Nussbaum and Vitek provide a careful examination of the fluid and nuanced differences between terrorist actions and hate or bias-motivated acts aimed at the Muslim community. Chapter 4, "Attacking Muslims in North America: An Empirical Analysis of Terrorist Attacks and Plots from 1970 to 2016," describes an escalation in violence, termed "high-intensity violence," perpetrated against Muslims in the United States and North America. Using the Study of Terrorism and Responses to Terrorism (START) Center's Terrorism Database, these authors describe the nature of planned assaults that have occurred and likely ongoing in this country. Moreover, this chapter provides a subtle reminder that while some anti-Muslim stereotypes include that of "terrorist," some American citizens plan similar "terrorist" activities to be perpetrated against Muslim Americans. Nussbaum and Vitek also warn that the frequency and intensity of attempted, foiled, or executed violence against the Muslim community have escalated in recent years and warrant comprehensive and impactful responses.

Engy Abdelkader turns our attention to the sociopolitical dynamics involving the contextualizing of Muslim American women in Chapter 5, "The Victimization of Muslim American Women and the Challenges of Imperial Feminism in Comparative Context." Her analysis, which utilizes a critique of imperialist feminism, suggests that views of Muslim American women serve the purpose of furthering their marginalization by employing formal and informal systems of oppression and narrative framing meant to "liberate" them. Her observations and insights are wholly informative, revelatory, and perhaps somewhat unanticipated.

Even in the distant past, suspicion toward Islam, Muslims, and people from the Middle East centered upon situating Islam itself as anti-Western, and in fact, a threat to the West. This tendency is exacerbated by Muslim terrorists' referral to the Qur'an as the source that justifies their violence. Jabbar Al-Obaidi takes on this very important and underrepresented issue in academic circles and leads readers through a thorough explication on how Islamists misuse and misinterpret Islamic scripture to rationalize and justify their schemes. Chapter 6, "An Opinion: What the Qur'an Says That Disqualifies the Perspectives of Militant Radical Muslims," also informs us on how much Muslim terrorists disrespect and exploit the very religion that they claim to hold sacred. Al-Obaidi unpacks how extremists pervert the theological tenets and principles of Islam to justify a self-serving violent agenda. Also discerned is the symbiotic relationship between the efforts of Muslim radicals to conspire and carry out terrorist acts and the equally questionable reaction by Islamophobes to justify the overall suppression of Muslim culture and civil liberties brought about by fear.

Levin summarizes for us, in Chapter 7, "Trends and Catalysts of Anti-Muslim Hate Crime and Bigoted Attitudes: A Multidecade Analysis," a comprehensive view of the rise and fall of anti-Muslim hate crime rates according to national and other statistics. In addition, he references some of the more aggressive legislative efforts to suppress representations of Islamic culture in the United States. For example, the robust proposals to prohibit Sharia law. Sharia Law which primarily serves to provide spiritual guidelines to practicing Muslims. and has no ability to replace or subvert existing laws in a given jurisdiction in the United States. Or the efforts to thwart plans to construct mosques, which have occurred in several states. Such actions are driven by the fear of a culture perceived as threatening by its very existence. But Levin's piece also examines those catalytic drivers, such as highly publicized jihadist terrorist attacks, that correlate with anti-Muslim-motivated hate crime; however it is also true that anti-Muslim hostilities at times scale up in the absence of such provocations. The point is there are several possible explanations helpful in understanding the patterns and trends in anti-Muslim-motivated crimes.

Finally, this volume wraps up with Chapter 8—"Conclusions: Veils Uncovered and Veils That Remain." Here I summarize some of the highlights I observed in the contributed chapters and use these summaries to make theoretical connections or suppositions and raise other critical questions that suggest a need for further investigation.

I am deeply appreciative of the collective works of the contributing authors. Their work further informs us on the complexities of Islamophobia and anti-Muslim hate crimes as they exist in the United States. As a result, readers of this issue will be both better informed and disturbed by this critical content.

References

Intelligence Report. (2008). Prejudice against Jews and Muslims is increasing in Europe amid heightened worries about globalization and immigration, according to a new international poll. Southern Poverty Law Center. Retrieved from www.splcenter.org/fighting-hate/intelligence-report/2008/anti-muslim-attitudes-rise-europe

Oprea, M. G. (2017). Is the U.S. better at assimilating immigrants than Europe? Retrieved from https://nationalinterest.org/feature/america-better-assimilating-immigrants-europe-21846

Strabac, Z., & Listhaug, O. (2008). Anti-Muslim prejudice in Europe: A multilevel analysis of survey data from 30 countries. *Social Science Research, 37*(1), 268–286.

Engy Abdelkader, a fellow with the German Marshall Fund and Public Religion Research Institute, teaches at Rutgers University, where her research explores race, gender, and religion at the intersection of law, politics, and society.

Jabbar A. Al-Obaidi, PhD, is a professor of media studies and communication technologies at the Department of Communication Studies at Bridgewater State University (BSU). He received his PhD in communication from the University of Michigan, Ann Arbor, a master's of art education from Hartford University, and completed his undergraduate studies at Baghdad University. He is the founder and former director of the Center for Middle East Studies (renamed as MENA Studies Program) and the former chairperson of the Department of Communication Studies at BSU. Currently, Professor Al-Obaidi serves as the Academic Director of Global Programs at BSU. In addition to his extensive teaching and administrative experiences in Iraq, Yemen, and the United States, he has taught in Iraq, Jordan, Yemen, United Arab Emirates, and China. In addition to his extensive scholarly research and publications, Al-Obaidi is the author of *Media Censorship in the Middle East* (2007) and the coeditor of *Broadcast, Internet, and the Media in the Arab World and Small Nations* (2010). He is certified by Quality Matters for online teaching. Al-Obaidi's contribution also includes producing documentary films and serving as a producer and the host of InFocus television program, BTV Access Corporation or Cable 9.

Zainab Arain serves as a research and program manager at the Horizon Forum. She provides direct services to community foundations, affiliation networks, and other philanthropic entities related to DEI policy and DAF management. Prior to joining the Horizon Forum, Zainab worked in the fields of civil rights and political economy. She has authored multiple authoritative reports on Islamophobia, hate funding in philanthropy, and American Muslim civil rights in the last few years, including *Hijacked by Hate* and *Targeted*. Zainab has appeared in ProPublica, HuffPost, The Congressional Quarterly, BBC Urdu, the New York Times, CNN, Voice of America, and Buzzfeed News, among others. She completed her undergraduate and master's degrees at the University of California Los Angeles in communications studies and Islamic studies, respectively.

Abbas Barzegar, PhD, serves as the director of the Horizon Forum, where he stewards its collaborative and stakeholder-centered research programming. He is a term member of the Council on Foreign Relations and maintains research and teaching affiliations with Indiana University's Lilly Family School of Philanthropy, Emory University's Master's in Development Program, and George Mason's Ali Vural Ak Center for Global Islamic Studies. He has years of applied research experience covering transnational Muslim civil society at the intersection of global Islamic revival and geopolitical conflict. Recent projects he has led include the European Union–funded "Bridging Transatlantic Voices" initiative at the British Council USA, the digital archive, "After Malcolm" at George Mason, and the Hijacked by Hate study on US philanthropy and anti-Muslim special interest groups. In addition to numerous articles and book chapters, he is the coauthor of *Islamism: Contested Perspectives on Political Islam* (Stanford University Press). His work has been supported by The European Union, The British Council, The US Institute of Peace (USIP), the Mellon Foundation, The National Endowment for the Humanities (NEH), and The American Council of Learned Societies (ACLS). His commentary and analysis can be found in a variety of print and broadcast media outlets, including CNN, Fox News, The Guardian, The Hill, The Huffington Post, and Aljazeera.

Randy Blazak earned his PhD at Emory University in 1995 after completing an extensive field study of racist skinheads that included undercover observations and interviews across the world. He is on the faculty of the University of Oregon Sociology Department and serves as the chair of the Coalition Against Hate Crimes. His current work with the Oregon Department of Justice centers on the implementation of the state's trauma-informed bias crime law.

Brian Levin is a professor of criminal justice and director of the Center for the Study of Hate and Extremism at California State University, San Bernardino, where he specializes in analysis of hate crime, terrorism, and legal issues. Previously, Professor Levin served as Associate Director–Legal Affairs of the Southern Poverty Law Center's Klanwatch/Militia Task Force in Montgomery, Alabama. He is the author or coauthor of books, scholarly articles, manuals, studies, and Supreme Court briefs and is the 2020 Wang Family Excellence Award recipient for Outstanding Scholarship in the California State University system.

Brian Nussbaum, PhD (University at Albany, 2009), is assistant professor at the College of Emergency Preparedness, Homeland Security and Cybersecurity (CEHC), University at Albany. Dr. Nussbaum is a former intelligence analyst, whose work has been published in *Global Crime*, *Studies in Conflict and Terrorism*, the *Journal of Cyber Policy*, and the *Journal of Financial Crime*.

Carolyn Turpin-Petrosino is Professor Emerita of criminal justice at Bridgewater State University in Massachusetts. She received her PhD from Rutgers University School of Criminal Justice. Her publication record includes journal articles, book chapters, and several books in the areas of institutional corrections, criminal justice policy, and hate crimes. She is the author of Understanding Hate Crimes: Acts, Motives, Offenders, Victims, and Justice, co-author of American Corrections—The Brief; and editor of Introduction to Criminal Justice: Structure, Process, Principles and Morality. Her current research examines how African Americans construct understanding of anti-Black-motivated hate crime and how these views might impact their sense of social place, personal safety, and attitudes toward patriotism.

Andrew Vitek currently serves as an assistant teaching professor in the Penn State University Park Department of Political Science as well as the director of the Counter-Terrorism Option of Penn State's Homeland Security MPS program. His research focuses primarily on the divergence between violent and nonviolent domestic extremist actors, the ongoing evolution of extremist violence, and pathways of radicalization.

The Nature and Scope of Islamophobia and Anti-Muslim Hate Crime in Contemporary America

CAROLYN TURPIN-PETROSINO■

ISLAMOPHOBIA AND ANTI-MUSLIM ACTS

Identifying the Problem

America has an egregious and protracted history involving violent and cruel practices used to dehumanize communities deemed to be the "Other." These documented acts began with the Indigenous People of the New World (theft of land and near genocide), the enslavement and legal constriction of African people for 350 years (theft of labor, freedom, and life), followed by the subjugation of Asian immigrants and Hispanic migrant workers (exploiting their labor and the nullification/denial of their entrepreneurship). These oppressive practices were introduced and initially sustained in the New World by White European colonizers primarily from England. Other European ethnic groups that immigrated to America and viewed as *lesser* or inferior, such as the Irish, Germans,

Carolyn Turpin-Petrosino, *The Nature and Scope of Islamophobia and Anti-Muslim Hate Crime in Contemporary America*
In: *Islamophobia and Acts of Violence*. Edited by: Carolyn Turpin-Petrosino, Oxford University Press. © Oxford University Press 2022. DOI: 10.1093/oso/9780190922313.003.0001

Italians, and those from Eastern European nations, experienced 'otherness' but navigated the American social vetting system until they were deemed White and thus accepted (Ignatiev, 1995; Roediger, 2006). Within this sociopolitical crucible, racial identity, acceptance, or rejection are determined and managed as commodities or indicators of social worth. Both then and now, the social construction of group identities is designed to benefit White majority groups in various ways that yield cumulative advantages. However, to those groups deemed "Other," the process yields corresponding disadvantages. The process of labeling and the structural systems in place to maintain these designations and their subsequent effects continue to strongly impact communities of color and those groups viewed as substantially different from the White, male, Christian, heterosexism hegemony long established in the United States (Branscombe et al., 1993; Cadinu & Rothbart, 1996; Tajfel et al., 1971). The U.S. Muslim community, currently estimated at 3.45 million (Pew Research Center, 2018), has been made to feel the consequences of their perceived differentness, their otherness, sharply. Numerous incidents communicate to them and the public that there is a price exacted for Muslim differentness. The price includes the view of being perpetually foreign, culturally backward, violence-prone, misogynistic, espousing or agreeing with terrorist ideology, and representing an ongoing threat to America and Americans. Those who require this price may be acting from anti-Muslim sentiments, an aspect of Islamophobia. A multifaceted form of bigotry, the attributes of Islamophobia are discussed later in this chapter. However, the "price" of Islamophobia is examined throughout this entire volume, and with that, the various faces of Islamophobia become more recognizable.

A widely publicized incident that suggests a normalization of Islamophobia involves former President Donald Trump's retweeting of a photoshopped image of two Democrat Party leaders dressed in Muslim attire with his added assertion that Democrats support *terrorists* (Sargent, 2020). Trump's unsubtle allusion equating traditional Muslim dress with terrorism evoked both fear and anger, particularly among the Muslim community, as reported by the Council on American Islamic Relations (CAIR) (Samuels, 2020). Besides the political gains that President Trump hoped for in this effort, a larger question is why such messaging is effective. The short answer is that Islamophobia is all too real and does not exist as an aberration. On the contrary, what it conveys is recognized, understood, and accepted by many, and its worse manifestations result in the targeting of Muslims for physical violence.

This chapter distinguishes the term "Islamophobia" from "anti-Muslim hate crime" and does not use them interchangeably, as there is a clear distinction between the terms. Islamophobia represents negative attitudes such as generalized hostility, suspicion, and general animus toward Islam, and its followers, that is, Muslims. However, Islamophobic beliefs do not necessarily lead to unlawful or criminal behavior. In contrast, anti-Muslim hate crime requires a violation of the law, usually an act of commission, motivated by bigoted notions toward Muslims or Islam. This act is evident when the perpetrator deliberately selects a target believed to represent the Muslim community. Thus, anti-Muslim hate crimes reflect Islamophobic inspired motives, but such motives do not always result in anti-Muslim hate crimes. Bakali (2016) offers a concise definition of Islamophobia: "discriminatory practices toward Muslims in Western nations" (p. 2), including individual or institutionalized actions. A widely recognized explanation of the origins of Islamophobia is Orientalism. According to scholar Edward W. Said (2001) and others, Orientalism is foundational to understanding Western nations' sociological and geopolitical perspectives toward the East. Orientalism concerns the entrenched suspicion toward and the diminution of the religions, cultures, and peoples of the Near East, Middle East, and Far East nations. The depiction of Eastern religions as barbaric and explicitly framing Islam and its adherents as prone to exoticism, extremism, violence, and as adversarial to the West dates to the time of the Ottoman Empire. Given this perspective, Islamophobia represents an element of Orientalism, a perspective that came into existence hundreds of years ago (Thomas, 2014).

In the more recent past, the term "Islamophobia" and its recognition as a significant social problem became more widely known through the United Kingdom's Runnymede Trust Commission (1997) report, *Islamophobia: A Challenge for Us All.* As described in the report (p. 10):

The word "Islamophobia" has been coined because there is a new reality which needs naming: anti-Muslim prejudice has grown so considerably and so rapidly in recent years that a new item in the vocabulary is needed so that it can be identified and acted against.

In a similar way there was a time in European history when a new Word, anti-semitism, was needed and coined to highlight the growing dangers of anti-Jewish hostility. The coining of a new word, and with it the identification of a growing danger, did not . . . avert eventual tragedy. By the same token, the mere use of the new word "Islamophobia" will not in itself prevent tragic conflict and waste. But, we believe, it can play a valuable part in the long endeavor of correcting perceptions and improving relationships.

The Commission sought to distinguish Islamophobia from a legitimate debate about Muslim communities' theological issues and cultural practices. Of the Commission's eight findings (or lines of inquiry), I emphasize three here that may help distinguish philosophical debate from everyday bias. First, whether Islam is viewed as inferior or merely different and equal to other faiths; second, whether Muslims are viewed as inferior persons or simply as followers of another faith; and finally, whether discriminatory behavior against Muslims is broadly accepted or denounced (Runnymede Trust, 1997, p. 10). A systematic investigation of these questions would uncouple valid from invalid interrogatories.

The tragic occurrence of September 11th fuels the misperception that Islam itself justifies the perpetuation of violence against the Muslim community. For example, some believe that Muslims use their faith more to achieve political aims than for worship and spiritual growth ultimately. In response to such assumptions and misjudgments toward Islam, some Islamic leaders question whether the 9/11 hijackers were, in fact, true Muslims. According to their views, faithful adherents of Islam would not drink alcohol, gamble, patronize strip clubs, or consume pornography, as several attackers reportedly did (Griffen, 2016). It is likely as offensive to mainstream Muslims to be grouped with the hijackers as it is for Christians to be grouped with the Ku Klux Klan, who claim to honor Christ by burning a cross with fire.

The Runnymede Trust published a 20th Anniversary report, which compared the state of Islamophobia in the United Kingdom with where it was 20 years before. It concludes that there has been little progress, and the government should consider the following policy approaches (Runnymede Trust, 2017, p. 7):

> The government should adopt our definition of Islamophobia as anti-Muslim racism. As with many Black and minority ethnic groups, Muslims experience disadvantage and discrimination in a wide range of institutions and environments, from schools to the labour market to prisons to violence on the street. Policies to tackle Islamophobia should be developed in line with policies to tackle racial discrimination more generally, with the focus also on the real effects on people. Islamophobia is a complex issue, but so too are all forms of prejudice and discrimination.

The Department of Justice issued a report in 2011, *Confronting Discrimination in the Post-9/11 Era: Challenges and Opportunities Ten Years Later, a Report on the Civil Rights Division's Post-9/11 Civil Rights Summit*, on the state of Islamophobia and anti-Muslim hate crime in the United States. It outlines in broad strokes the problem of Islamophobia in the United States and the federal programs and policies in place to address it. Likewise, nonprofit organizations such as the Muslim Public Affairs Council, the Constitutional Law Center for Muslims in America, the Council on American Islamic Relations (CAIR), and the American-Arab Anti-Discrimination Committee produce annual reports on the state of Islamophobia in the United States. These annual assessments describe the scope and breadth of anti-Muslim motivated behaviors reported in the United States, not unlike the Southern Poverty Law Center and Anti-Defamation League publications, which report occurrences of anti-Semitism and bias crimes in general.

Although there are nuanced differences between Islamophobia and other categories of bias, the basic mechanics are the same. Islamophobia represents the stereotyping, marginalization, and devaluing of Muslims as a group deemed unassimilable and undeserving of equal protection and equal rights. Islamophobic attitudes exist and have for some time, as mentioned earlier. The question is just how prevalent is it in American society today?

Since the blatant expression of prejudice is sometimes met with disapprobation, those who hold such views may instinctively keep them close to the vest. Still, some metrics approximate how widespread Islamophobic attitudes may be. Three are discussed here: self-reported attitudes of non-Muslims toward Muslims, the Muslim community's perception of safety in the United States, and finally, the nature and frequency of anti-Muslim hate crimes.

How the U.S. Public Views Muslims and Islam

The Pew Research Center conducted a series of surveys and interviews in 2017 of U.S. adults on their perceptions of Muslim Americans. Overall, Americans continue to express contradictory views of Muslims and Islam. However, the reports also note a trend toward more favorable opinions in comparison to prior years. Negative views, however, are still apparent and quite strident. Generally, Americans rate Muslims and Islam more negatively than any other widely recognized faith. In addition, at least half of the public believes that some U.S. Muslims are anti-American, with 25% reporting that almost all U.S. Muslims are anti-American. Those Americans who self-identify as adherents or followers of traditional faiths all report awareness of anti-Muslim discrimination. Nearly half of White evangelicals and White Protestants state that there is much discrimination against Muslims in the United States. Discrimination awareness is higher among Catholics (61%) and Black Protestants (67%). Up to three quarters of White evangelicals believe that the tenets of Islam are antithetical to democracy itself. What is unclear is whether White evangelicals (or adherents of other faiths) are active participants in demonstrative discrimination against Muslims. This type of information regarding the religious faith of those who admit to discriminating against Muslims, or any other group for that matter, is not often reported, making it difficult to determine whether religious beliefs drive some aspects of Islamophobia or anti-Muslim hate crime.

Awareness of anti-Muslim discrimination is at 73% among those who self-identify as nonreligious. Some may interpret the fact that nonreligious respondents seem more aware of anti-Muslim discrimination as unfavorable. There is a presumption that the faith community is likely more sensitive to and aware of social injustice than the nonfaith community. However, here we see that those unaffiliated with any faith community report higher awareness of discrimination against Muslims. Potential causes of this difference should be explored to understand better the role of religion or some other factors in the awareness, rejection, or tolerance of anti-Muslim discrimination, as previously mentioned.

Political ideology also impacts perceptions of Muslims. Pew reports that Republicans and those who lean toward traditional GOP beliefs view Muslims *far less positively* than those who hold other political perspectives. This question was first posed in 2002 and resulted in an 11-point difference between Republicans and Democrats. However, by 2016, the gap increased to 44 points. Another striking statistic, "70% of Republicans say Islam is more likely than other religions to encourage violence, compared with 26% of Democrats who say the same" (p. 5).

Finally, half of U.S. adults say Islam is not part of mainstream American society. These trends are concerning and suggest that institutional practices and cultures may partly drive anti-Muslim sentiments.

Overall, perceptions of Muslims have improved in some areas. An example of a more positive change is the acknowledgment by most U.S. adults that there is little to no support for extremism within the Muslim community. This shift is significant and perhaps signals a softening of the widely held presumption that Islam itself is synonymous with tendencies toward terrorism. This departure from some stereotypical notions seems to be going in the right direction. Still, increased awareness does not always result in a behavioral change. As these slight changes are occurring, unfortunately so are Islamophobic attitudes and anti-Muslim hate crimes. The following section describes how the Muslim community understands its safety and its state of security in the United States.

Muslims' Perceptions of Safety in the United States

Nearly two thirds of Muslim Americans reported being dissatisfied with the way things were going in the United States in 2017, noting that three quarters of them saw Donald Trump as unfriendly toward Muslims in America. This opinion changed significantly since 2011. When President Obama was in office, most Muslims were satisfied with where the country was heading, and they also viewed the President as friendly toward their community (Pew Research Center, 2017b). Still, Muslims in the United States perceive much discrimination against their religion and believe that their fellow Americans do not see Islam as part of mainstream U.S. society. Nearly half reported experiencing at least one incident of discrimination in the past 12 months, up from 43% in 2011. One in five reported seeing anti-Muslim graffiti in their local community in the last 12 months. The same number state that they have been called offensive names or singled out by airport security, with at least 6% describing being physically threatened or attacked. There is a gender difference in the perception of safety in the Muslim community. Muslim women report a higher level of concern than Muslim men about the security of Muslims in U.S. society. Muslim women more frequently report a good deal of discrimination against Muslims in the United States and have personally experienced such acts.

Despite the more distressing observations, Muslim Americans overall remain optimistic. They believe in the promise of America: that hard work generally brings success in this country, and they are satisfied with the way things are going in their own lives despite being uncomfortable with the direction of the country. One takeaway from the Pew studies is that even in a climate that does not fully welcome Muslims, there are still enough opportunities to pursue goals and create a fulfilling life in the United States. While Muslims adjust to living more cautiously while making progress, it is life without access to a full and unfettered freedom. The following section describes the frequency of Islamophobic-motivated hate crime in America.

The Nature and Frequency of Anti-Muslim Hate Crimes in the United States

Anti-Muslim motivated crime ranges significantly, not unlike those actions aimed at other targeted groups. However, some qualities of anti-Muslim hate crime may be distinctive.

The Derogation of Islam

On April 7, 2007, in Clarksville, Tennessee, a defaced copy of the Koran, also smeared with strips of bacon, was found on the steps of the Islamic Center of Clarksville. Authorities labeled the incident a hate crime, and officials from the F.B.I. were involved in the investigation. (Human Rights First, 2007, p. 5)

Here the perpetrator(s) were clearly aware that smearing the Koran with pork would be particularly disturbing and repugnant to practicing Muslims. Among Islamic teachings are rules forbidding the eating of pork or the use of pork products (Stacey, 2009). The intentional use of pork in this desecration is an added effort of cruelty to inflict hurt upon the Muslim community.

The Conflation of Race, Immigrant Status, and Religious Identity With Terrorism

A group of teenagers assaulted Shahid Amber, a 24-year-old Pakistani immigrant, while hurling anti-Muslim and anti-immigrant slurs at him, calling him a "terrorist," and shouting "Go back to your country." This attack occurred on October 29, 2006, in Brooklyn,

New York. The attackers reportedly spit on him, knocked him to the ground, kicked him, and punched him in the head and body with brass knuckles. Police arrested the suspects and charged them with assault as a hate crime, gang assault, and possession of a deadly weapon. (Human Rights First, 2007, p. 6)

The attackers' perception of the victim reveals the bias motives at work here. They assumed much about the victim. For example, it is not uncommon for Middle Eastern people to possess skin pigmentations that range from tan to dark brown or wear attire distinct from Western fashion. Thus, the attackers may have surmised that the multiple social identities ascribed to the victim, justified this brutal assault. While race, ethnicity, immigrant status, and religion are among suitable social identity characteristics, the assumption of terrorism is not. Therefore, to equate these characteristics with the possibility of being a terrorist is a unique feature in Islamophobic attitudes and anti-Muslim-motivated hate crime. What is distinct here is the establishment of multiplied risk factors attributed to Muslims or those perceived to be Muslim through the intersectional biases held by bigots and hate crime perpetrators.

Plans for Escalated Violence Against Muslims

Three members of a militia group known as "the Crusaders" were sentenced on January 25, 2019, to 81 years in prison for plotting to bomb Somali and Muslim communities in Garden City, Kansas. Their mission was to start a war against Muslims. (SPLC, 2019)

In the more common categories of hate crime, we see assaultive behaviors committed upon individuals, defacing property symbolic of the targeted group, or graffiti messages of hate. The planned attack against the Somali and Muslim communities in Kansas indicates a more formidable threat by anti-Muslim conspirators. Recognized as a long-standing strategy expressed in hate ideology is the desire to incite a race war. In the crime mentioned earlier, the Crusaders' intention was to play a role in igniting a war against Muslims. The plan to bomb communities reflects the desire to kill scores of individuals, which surpasses the more common occurrences of property defacement or spontaneous assault on others noted in hate crime offenses. The planning of pogrom-like acts targeting vast numbers of individuals, such as in Kansas, may be a distinctive element in the criminality of anti-Muslim hate crime should such planned attacks be effectively documented by law enforcement.

The Center for the Study of Hate and Extremism reported a trend toward increasingly violent anti-Muslim hate crime. Center Director Brian Levin reported a drop in the number of these crimes, but a higher degree of violence perpetrated against the Muslim community is discernible (Treisman, 2019). Between 2010 and 2014, the average number of anti-Muslim bias incidents totaled 147. Using that number as a yardstick, the years since then (2015–2018) show a marked increase in these events, which have not regressed thus far. Figure 1.1 shows the number of anti-Muslim acts reported by law enforcement agencies for the last 18 years. This sample of anti-Muslim-motivated crimes reveals a degree of calculated harm and lethal violence aimed at symbols of Islam or upon persons perceived to be Muslim, resulting in multiple deaths.

In addition to the derision of Islam, the compounding of risk factors that lead to allegations of terrorism and the subsequent planning of mass

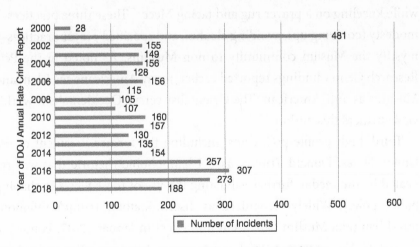

Figure 1.1 Reported Anti-Muslim/Islam Incidents in the United States
SOURCE: ucr.fbi.gov/hate_crime

killings of Muslims by right-wing extremists is the politicization of anti-Muslim sentiments that influence policing and surveillance of the Muslim community. Some Islamophobic arguments are offered to explain suspect public policies, but none of them are justified. First, ongoing extremist factions periodically claim Islamic justification for an agenda of political violence by terrorism. The National Consortium for the Study of Terrorism and Responses to Terrorism (START) published a report on the number of jihadist plots in the United States between 1993 and 2017. There were 121 such plots, and 82% were foiled or successfully intercepted (Crenshaw et al., 2017). The reality of terrorists that claim a theological identity with Islam fuels Islamophobia as the proper lens to view and understand the policing of the Muslim community.

Second, the Muslim community is demeaned by some for practicing cultural values that are distinct from mainstream cultural norms thus fueling suspicion. For example, Islam highly values modesty, particularly for Muslim women who are encouraged to adopt clothing that covers the body. They frequently wear items such as the hijab, face veils, the abaya, and the burqa. Each of these articles serves to cover a woman's body to protect and symbolize her chastity. Some Muslim men also avoid wearing form-fitting attire. The use of alcoholic beverages is also discouraged. Finally, the daily prayer life in Islam is different. Prayers occur 5 times a day while kneeling on a prayer rug and facing Mecca. These three practices—modesty (covering up), avoiding alcohol, and specified prayer practices—mystify the Muslim community to non-Muslims. As noted in the Pew Research Center findings reported earlier, many Americans see Islam and Muslims as anti-American. The Orientalist versus Occidentalism worldview furthers this notion.

Third, high-profile politicians, including the former President of the United States, Donald Trump, used Islamophobic rhetoric that was repeated by the media, further validating the use of these views in shaping public policy. Widely recognized as discriminatory, Trump's infamous travel ban (aka Muslim ban) went into effect in January 2017. Following a great deal of protest, federal courts rejected the executive order (and its various iterations) for a period, finding that the ban unfairly targeted

Muslims and that it was an abuse of executive power. The Muslim community and civil rights advocates were alarmed over the travel ban for several reasons. Candidate Trump made highly inflammatory remarks against the Muslim community that left no doubt of bias. For example, his formal pronouncement calling for "a total and complete shutdown of Muslims entering the United States" sounded an alarm. Other remarks, such as "Islam hates us" and that the United States was having problems with Muslims entering the country (Blake, 2018), further heightened suspicions. The U.S. Supreme Court upheld the most recent version of the travel ban with a 5-4 opinion in June 2018. The Court noted that the ban did not include all Islamic countries, nor did it mention Islam as a religion. It only included countries previously identified as posing a national security risk. However, given a social climate where Islamophobic attitudes existed among the public, this action by the Trump administration likely exacerbated anti-Muslim sentiments.

Additional examples of Islamophobic rhetoric in political speech include the former President's referral to newly elected Congresswoman Ilhan Omar, a Muslim, as a "terrorist sympathizer." He did so by retweeting a video clip that depicted the Congresswoman, making a statement downplaying the 9/11 attack. Following Donald Trump's highlighting this video, Congresswoman Omar received numerous death threats (ABC News, 2019). Even more toxic were the remarks of former Congressman Peter King. As chairman of the Homeland Security Committee, he announced that the committee's work would include the investigation of Muslim Americans due to the potential threat they pose for radicalization and homegrown terrorism. King also said there were "too many mosques" in the United States (Fang, 2011).

Lastly, the intersectionality of difference—an unfamiliar religion equated to terrorism, an immigrant status (real or imagined), and distinctive physical appearances (attire) accompanied by brown skin—promotes redundant justifications for bigotry. Referred to earlier as a compounding of risk factors, this trifecta of characteristics ascribed to Muslims by right-wing extremist groups, or just haters of anything Muslim, establishes Muslims as high-value targets.

The vulnerability of the Muslim community is further exacerbated by the echo chamber created by the talking points of extremist groups and the themes promoted by ultra-conservative media associations which mirror one another (Bakali, 2016). ACT for America, a nonprofit organization headquartered in Washington, DC, describes itself as a *national security* grassroots organization. ACT identifies the terrorist threat in the United States as comprised of extremist jihadist groups and fails to distinguish that imputed status from Muslims in general. This position permits the mainstreaming and legitimizing of Islamophobic viewpoints, which have detrimental public policy implications. ACT aligns itself with the Republican Party and has interfaced with Republican leaders periodically. *The Atlantic* reported that ACT's founder, Brigitte Gabriel, is linked to former National Security Advisor Michael Flynn, Secretary of State Mike Pompeo (then Director of the CIA), and Sebastian Gorka, an advisor to the former President Trump on counterterrorism (Beinart, 2017). However, according to the Anti-Defamation League and the Southern Poverty Law Center, ACT is an anti-Muslim hate group advocating conspiracy theories concerning Muslims as dangerous radicals who harbor anti-American sentiments. According to ACT, the very wearing of a hijab is a signifier of extremism (SPLC—ACT; ADL—ACT). In addition to the existing relationships between political figures and groups like ACT, major news media outlets and social media sites are also viewed as propagating this convergence, which furthers negative perceptions of Islam and Muslims (Dixon & Williams, 2014; Rahim, 2010). Terrorist Brenton Tarrant murdered 51 persons on March 15, 2019, during worship services at two mosques in Christchurch, New Zealand. He used social media, such as Facebook, to live-stream his slaughter. The video was 17 minutes long and taken down within the hour, but by that time, it was reportedly reuploaded more than 2 million times on Facebook, Twitter, Instagram, and on dark platforms such as 8chan. Even more unsettling is the amount of supportive comments applauding the attacks on these media platforms (Williams et al., 2020).

Now that we have presented an abridged overview of anti-Muslim attitudes and anti-Muslim-motivated hate crime, we focus next on examining the principal source of animus against the Muslim community. Is it driven primarily by religious bias or by racial hostility? Is it possible to unpack these intertwined hostilities?

IS ISLAMOPHOBIA PREDOMINATELY RELIGIOUS OR RACIAL BIAS?

The Runnymede Trust, mentioned previously, sought to address racial injustice and the struggle for civil rights for People of Color in Great Britain. It pioneered recognizing Islamophobia as a significant social problem and brought attention to that reality by publishing critical white papers. Its 1997 report asserts that Islamophobia encompasses religious bias *and* racism since many Muslims (or Middle Easterners in general) also have darker complexions. The report includes a list of murders in the United Kingdom from 1992 to 1993 of Black and Brown individuals (p. 46):

Ruhullah Aramesh, murdered in London, July 1992

Saddik Dadaa, murdered in Manchester, January 1992

Rohit Duggal, murdered in London, July 1992

Ashiq Hussain, murdered in Birmingham, August 1992

Ali Ibrahim, murdered in Brighton, November 1993

Stephen Lawrence, murdered in London, April 1993

Iftiqar Malik, murdered in Newcastle, June 1993

Khoaz Miah, murdered in Newcastle, August 1992

Fiaz Mirza, murdered in London, February 1993

Navid Sadiq, murdered in London, January 1992

Sher Singh Sagoo, murdered in London, October 1992

Nimal Samarasinha, murdered in London, January 1992

Mohammed Sarwar, murdered in Manchester, January 1992

Nine of the 13 victims were Muslim. These crimes raised the question of whether most brown or black complexioned people in the United Kingdom at that time were coincidentally Muslim or not. During the

Gulf War, law enforcement officials in West Yorkshire reported that attacks on brown-skinned people escalated. Attackers believed that these victims were supporters of Saddam Hussein, regardless of their attire (Runnymede Trust, 1997). In contrast, white-skinned Muslims were harassed and attacked *when wearing the hijab*. According to the report, for "racist offenders a seamless convergence of anti-Muslim, anti-foreigner, anti-immigrant and anti-Black hostilities 'merges' . . . reinforcing each other in complex ways" (Bakali, 2016; Runnymede Trust, 1997, p. 46).

Perhaps just as relevant is the racialization of cultural practices. Ethnic identity often intertwines with religious customs, a significant constituent of culture and social identity. Even though Islam is the fastest-growing religion globally and, as of 2015, comprises 1.8 billion followers who reside in many nations (Lipka, 2017), most followers remain Middle Eastern. In the United States, 41% of Muslims are Caucasian, via the U.S. Census Bureau's outdated racial categorization system. There are indications that the Bureau is moving toward creating a more meaningful racial category option for Middle Eastern persons, that is, "MENA" (Middle Eastern, North American) for self-identification (Pew Research Center, 2017b). However, this accommodation did not make the 2020 census. An additional 28% of U.S. Muslims self-identify as Asian, 20% as Black, and 8% as Hispanic. Therefore, 56% of U.S. Muslims self-identify as People of Color. Even though the Muslim world consists of many different ethnic groups and races, the myopic view of Muslims as brown-skinned backward people continues to prevail. It appears that it is the status of being Muslim that also categorizes them *racially*.

Many in the Muslim community view 9/11 as the watershed moment in which the "War on Terrorism" legitimized Muslim racial profiling by law enforcement. We saw similar reactions by Hispanics due to Arizona's 2010 Immigration Enforcement Law which gave police wide discretion to stop and question individuals 'suspected' to be in the country illegally. Many argued that merely appearing Hispanic resulted in an assumption of illegitimacy. Individuals who *appeared* to be Muslim, via skin color, attire, or language, primarily visual cues, were treated likewise following the 9/11 attacks (Rana, 2007). These characteristics draw the attention of hate crime perpetrators as well. Despite the ethnic and religious diversity among individuals from the Middle East and North Africa (i.e., Syrian, Pakistani, Lebanese, Israel, India, Morocco, Islam, Hinduism, Sikh, Jainism, Buddhism, Judaism, Christianity), bias-motivated perpetrators view them through the lens of race (Love, 2009). Moreover, immigrants are often marginalized due to xenophobic postures until or unless they are assimilated and viewed as less different.

We are also mindful of the conflation of race and religion merged with the characterizations of terrorism and terrorists. Mamdani (2004) refers to Islamophobia as a politicized theology that situates Islamic teachings as inhabiting themes of aggression, misogyny, primitiveness, and violence. Although such stereotypes are long-standing, they were invigorated with the September 11 tragedy. In the West, the conceptualizations of terrorists and terrorism are often connected to Islam. The use of the terms "jihad" and "jihadist" has become synonymous with terrorism and terrorist, respectively, despite the long-standing meaning of the terms in the Islamic world. Jihad refers to the lifelong spiritual struggle engaged in by adherents as they seek to become more reflective of God's goodness. There is also a more literal interpretation that identifies the right to defend oneself against an enemy interfering with the right to practice Islam. However, this defense never includes the perpetration of violence or any type of insurrection (al-Islam.org).

Islamophobia is a complex construct that is neither explained nor understood in an elemental way. It is anchored in a centuries-old intentional misrepresentation of the Middle Eastern world that continues today and results in skewed perceptions and public policies. Under some circumstances, Islamophobia is used as a political tool to accommodate foreign and domestic policy objectives. Opportunistic political leaders hold that Islam promotes the subjugation of women and weaponizes the threat of violence for the non-Muslim world. The reality of extremists in the Muslim world permits the generalizing of such misjudgments. Nevertheless, incautious leaders exploit the fears and ignorance of others who believe that Muslims are a perpetual threat to native-born Americans and the West. Muslim "inferiority" is also determined by the dominance of White Christian hegemony. Thus, Islamophobia is not easily unpacked as it presents to be an amalgamation of xenophobia, religious, and cultural bias, as well as racism.

MUSLIM (INTERNATIONAL) TERRORISTS VERSUS NON-MUSLIM (DOMESTIC) TERRORISTS: PERCEPTIONS OF THREAT

Few would disagree with the assertion that federal law enforcement maintains focus on disrupting any al-Qaeda or ISIS-inspired terrorism plots. After the 9/11 attack, several governmental agencies and divisions were formed for that purpose: the Department of Homeland Security, the National Security Division (NSD), and the FBI National Security Branch, field intelligence groups, Fusion centers, and the National Joint Terrorism Task Force (NJTTF), to name a few.

The emphasis on terrorism committed by actors or jihadists wrongly inspired by Islam was the primary interest of the federal law enforcement system, even while acts of terror occurred that were perpetrated by home-grown domestic terrorists, such as white supremacists. The FBI reported that far-right extremists were responsible for 3 times as many attacks on the homeland as Islamic terrorists. From 2009 to 2018, 73% of domestic extremist killings link to white nationalists or other white suprema-cist factions, according to the Anti-Defamation League (Bergengruen & Hennigan, 2019). H.R. 3162 in the USA Patriot Act expands the definition of *terrorism* beyond that of international terrorism:

> A person engages in domestic terrorism if they do an act "dangerous to human life" that is a violation of the criminal laws of a state or the United States if the act appears to be intended to: (i) intimidate or coerce a civilian population; (ii) influence the policy of a gov-ernment by intimidation or coercion; or (iii) to affect the conduct of a government by mass destruction, assassination, or kidnapping. Additionally, the acts have to occur primarily within the territorial jurisdiction of the United States and if they do not, may be regarded as international terrorism. (Sec. 802)

Federal authorities did not ignore domestic terrorism, but the acknowledg-ment of its potential lethality was made public only recently. FBI officials stated in May 2019, before the House Homeland Security Committee, that "domestic terrorists cause more arrests and deaths than international terrorists in recent years" (FBI, 2019, para. 4). There are several plausible explanations for why foreign terrorism is viewed as more threatening than domestic terrorism. First, the September 11 attack was unprecedented, the cost in lives was stunning, and even more disturbing was its level of sophistication and that such planning went undetected. Second, that foreign actors caused such devastation shook the nation's sense of security and safety. However, one may also ask whether aspects of preexisting Islamophobic attitudes exacerbated the alarm set off by this horrific act. We are aware of the impact of using a racial lens in the determination of bona fide threats. There is no greater example of this absurdity than the remarks recently made by U.S. Senator Ron Johnson. On a conservative radio talk program, Johnson stated that he would have been more frightened if the rioters who stormed the U.S. Capitol on January 6 were supporters of Black Lives Matter or Antifa supporters (Leonard, 2021). His racialized threat analysis concluded that violent white mobs who broke through mental fencing, windows, and doors, violently attacked law enforcement officers, defecated and urinated in the halls of the Capitol, built makeshift gallows on federal property, while chanting "Hang Mike Pence" and wearing tee-shirts that said, "6 Million Wasn't Enough," was *less* of a threat than Brown, Black, and White protestors demonstrating for the equal rights of Black Americans. Since right-wing extremist groups are viewed as less dangerous than Muslim jihadists, it appears that race may be a critical determinative factor causing brown complexions to represent danger far more than white ones.

Kanji and Palumbo-Liu (2019) write about the effects of settler colonialism on how violence is perceived and rationalized according to the actors involved. Settler colonialism involves replacing, subjugating, and annihilating indigenous populations by an invasive settler society. It requires an installment of the colonizer's authority via acts of violence and then forming state institutions that ensure the invasive settler of long-term power and domination. Many Western nations were established through settler colonialism, including the United States. Kanji and Palumbo-Liu analyzed the Christchurch massacre of Muslims through this lens. Their thesis is straightforward. The terrorist rationalized his killings by stating that Muslims were attempting to replace White (male) New Zealanders. This claim made by various white nationalists is known as the "Replacement theory." To some extent, this theory is an extension of settler colonialism. When "colonizers" sense growth in numbers of minoritized communities, or their increased political and economic power, it is perceived as a threat, prompting the fear of being "replaced." New Zealanders, including government officials, strongly denounced the killings and enacted significant gun policy changes, but failed to connect the tragedy with New Zealand's history of settler colonialism. To understand why Muslim acts of violence are resoundingly condemned as terrorism, but similar acts committed by Western White males tend not to be labeled as such or viewed as *less concerning*, may be evidence of settler colonialism perspectives. As a result, it is also possible to argue that this legacy encompasses a plethora of biases and reflections of white entitlement and white supremacy, including Islamophobia, that have become normalized.

IMPACT OF ISLAMOPHOBIA ON THE AMERICAN MUSLIM COMMUNITY

Living a Cautious Life in the Land of the Free

Members of groups often targeted for discrimination or hate crime learn to live life in a circumspect way and develop a sixth sense for safety. Because of the reality of Islamophobic-motivated acts, Muslims are taxed with this extra burden. What should be a worry-free act familiar to many, if not most Americans, is worshiping as one chooses. However, worshipping in mosques is laced with anxieties. What is becoming increasingly common in American mosques are the warnings and frequent reminders to take precautions when traveling to, during, and departing from worship services. The mere existence of the First Amendment's freedom of religion does not guarantee that one is safe while practicing it, particularly when the mosque itself symbolizes a threat to bad actors. CNN reported 63 incidents targeting mosques, averaging 9 per month, ranging from threats to arson from January to July 2017. What follows is a list of the states where these incidents occurred (Coleman, 2017):

Alabama	Arizona	California	Colorado	Florida	Georgia
Hawaii	Illinois	Iowa	Kentucky	Louisiana	
Maine	Maryland	Michigan	Mississippi	Montana	
New Jersey	New York	Ohio	Oregon	Pennsylvania	
Tennessee	Texas	Virginia	Washington	West Virginia	

What is most noticeable is that these threats occur across the country, increasing the Muslim community's stress level and denying them the ability to worship anxiety-free. Some Imams report decreases in worship attendance and the need to acquire security details for mosques. Whether one is part of the Muslim community or not, the misperception by an anti-Muslim bigot could bring about harmful consequences. Recently, a brown-skinned University of Minnesota student had profanities yelled at him by a passing motorist who shouted, "a [expletive] ISIS" . . . "go back to Africa" (Montemayor & Mahamud, 2017, para. 15). Ironically, the student is Christian, not Muslim.

It is not infrequent that others are misidentified as Muslims. Sikhism of Sikh Dharma is a spiritual practice that is not linked to Islam. However, because male Sikhs often wear a headdress or turban, they are mistaken as Muslim. The Sikh Coalition, a community-based civil rights organization, published findings in 2008 of their study on the treatment of Sikh students in the United States. Their study included surveys, focus groups, and student interviews in four states: Massachusetts, Indiana, Washington, and California. In addition to the verbal harassment experienced by nearly two thirds of study participants, especially those who wore turbans, several students relayed that insults hurled included "Bin Laden," "terrorist," and "go back to your country" (Sikh Coalition, 2014, para. 4). The report asserts that "Brown skin and turbans have popularly become associated with terror" (para. 5). The results of such ignorance can lead to tragedy. In

Oak Creek, Wisconsin, a Sikh temple was targeted and invaded by armed white supremacist Wade Michael Page in 2012 and resulted in the murder of six worshippers and the injury of several others, including responding law enforcement. With great generosity, the targeted community, the Sikhs in Oak Creek, extended the hand of grace to the greater surrounding community in Wisconsin, expressing forgiveness and understanding. Despite such tragic lessons, the Muslim community continues to be the recipient of abuse and harmful behaviors. The most recent example is the significant increase in online chatter of those advocating a conspiracy theory accusing the Muslim community of spreading the COVID-19 virus (Mahmood, 2020). Exploiting the frustration of some, these groups push the falsehood of Muslims ignoring CDC guidelines of social/physical distancing and holding worship services in mosques, mainly due to Ramadan, which fits the pattern of scapegoating marginalized groups to justify their victimization. In addition, economic,and additional uncertainties caused by the pandemic create the possibility of aggression waged against Muslim Americans, Asian Americans, and other historically targeted groups.

Law Enforcement Identified as Participants in Anti-Muslim Discrimination

Muslim Americans understood that the Trump administration's national security policies left their community vulnerable to intrusive surveillance practices during ordinary activities. However, newly elected President Joe Biden removed the infamous Muslim ban the day after his inauguration, hoping to end the formalized scapegoating of Muslims.

As mentioned earlier in this paper, CAIR invites public reporting of alleged civil or criminal offenses motivated by anti-Muslim bigotry. Interestingly, several of such acts reported are allegedly committed by federal agents. CAIR reports that from 2015 to 2019 a total of 10,015 anti-Muslim bias incidents were reported, and 2,783 were within federal agencies (CAIR, 2019). The Federal Bureau of Investigation (FBI) is reported as the biggest offender with 1,177 incidents. Customs and Border

Protection (CBP) had 635 incidents, and the Transportation Security Administration (TSA) had 290 incidents. The category of "Multiple Federal Agencies" is reported to have 298 incidents. It is important to note here that the Muslim community identified interactions with federal agents as demeaning, harassment, and the perpetuation of aggressive treatment, but whether these incidents rose to the level of criminality is unknown.

For some, the potential threat of anti-Muslim violence causes a distancing from Islam. Many younger Muslims are electing to deny or to leave their faith altogether to escape public suspicion. Some frame this painful dilemma as choosing between being a Muslim and being an American (Meyer, 2007, as cited in Rahim, 2010). Rethinking one's self-identity is an inevitable development due to the pressures from constant scrutiny. A recent opinion piece published in *USA Today* (2018) captures a traumatizing event suffered by Muna Hussaini, a Muslim American woman. She writes:

> I was 22 the first time I was attacked for being Muslim. After 9/11,
>> I was run off the road while driving, yelled at and humiliated on
> a plane,
>> spit on and cursed at. My crime was being a visible Muslim
> woman who
>> wore a headscarf. I was attacked in this way in public, in broad
> daylight,
>> surrounded by people, in good neighborhoods.
>> I sometimes think about the old man who verbally attacked me and
>> mostly humiliated me on that plane. I also wonder about the flight
>> attendants and all of the people who watched and did nothing. But I
>> mostly wonder about the woman who held me in the aftermath
> of that
>> threatening confrontation. I can't even remember her face, just
> the view
>> of her lap as I cried in her arms. Her kindness saved me from
> breaking.

Why did she help me and how had she become that way? And
why did
    that older man hate me when we had never met before? (para. 4–6)

Faced with the daunting crosswinds of freedom of religion, freedom of
speech, group identity, patriotism, the surveillance and policing of Muslim
communities, and the ebb and flow of everyday Islamophobia, the Muslim
community has developed constructive strategies to combat Muslim bigotry such as (1) educating fellow Muslims on their civil rights; (2) development of advocacy organizations; (3) data collection and dissemination
of reports on anti-Muslim incidents and hate crimes in the United States;
(4) establishment of lobbying organizations; (5) building coalitions with
allies; and (6) the development of political capital.

What follows is a brief description of how the aforementioned strategies
are operationalized among community-based Muslim advocacy groups
and collaborations with partner organizations.

Educating Muslims on Their Civil Rights

The Creating Law Enforcement Accountability and Responsibility
(CLEAR) project is a New York–based legal aid organization located
within the CUNY School of Law. It provides legal services to Muslim
Americans and others subjected to discriminatory policing and law enforcement tactics. Similarly, the Council on American-Islamic Relations
(CAIR) is a highly active advocacy group. It provides several educational
services to the Muslim community, such as civil rights guidelines that include protections at the workplace and educational settings (https://www.
cair.com/resources/know-your-rights).

Development of and Collaborations With Organizations to Advocate for Muslims With Allegations of Civil Rights Violations

The American Civil Liberties Union (ACLU) has taken up many issues
that impact the Muslim community. For example, some states are focusing
on preventing the installment of "Islamic or Sharia" law. Sharia law is a set

of religious laws or a code of conduct applicable to followers of Islam. The ACLU's position is that state laws desiring to criminalize Sharia violate the First Amendment rights of Muslims. The ACLU also worked to ensure religious accommodation for a female Muslim Air Force officer slated to join the Judge Advocate General Corp. Her faith requires that she wear the hijab even during basic and officer training. The Air Force gave conflicting orders, approving the first accommodation but then later denying a second. The ACLU and other organizations intervened, requesting the Air Force to reconsider their policy. This action finally resulted in approval for religious accommodation (Weaver, 2018).

DATA COLLECTION AND PERIODIC DISSEMINATION OF REPORTS ON ANTI-MUSLIM BIAS INCIDENTS AND HATE CRIMES IN THE UNITED STATES

CAIR published "The Bias Brief: Trump's Impact on Anti-Muslim Bias" in September 2019. The report describes trends in bias incidents and hate crimes from January 2014 through June 2019. (See Cair-ohio.org.) The American Islamic Congress also provides information on anti-Muslim hate speech occurrences. (See AIcongress.org/.)

ESTABLISHMENT OF LOBBYING ORGANIZATIONS

The Arab American Institute (AAI) encourages Arab Americans to recognize and participate in civic and political life opportunities. It also functions as a resource to government officials and community groups on matters of interest to the Arab American community. It performs as a lobbying organization through its consistency in meeting with Congress and various policymakers on issues of interest to their constituents. (See AAIUSA.org.)

BUILDING COALITIONS WITH ALLY GROUPS

The American-Arab Anti-Discrimination Committee (ADC) combats bias and cultural illiteracy through its ADC Research Institute, and its "Reaching the Teachers" program offers educational resources (e.g., bibliographies, articles, and lesson plans) and consultations with public school teachers and others that provide an unbiased view of Middle Eastern ethnic groups. The Muslim-Jewish Advisory Council represents an alliance between Muslims and Jews, which serves as a coalition-building model between groups often presented as oppositional. Members represent a cross-section of leadership positions in both communities and are committed to identifying and advocating for their common concerns. (See MUSLIMJEWISHADVOCACY.org/.)

DEVELOPMENT AND EXERCISE OF POLITICAL CAPITAL

CAIR provides vital information regarding voter eligibility. (See cair/register-to-vote.com.) Topics covered include registration deadlines, information on registration locations, and vote-by-mail guidelines. This educational service to the Muslim community is critical considering recent efforts by state legislatures to restrict voting, particularly in districts of color. Currently, there are over 350 bills in 47 states seeking to restrict voting measures (www.brennancenter.org).

The American-Arab Anti-Discrimination Committee (ADC) takes a different approach. Through the ADC Research Institute, more than 500 students have participated in an internship program that exposes students to an impressive experiential learning experience that centers on government, policy, and nonprofit work. The Anthony Shadid Internship Program also incorporates civil rights training, media functions, community organizing, and case handling. All are critical for developing skill sets that advance political agency. (See ADC.org.)

CONCLUSIONS

This chapter discusses the broad contours of Islamophobia. It is a social issue steeped in the historical legacies of ignorance, intolerance, racism, xenophobia, religious bias, classism, and cultural illiteracy. It is contemporized today by the added bigoted notions of terrorism and terrorists as synonymous with Islam and Muslims. As a result, the Muslim community (or those thought to be Muslim) is subjected to abuses committed by hate groups, ordinary American citizens, and sometimes by well-meaning government agencies and their respective agents. Despite the discriminatory treatment experienced by many American Muslims, they continue to define what it means to be both Muslim and American. They exercise their constitutional rights as U.S. citizens while proclaiming their cultural and religious traditions. They have educated members of their community to know their rights while developing agency regarding how to use the law, political leverage, and the court system to protect their rights. Due to the hostilities they face, Muslims have developed collaborative relationships with some law enforcement and public officials to improve Muslim quality of life. Thus, they have identified paths forward to live less encumbered as Muslim Americans. However, until such time that there is no longer a social tax exacted upon them, their ability to live freely, with all the entitlements of liberty as ascribed by the Constitution, will continue to be compromised.

REFERENCES

ABC News. (2019). Donald Trump's tweet about Ilhan Omar, a Muslim congresswoman, led to death threats, she says. ABC News. Retrieved from https://www.abc.net.au/news/2019-04-15/ilhan-omar-death-threats-donald-trump/11005094

Bakali, N. (2016). *Islamophobia: Understanding anti-Muslim racism through the lived experiences of Muslim youth*. Sense Publishers.

Barrouquere, B. (2019). 3 members of a Kansas militia once plotted to bomb a mosque, now are going to prison. Southern Poverty Law Center. Retrieved from https://www.splcenter.org/hatewatch/2019/01/25/3-members-kansas-militia-once-plotted-bomb-mosque-now-are-going-prison

Beinart, P. (2017). America's most prominent anti-Muslim activist is welcome at the White House. Retrieved from https://www.theatlantic.com/politics/archive/2017/03/americas-most-anti-muslim-activist-is-welcome-at-the-white-house/520323/

Bergengruen, V., & Hennigan, W. J. (2019). "We are being eaten from within": Why America is losing the battle against white nationalist terrorism. *Time Magazine, 194*(6). Retrieved from https://time.com/5647304/white-nationalist-terrorism-united-states/

Blake, A. (2018). The Supreme Court's ruling that Trump's travel ban isn't a "Muslim ban," annotated. Retrieved from https://www.washingtonpost.com/news/the-fix/wp/2018/06/26/the-supreme-courts-rejection-of-the-trump-muslim-ban-argument-annotated/

Branscombe, N. R., Wann, D. L., Noel, J. G., & Coleman, J. (1993). In-group or out-group extremity: Importance of the threatened social identity. *Personality and Social Psychology Bulletin, 19*, 381–388.

Brennan Center. (2021). State voting bills tracker 2021. Retrieved from https:// www. brennancenter.org/our-work/research-reports/state-voting-bills-tracker-2021

Cadinu, M. R., & Rothbart, M. (1996). Self-anchoring and differentiation processes in the minimal group setting. *Journal of Personality and Social Psychology, 70*(4), 661–677.

CAIR. (2019). The bias brief: Trump's impact on anti-Muslim bias. Research and Advocacy Department. Retrieved from http://www.Islamophobia.org/images/2019/ Bias_Brief/BB_2_-_FINAL.pdf

Coleman, N. (2017). On average, 9 mosques have been targeted every month this year. Retrieved from https://www.cnn.com/2017/03/20/us/mosques-targeted-2017-trnd/ index.html

Congress.Gov. (2001). H.R.3162. Uniting and strengthening America by providing appropriate tools required to intercept and obstruct terrorism (USA PATRIOT ACT) act of 2001. Retrieved from https://www.congress.gov/bill/107th-congress/house-bill/ 3162

Crenshaw, M., Dahl, E., & Wilson, M. (2017, December). Jihadist terrorist plots in the United States. START. Retrieved from https://www.start.umd.edu/pubs/START_ JihadistTerroristPlotsUS_Dec2017.pdf

Department of Justice. (2011). Confronting discrimination in the post-9/11 era: Challenges and opportunities ten years later. A report on the Civil Rights Division's Post-9/11 Civil Rights Summit. Retrieved from https://www.justice.gov/sites/default/files/crt/ legacy/2012/04/16/post911summit_report_2012-04.pdf

Department of Justice. (2015). Justice news. Assistant Attorney General John P. Carlin's remarks on domestic terrorism. Retrieved from https://www.justice.gov/opa/speech/ assistant-attorney-general-john-p-carlin-delivers-remarks-domestic-terrorism-event-co

Dixon, T. L., & Williams, C. L. (2014). The changing misrepresentation of race and crime on network and cable news. *Journal of Communication, 65*(1), 24–39. doi:10.1111/ JCom.12133

Fang, L. (2011). Rep. Peter King says Muslims aren't "American" when it comes to war. Retrieved from https://thinkprogress.org/rep-peter-king-says-muslims-arent-american-when-it-comes-to-war-a9923a82f85d/

Federal Bureau of Investigation. (2019). Confronting the rise of domestic terrorism in the homeland. Retrieved from https://www.fbi.gov/news/testimony/ confronting-the-rise-of-domestic-terrorism-in-the-homeland

Griffen, D. R. (2016). Was America attacked by Muslims on 9/11? *Global Research.* Retrieved from https://www.globalresearch.ca/was-america-attacked-by-muslims-on-9-11/10142

Human Rights First. (2007). Islamophobia. 2007 Hate Crime Survey. Retrieved from https://mafiadoc.com/companion-survey-on-Islamophobia-human-rights-first_ 5a0177a91723dd9c1703af90.html

Ignatiev, N. (1995). *How the Irish became white.* Routledge.

Kanji, A., & Palumbo-Liu, D. (2019). Settler colonialism lurked beneath the Christchurch massacre. *Turnout.* Retrieved from https://truthout.org/articles/ settler-colonialism-lurked-beneath-the-christchurch-massacre/

Leonard, B. (2021). Ron Johnson says he didn't feel threatened January 6. If B.L.M. or Antifa stormed Capitol, he "might have." Retrieved from https://www.politico.com/news/2021/03/13/ron-johnson-black-lives-matter-antifa-capitol-riot-475727

Lipka, M. (2017). Muslims and Islam: Key findings in the U.S. and around the world. Retrieved from https://www.pewresearch.org/fact-tank/2017/08/09/muslims-and-islam-key-findings-in-the-u-s-and-around-the-world/

Love, E. (2009). Confronting Islamophobia in the United States: Framing civil rights activism among Middle Eastern Americans. *Patterns of Prejudice, 43*(3–4), 401–425.

Mahmood, B. (2020). Rise in anti-Muslim hatze crimes as Islam wrongly blamed for coronavirus. Retrieved from https://www.newsweek.com/islam-muslims-coronavirus-lockdown-ramadan-Islamophobia-1498499

Mamdani, M. (2004). *Good Muslim, bad Muslim: America, the Cold War, and the roots of terror.* Three Leaves Press.

Montemayor, S., & Mahamud, F. (2017). Rattled by hate incidents here and abroad, Minnesota Muslims take new precautions. Retrieved from http://www.startribune.com/rattled-by-hate-incidents-here-and-abroad-minnesota-muslims-take-new-precautions/430584913/

Pew Research Center. (2017a). How the U.S. general public views Muslims and Islam. Retrieved from https://www.pewforum.org/2017/07/26/how-the-u-s-general-public-views-muslims-and-islam/

Pew Research Center. (2017b). U.S. Muslims concerned about their place in society, but continue to believe in the American Dream. Retrieved from https://www.pewforum.org/2017/07/26/findings-from-pew-research-centers-2017-survey-of-us-muslims/

Pew Research Center. (2017c). Demographic portrait of Muslim Americans. Retrieved from https://www.pewforum.org/2017/07/26/demographic-portrait-of-muslim-americans/

Pew Research Center. (2018). New estimates show U.S. Muslim population continues to grow. Retrieved from https://www.pewresearch.org/fact-tank/2018/01/03/new-estimates-show-u-s-muslim-population-continues-to-grow/

Rahim, E. (2010). The growing epidemic of "Islamophobia" in America: Social change through appreciative inquiry. *The International Journal of Diversity in Organisations, Communities and Nations, 10*(1), 239–246.

Rana, J. (2007). The story of Islamophobia. *Souls, 9*(2), 148–161. doi:10.1080/10999940701382607

Roediger, D. (2006). *Working toward whiteness: How America's immigrants became white: The strange journey from Ellis Island to the suburbs.* Basic Books.

Runnymede Trust. (1997). *Islamophobia: A challenge for us all.* Report of the Runnymede Trust Commission on British Muslims and Islamophobia. Retrieved from https://www.runnymedetrust.org/companies/17/74/Islamophobia-A-Challenge-for-Us-All.html

Runnymede Trust. (2017). *Islamophobia still a challenge for us all.* Report of the Runnymede Trust Commission on British Muslims and Islamophobia. Retrieved from https://www.runnymedetrust.org/uploads/Islamophobia%20Report%202018%20FINAL.pdf

Said, E. W. (2001). *Orientalism: Western conceptions of the Orient.* Penguin.

Samuels, B. (2020). Trump criticized for retweeting image of Pelosi, Schumer in Muslim attire. Retrieved from https://thehill.com/homenews/administration/478017

Sargent, G. (2020, January 13). Trump retweeted Pelosi in Muslim garb. The White House made it worse. Retrieved from https://www.washingtonpost.com

Sikh Coalition. (2014). *Go home terrorist.* A report on bullying against Sikh American school children. Retrieved from http://www.sikhcoalition.org/documents/pdf/go-home-terrorist.pdf

Southern Poverty Law Center. A.C.T. for America. Retrieved from https://www.splcenter.org/fighting-hate/extremist-files/group/act-america

Southern Poverty Law Center. (2019). Hatewatch. Retrieved from https://www.splcenter.org/hatewatch/2019

Stacey, A. (2009). Why pork is forbidden in Islam. https://islamreligion.com

Tajfel, H., Billig, M., Bundy, R., & Flament, C. (1971). Social categorization and intergroup behavior. *European Journal of Social Psychology*, 1, 149–178.

Thomas, M. C. (2014, November 11). Orientalism. *Encyclopedia Britannica*. https://www.britannica.com/science/Orientalism-cultural-field-of-study

Treisman, R. (2019). F.B.I. reports dip in hate crimes, but rise in violence. Retrieved from https://www.kcrw.com/news/shows/npr/npr-story/778542614

USA Today. (2018, October 1). As a mother—and a Muslim—in America, I see our flaws and failures, but also our potential. Retrieved from https://www.usatoday.com/story/opinion/voices/2018/10/01/muslim-hate-crime-adl-family-column/1472702002/

Weaver, H. L. (2018). A.C.L.U. client makes history as first Air Force J.A.G. Corps officer to wear hijab. Retrieved from https://www.aclu.org/blog/religious-liberty/free-exercise-religion/aclu-client-makes-history-first-air-force-jag-corps

Williams, M. L., Burnap, P., Javed, A., Liu, H., & Ozalp, S. (2020). Hate in the machine: Anti-black and anti-Muslim social media posts as predictors of offline racially and religiously aggravated crime. *The British Journal of Criminology*, 60(1), 93–117. https://doi.org/10.1093/bjc/azz049

2

The Structure, Impact, and Power of the American Islamophobia Network

ZAINAB ARAIN AND ABBAS BARZEGAR■

INTRODUCTION

The American Islamophobia Network is a close-knit family of individuals and organizations that share an ideology of extreme anti-Muslim animus and work with one another to negatively influence public opinion and government policy about Muslims and Islam. Once on the fringes of the public sphere, they now help shape federal policy and influence local municipalities. The Network operates across media and political spaces, using dark money to advance hateful attitudes, behaviors, and policies toward a marginalized minority in the country.

Given the Trump administration's embrace of xenophobic policies and personalities, there has been greater public attention on the sources and structures enabling hate speech and the funding of hate groups. As a result, there has also been a considerable rise in advocacy and research networks' efforts to curb the impact of hate groups. This chapter provides an overview of the Islamophobia Network's structure, impact, and funding sources to bring greater attention to its influence on mainstream American

Zainab Arain and Abbas Barzegar, *The Structure, Impact, and Power of the American Islamophobia Network* In: *Islamophobia and Acts of Violence*. Edited by: Carolyn Turpin-Petrosino, Oxford University Press. © Oxford University Press 2022.
DOI: 10.1093/oso/9780190922313.003.0002

politics and society. It begins by providing a definition and framework for understanding anti-Muslim bigotry and the actors and institutions that make up the Islamophobia Network. It then reviews how these actors use law, media, and advocacy to influence society and politics. The chapter then closes by analyzing the funding sources and mechanisms used to fuel the Network's activities. In this section, it becomes clear that anti-Muslim special interest groups regularly abuse tax-exempt charitable foundations and institutions to perpetuate their xenophobic agendas at the public's expense. It also becomes clear that given the sheer power and complex configuration of the Islamophobic Network, advocates and researchers interested in countering its influence will require a sustained, strategic, and long-term response.

DEFINING ISLAMOPHOBIA AND THE NETWORK

To allow for a clear determination of which individuals or what institution may or may not be part of the Network that perpetuates and advances Islamophobia, it is important to develop a standard of measure. For this purpose, the Research and Advocacy Department at the Council on American-Islamic Relations (CAIR) has created a four-point model to allow for transparency and consistency. If an individual or group engages in any one of the four indicators or funds, partners with, or presents individuals or groups that do so, it is part of the Islamophobia Network. This model is based on the definition of Islamophobia that incorporates both personal animus and structural/institutionalized forces of anti-Muslim discrimination. Islamophobia is a fear, hatred, or prejudice toward Islam and Muslims that results in a pattern of discrimination and oppression. Islamophobia creates a distorted understanding of Islam and Muslims by transforming the global and historical faith tradition of Islam, along with the rich history of cultural and ethnic diversity of its adherents, into a set of stereotyped characteristics most often reducible to themes of violence, civilizational subversion, and fundamental otherness. Islamophobia must also be understood as a system of both religious and racial animosity perpetrated by private citizens and cultural and political structures (Islamophobia Research and Documentation Project).[1]

The first indicator of the four-point model is that a group or individual alleges that Islam and Muslims demonstrate at least one or more of these characteristics: being inherently or uniquely violent, misogynistic, inferior, intolerant, primitive, static, authoritarian, homophobic, manipulative, self-righteous, devious, or that Islam is the antithesis of civilization. Moreover, these characteristics are presented as immutable aspects of being Muslim and an expression of Islamic religiosity. For example, in the worldview of the vociferous anti-Islam activist Ayaan Hirsi Ali, Islam is the source of misogynistic practices around the world, from sexual violence to forced marriages. In a display of pristine imperial and Islamophobic feminism, she demanded that when men of Muslim background are suspected of rape in the West, "the culture and religion of the rapist . . . must be addressed if we want to end this primitive behavior" (Ali, 2018). This rhetoric is echoed by Brigitte Gabriel, founder and president of ACT for America, the largest anti-Muslim grassroots organization in the country. In an interview with Charisma News, Gabriel states, "When you look at the Islamic world, or even the Islamists that are now coming to our Western nation, we are seeing a rise in child marriages." She continues, "We are seeing a rise in child rape. We are seeing a rise in honor killings. We are seeing a rise in female genital mutilation" (Bergland, 2019). The American Freedom Defense Initiative (AFDI), led by notorious Islamophobe Pamela Geller, has taken out ads in New York, Washington, DC, and San Francisco that demonize Muslims. One series

---

1. This definition was developed by drawing on two existing definitions: one by UC Berkeley's Islamophobia Research and Documentation Project and the second by Professor Khaled Beydoun in his paper, "Islamophobia: Toward a Legal Definition and Framework." UC Berkeley's definition reads: "Islamophobia is a contrived fear or prejudice fomented by the existing Eurocentric and Orientalist global power structure. It is directed at a perceived or real Muslim threat through the maintenance and extension of existing disparities in economic, political, social and cultural relations, while rationalizing the necessity to deploy violence as a tool to achieve 'civilizational rehab' of the target communities (Muslim or otherwise). Islamophobia reintroduces and reaffirms a global racial structure through which resource distribution disparities are maintained and extended."

of ads equated Muslims with being "savage." They read, "in any war between the civilized man and the savage, support the civilized man. Support
Israel. Defeat Jihad." In another instance, Geller wrote that Ramadan was
the "month of conquest and jihad." On her website she stated, "Muslim
religious leaders have long exhorted devout (active) Muslims to use the
holy month of Ramadan as a sacred opportunity to attack non-Muslim
infidels in the United States and Europe" (Geller, 2019). The link between
Islam and violence is repeated ad nauseum by David Horowitz, founder
of the David Horowitz Freedom Center (DHFC). In a speech to Brooklyn
College in 2011, Horowitz stated: "when you have a religion [Islam] which
preaches war and violence and hate, rationality is never gonna take over"
(Horowitz, 2011). These examples of hateful rhetoric demonstrate how
tropes of the inability of Muslims to assimilate dominate their representation within the Islamophobia Network.

A second indicator that qualifies someone to be counted as part of the
Islamophobia Network is the allegation that Islam is an existential threat
to the United States and the "West" and that Muslims, or their representative institutions, are part of a plot to overthrow the "West" or America.
Referred to as "civilizational Jihad," this anti-Muslim trope often posits
that Islam and the West are on a civilizational collision course and that
Muslims in North American and European countries are merely a fifth
column in protracted existential war.

This belief is clearly visible in the work of DHFC, which, in 2007,
launched its "Islamofascism Awareness Week" on at least 100 college
campuses across the country. As billed, the events were to alert Americans,
particularly students, about the alleged threat posed by Islam. The same
year, Gabriel stated that a "practicing Muslim who believes the word of
the Quran to be the word of Allah . . . who goes to mosque and prays
every Friday, who prays five times a day—this practicing Muslim, who
believes in the teachings of the Koran, cannot be a loyal citizen of the
United States" (Ali, 2017). She has also claimed that radical Muslims have
infiltrated America at "the C.I.A., the F.B.I., at the Pentagon, at the State
Department" (Goodstein, 2011). In another instance, Gabriel called the
"peaceful majority" of Muslims "irrelevant" and stated the baseless claim

that 15%–25% of Muslims are "dedicated to the destruction of Western civilization" (LaCasse, 2015). Another group in the Islamophobia Network, the American Center for Law and Justice, founded by Trump's attorney Jay Sekulow, published a report entitled, "Shari'a Law: Radical Islam's Threat to the U.S. Constitution." It states that "devout Muslims cannot truthfully swear the oath to become citizens of the United States of America." Geller and Robert Spencer also cofounded the organization Stop Islamization of America on the very premise that Islam is an existential threat. The group seeks to provoke fear in the public space through constant vilification of Islam as the antithesis of "American values." The notion that Muslims intend to undermine "Western civilization" or are actively plotting to overthrow the U.S. government through subversion and subterfuge is particularly dangerous. Such rhetoric often motivates individuals and groups to take up arms to defend what is seen as an attack on their culture.

The third measure of a group or individual's inclusion in the Islamophobia Network is that they support unequal treatment under the law for Islam or Muslims. Hirsi Ali, for example, has suggested that the U.S. Constitution be amended to allow for discrimination against Muslims (Van-Bakel, 2007). Guy Rodgers, the executive director of ACT for America, has said that Muslims should be treated differently because their legal system is inherently flawed (Ricarrdi, 2010). The American Family Association's Bryan Fischer argues that the First Amendment's religious freedom protections apply only to Christians. He writes, "Islam has no fundamental First Amendment claims, for the simple reason that it was not written to protect the religion of Islam. Islam is entitled only to the religious liberty we extend to it out of courtesy. . . . From a constitutional point of view, Muslims have no First Amendment right to build mosques in America" (Fischer, 2011). The most dangerous aspect of this rhetoric is that it undermines the U.S. Constitution and thus threatens to erode the universal rights guaranteed to all U.S. citizens.

The final indicator that a group or individual is part of the Islamophobia Network is that they allege that violent groups such as al-Qaeda or ISIS, which perversely claim a religious cover, in fact, possess the correct understanding of Islam as opposed to the mainstream Islamic theological and legal traditions practiced by Muslims around the world. As an example, in her book *They Must Be Stopped*, Gabriel writes, "We must realize that the portent behind the terrorist attacks is the purest form of what the Prophet Mohammed created. It is not radical Islam. It's what Islam is at its core" (Gabriel, 2008). This rhetoric is designed to instill fear and misunderstanding in audiences unfamiliar with world affairs and contemporary geopolitical history.

The examples here are not meant to be exhaustive but rather illustrative of how such discourse has been and continues to be instrumental in the social construction of Islam in America as irreconcilably evil.

ANTI-MUSLIM BIGOTRY IN ACTION

That Islamophobia reached a normative, mainstream level in American society can be best conveyed through the remarks and actions of then-president Donald Trump, both before and during his first administration. While a candidate, he said simply and unequivocally (even if nonsensically): "Islam hates us" (Schleifer, 2016). He declared his support of developing immigration policies that prevented the entry of "Islamic extremists to our country who suppress women, gays and anyone who doesn't share their views" (Matthews, 2016). Later, in his presidential nomination acceptance speech about "brutal Islamic terrorism," he said, "I will do everything in my power to protect our LGBTQ citizens from the violence and oppression of a hateful foreign ideology" (Scott, 2018). The Islamophobia Network has become so mainstream as to integrate into the very government itself explicitly. As CAIR's 2019 Islamophobia report, *Hijacked by Hate: American Philanthropy and the Islamophobia Network*, documents, more than a dozen high-ranking individuals in the Trump administration have held close ties to multiple nodes in the Network (Arain & Barzegar, 2019).

However, before diving into the reach and impact of the Islamophobia Network, it is essential to consider where and how this Network arose. Although Islamophobia in America itself has a long history, arriving on the shores with the early European settlers, the Islamophobia Network became more formalized following the tragic events of September 11, 2001 (Marr, 2006). It has since grown more sophisticated and expansive, entrenching itself across multiple sectors in the American public sphere. Nodes in the Network include everything from crude blogs like Bare Naked Islam, whose tagline reads "It isn't Islamophobia when they really A.R.E. trying to kill you," to well-organized policy think tanks like the Gatestone Institute, which makes absurd claims like "Muslim mass-rape gangs" are transforming the United Kingdom into "an Islamist Colony" (Kern, 2018). The Network's ability to both disseminate hateful ideology and affect policy has contributed to the mainstreaming of Islamophobia in the last two decades.

Public scholar and UCLA law professor Khaled Aboul El Fadl argues that Islamophobia has flourished in the mainstream at a time when the United States has prepared to invest an enormous amount of resources into military activity against Muslim-majority countries. He cites the immense death tolls in Afghanistan and Iraq, among other places where the United States has sent military contractors or special forces, and argues that this slaughter would be impossible if not for the systemic dehumanization and demonization of Muslims advanced by the Islamophobia machine in the public sphere (Usuli Institute, 2018).

The impact of the Islamophobia Network's rise can be grouped around four themes: the targeting of local communities, abuse of the legal system, dissemination of false information, and clouding and confusing the mainstream and social media. The following pages will examine each of these, in turn, to fully draw out the effects of this organized industry of hate.

One way anti-Muslim hate groups in the country have fomented Islamophobia is by targeting local communities. This takes many forms, including anti-mosque rallies, anti-Islam and anti-Muslim demonstrations, and organized harassment efforts to prevent mosques and Islamic centers from getting zoning approval.

Many of these actions are organized by ACT for America, the self-proclaimed National Rifle Association of national security and the largest grassroots anti-Muslim group in the country. In 2017, for example, it organized nationwide marches against "sharia" in more than 20 cities. In the Richardson, Texas, rally, heavily armed men in army fatigues stood outside the Islamic Association of North Texas as terrified children fled into the mosque for their regularly scheduled weekend school (Ballor, 2017). One man yelled through a megaphone, "If Muslims have their way . . . there will be no justice for America's goats. Why do Muslims rape their goats so much?" He then continued, "It's because they're perverted, demonic, sex-crazed . . . sick perverts" (Tomaso, 2017).

Anti-Islam activist Jon Ritzheimer organized a similar demonstration in front of a Phoenix mosque in 2015. In his Facebook post announcing the protest, he wrote, "People are also encouraged to utilize their Second Amendment right at this event just in case our First Amendment comes under the much-anticipated attack." Attendees immediately picked up on the message, and of the approximately 250 protesters that day, many came heavily armed. They stood outside the mosque, intimidating and threatening local Muslim community members.

In another anti-Muslim demonstration organized by several anti-Muslim groups, including ACT for America, protestors rallied outside a fundraiser for women's housing and disaster relief organized by ICNA Relief, a nationally accredited charity that provides social services across the United States to the underprivileged. Protesters spewed local community attendees coming to the fundraiser in Yorba Linda, California, with hateful and bigoted statements, creating an unsafe environment of fear. In a video recording of the incident, one can see a small girl in a pink hijab walking toward the fundraiser, as a man's voice screams, "Muhammad was a child molester!" One can also see a woman shout at the cameraman, "You're a terrorist! . . . Do you beat your wife, too? Are you a molester? . . . You beat your women, your wife, and your children. Why don't you go beat up your wife like you do every night? Why not go have sex with a 9-year-old, marry her?"

In addition to these types of hateful demonstrations designed to intimidate and threaten the local Muslim communities, Islamophobia Network groups have also worked to shut down mosques, deprive American

Muslims of their First Amendment rights, and impede their practice of faith in their communities.

One of the most high-profile cases occurred in Murfreesboro, Tennessee. After county officials approved plans for the mosque in 2010, mosque opponents fought hard and protested the construction, eventually filing a lawsuit against the county to prevent construction. In the meantime, an arsonist set fire to construction equipment on the building site. Much of this opposition was led by Frank Gaffney's Center for Security Policy. Gaffney testified against the construction of the mosque, offering statements that describe mosques as furthering Sharia Laws which set the stage for acts of sedition (Grantham, 2010). He then falsely testified that allies of the Muslim Brotherhood finance 80% of mosques in America. The claim, put forth to drum up fear and mistrust, has been thoroughly debunked by academic experts (Kurzman et al., 2010).

In the 5 years from 2014 to 2018, CAIR documented 61 similar zoning cases targeting Islamic centers and institutions. The cases are everywhere from New Jersey to California and often take years in legal proceedings to address. Across the country, the Network targets local American Muslim communities and their practice of faith.

THE ANTI-SHARIA LEGISLATION MOVEMENT

In addition to targeting local communities, anti-Muslim hate groups advance Islamophobia by abusing the American legal system to publicly and politically malign American Muslims and American Muslim institutions. The Network's anti-Muslim legislation movement, which spans across the country, has been chiefly centered on promoting anti-Sharia laws in state legislatures. Sharia can be understood as a set of guiding religious principles on ethical living. The language of the introduced anti-Sharia or anti-foreign bills usually includes a clause that prohibits the use of "foreign law" in courts where it would result in a conflict with federal or state constitutional rights. The bill is legally pointless because the U.S. Constitution already denies authority to any foreign law.

However, it does serve a purpose. The purpose is best summed up by David Yerushalmi, a leading force behind the anti-Sharia movement, the architect of the model anti-Muslim legislation, "American Laws for American Courts" (ALAC), and the cofounder and senior counsel of the American Freedom Law Center. In an interview with the *New York Times*, Yerushalmi openly admitted the perverse intent behind the anti-Muslim legislation movement. "If this thing passed in every state without any friction, it would have not served its purpose," he said. "The purpose was heuristic—to get people asking this question, 'What is Shariah?'" (Elliot & Yerushalmi, 2011). In other words, the purpose of "foreign law" legislation is to function as a tool to foster fear of the unknown and vilify and create animosity toward an entire religious community. In addition, anti-Muslim legislation steals American Muslims' constitutional rights and stigmatizes community members who chose to use private, faith-based arbitrators for family disputes. This practice is comparable to that of American Jews and Catholics who opt to settle certain legal disputes with arbitrators who rely on Jewish law, also known as Halakha, or Catholic canon law.

Between 2010 and 2018, elected state representatives have introduced at least 218 anti-Muslim "foreign law" bills in 43 state legislatures. As of 2018, 14 of these bills were law in 12 states, covering nearly a quarter of the nation. Three hate groups who are a part of the Islamophobia Network lead the anti-Muslim legislation movement. One is the American Public Policy Alliance (APPA), an advocacy organization that first sponsored Yerushalmi's discriminatory "American Laws for American Courts" model legislation. APPA's fundamental mission is to advance legislation that demonizes Muslims.

ACT for America and Center for Security Policy (CSP) also influence and support state legislators to pass anti-Muslim legislation. In 2017, ACT chapter leader Caroline Solomon from Montana testified during the Senate hearing in support of anti-Muslim "foreign law" Senate Bill 97. In Iowa, Rep. Eric Redman worked with CSP's Chris W. Holton to introduce a series of anti-Muslim "foreign law" bills every year from 2016 to 2018.

Both anti-Muslim "foreign law" bills adopted into law in 2017—one in Alabama and one in Texas—were assisted in the process by individuals from CSP and ACT. CSP's Col. Paul Deckert (Ret.) helped Alabama State Rep. Brandt Smith (R-District 5) present and introduce HB 1041, which included in its title "To Declare American Laws for American Courts." Texas State Rep. Dan Flynn's (R-District 2) introduced anti-Muslim legislation in 2016 a second time, his first attempt having failed the year before. The language of the two acts matched 100%. After it became law, Flynn lauded ACT for their support, stating in a 2018 interview, "[the bill] was my number one priority because it had been offered before and gone down in flames . . . then the national association of ACT came back and they got 750,000 members and they selected our bill as their number one bill for promoting . . . and they were kind to me."

The anti-Muslim legislation movement also includes a more recent attempt to promote a statute known as Andy's Law. This law creates a civil cause for action in incidents of terrorism and allows private individuals to sue those who may be directly or indirectly involved in the act. The mechanism that allows for this type of civil liability comes from the material support statute, which is already a problematic threshold, given its definitional and prosecutorial ambiguity in the criminal code itself. In effect, this legislation can drag American Muslim individuals, institutions, and businesses into lawsuits and exert a chilling effect on American Muslim civic, political, and commercial life.

Redundant and unnecessary, Andy's Law has already become law in seven states. The law's redundancy is rooted in its anti-Muslim agenda: already under the federal Antiterrorism Act of 1992, individuals can bring civil suits "against third-parties for injuries purportedly resulting from violence committed by terrorist groups." These laws serve no purpose except to reinforce the notion that Islam and Muslims, in general, are connected to acts of international terror.

Like "foreign law" legislation, the original template of Andy's Law itself has been drafted by the anti-Muslim hate group American Public Policy Alliance. The legislation is also promoted by ACT, which actively displays Andy's Law on its state legislative webpage as a bill it is advocating. Additionally, C.S.P. Threat Information Office Director Kyle Shideler authored an article promoting Andy's Law in December 2014.

MISEDUCATION IN PUBLIC SCHOOLS

A third way the Islamophobia Network advances anti-Muslim animus is by spreading false information in the public sphere. One of the critical institutional spaces for this is American public schools. The Network has pushed school districts and textbook publishers to remove information that portrays Islam and Muslim culture in a neutral or positive light.

The process by which states decide on a list of approved textbooks for use in their public schools influences how publishers write educational material. Nineteen states are currently listed as "textbook adoption states," meaning that the state's Board/Department of Education selects a list of textbooks based on state-specific criteria from which individual school districts can choose. If these schools choose from the list of approved textbooks, the state pays for the books (Levinson, 2018). This process has its roots as far back as the Reconstruction period when most publishing houses were headquartered in the North. The ex-Confederate states distrusted Northern publishers and wanted to ensure that their children did not learn a history that vilified the South. Therefore, Southern states established statewide textbook adoption systems to ensure that "anti-Confederate books stayed out of their schools" (Thomas B. Fordham Institute, 2004). The majority of statewide textbook adoption states are still in the South and West.

California, Florida, and Texas, which comprise over one third of all public high school students in the country, are all textbook adoption states. As a result, publishers vie for the select spots on these lists of approved textbooks in the most populated states. Given that the biggest market for textbook sales occurs in these states, the textbooks made available to the entire nation, and thus the knowledge considered legitimate, are determined by what sells in Texas, California, and Florida (Levinson, 2018).

In this light, it is no surprise that the Network has focused its efforts in Texas. Truth in Texas Textbooks, led by former Lt. Col. Roy White, formerly chapter coordinator for ACT's San Antonio chapter, has inserted materials into Texas textbooks that portray Islam negatively or in a misrepresentative light. The group continuously reviews textbooks and submits dozens of revisions to publishers, including Pearson, McGraw Hill, and Worldview. Truth in Texas Textbooks's website publishes these revisions and the publishers' responses. Though the publishers do not always adhere to the suggestions made by the Islamophobia Network, even a few concessions lead to miseducation, misrepresentation, and ultimately dehumanization on a mass scale. In one of its reviews, Truth in Texas Textbooks rebuked Pearson for a statement that read, "For some, terrorism is connected to the concept of *jihad*, an Arabic word meaning 'struggle.' The word is most frequently used to describe an inner struggle in God's service. However, some extremist groups, such as Islamic Jihad, have interpreted the word to mean a violent holy war to defend or spread Islam" (Alfonsi, 2015). Truth in Texas Textbooks argued that "the primary meaning of *jihad* is mandatory, aggressive warfare to convert or subjugate infidels" (Alfonsi, 2015). Pearson capitulated and agreed to revise the text to: "Some Islamists support terrorism. Iran and Saudi Arabia have both provided financial support for terrorist organizations. For some, terrorism is connected to the concept of jihad. The word *jihad* in Arabic means 'struggle.' For some Muslims, it means a struggle against one's evil inclinations. For other Muslims, it refers to a struggle or violent holy war to defend or spread Islam. Muslim extremist groups in the region see European and American influence as a threat. Therefore, they support the use of violence against Westerners or Muslims who do not share the same interpretation of Islam" (Alfonsi, 2015). This example of a textbook revision demonstrates how a complex historical, legal, and theological concept in Islamic tradition is reduced to and dominated by a discussion about extremism, violence, and politics.

This type of revisionism imparts harmful, inaccurate, and misleading information about Islam to an entire generation of American children. In doing so, it cultivates the idea that Muslims are exceptionally violent and at odds with "the West." This generates an apprehension or fear of the looming "threat" in the readers' minds, thereby perpetuating anti-Muslim demonization and dehumanization at a generational scale.

In a "tag-team" effort, ACT has also produced a report titled "Education or Indoctrination: The Treatment of Islam in 6th Through 12th Grade

American Textbooks." The report reviews dozens of textbooks to point out what it deems are "inaccurate" statements. For example, it points out a statement in McDougal Littell's *World History—Patterns of Interaction* (2007), which reads, "The word *jihad* means 'striving' and can refer to the inner struggle against evil. However, the word is also used in the Qur'an to mean an armed struggle against unbelievers." The report castigates this sentence, arguing that "'armed struggle against unbelievers' specifically including aggressive warfare for the purpose of making Islam supreme over the entire world, was, and is, the predominant meaning of jihad" (Gabriel, 2011).

In instances where curriculum and textbooks have not been revised and molded to fit the Islamophobia Network's demands, the Network's legal nodes, led by the Thomas More Law Center, have sued school district for teaching about Islam. For example, in discussing his lawsuit against a New Jersey school district, Center president Richard Thompson said, "Our God is a loving God, Allah is a cruel God and they submit—Islam means submit, not love. . . . The school system witlessly turned their classrooms into Islamic indoctrination centers" (Careym, 2018).

LAW ENFORCEMENT AND "COUNTERTERRORISM"

In addition to targeting classrooms across the country, the Islamophobia Network also spreads false information that perpetuates anti-Muslim animus at an institutional level through its law enforcement training. Several groups, including the Strategic Engagement Group led by Stephen Coughlin and John Guandolo, the Counter Terrorism Operations Center led by Sam Kharoba, and the Forum for Middle East Understanding led by Walid Shoebat, conduct training sessions on Islam and Muslims that contain stereotypical contents and therefore promote dangerous speech.

Investigators attending a training session reported that Sam Kharoba told the audience, "When I look at the life of Muhammad, I get a very nasty image . . . I am talking about a pedophile, a serial killer, a rapist.

And that is just to start off with. Anyone who says that Islam is a religion of peace is either ignorant or flat out lying" (Stalcup & Craze, 2011). The Strategic Engagement Group speaks of Islamic centers as "potential military compounds" (Amons, 2012). The consequences of these anti-Muslim law enforcement trainings are far-reaching. For one, they undermine public safety and further institutionalize religious and racial discrimination as police officers pursue leads based on profiling. For another, they perpetuate a public discourse that paints Islam as an existential threat to America and demonizes, and thus dehumanizes, Muslims.

In 2019, the U.S. Army War College in Pennsylvania invited Raymond Ibrahim, former associate director of the Middle East Forum and then-Writing Fellow at M.E.F., to deliver a lecture in its prestigious 50th Annual Lecture Series (Hooper, 2019; Ibrahim, 2019). USAWC, one of the nation's oldest military institutions, provides instruction to military officers and civilians to prepare them for senior leadership assignments and responsibilities (U.S. Army, 2019). The title of Ibrahim's talk was the same as his most recent book, *Sword and Scimitar: Fourteen Centuries of War between Islam and the West*. In an interview with the David Horowitz Center's Frontpage Magazine, Ibrahim said, "[the book] sets the much-distorted historical record between the two civilizations straight, and, in so doing, demonstrates once and for all that Muslim hostility for and terrorization of the West is not an aberration but a continuation of Islamic history" (Ibrahim, 2018).

By inviting an anti-Muslim bigot like Ibrahim, the prestigious USAWC conferred legitimacy on an individual who advances prejudicial, inaccurate, inflammatory, and misleading information about Islam and Muslims through his books, writings, lectures, and media appearances (CAIR, 2019).

In response, the Philadelphia chapter of CAIR created a coalition. It worked with allied partners, including MPower Change, an online and offline organizing platform to build grassroots Muslim power; About Face, a network of post-9/11 service members and veterans organizing to end a foreign policy of permanent war; and Community Responders Network. This grassroots coalition works to prevent, confront, and respond to racism and bias incidents, to launch an online campaign highlighting Ibrahim's Islamophobic views and their negative impact.

The campaign encouraged concerned citizens of all faiths to sign a petition urging Commandant Major General John S. Kem and Provost Dr. James G. Breckenridge of USAWC to drop Ibrahim from the lecture series and denounce Islamophobia. The campaign drew more than 1,800 signatures and received widespread support from its interfaith allies. Additionally, CAIR-Philadelphia sent a letter to the College addressed to Gen. Kem and Breckenridge listing their concerns. They argued that Ibrahim's troubling views would skew American service members' perceptions of Islam and Muslims and fuel anti-Muslim hatred at home and abroad.

A few weeks later, the U.S. Army War College decided to "postpone" Ibrahim's lecture, though it declined to credit the community-wide campaign against the Islamophobic speaker. In a written statement to the news outlet PennLive, Army War College spokeswoman Carol Kerr wrote, "The presentation of Mr. Raymond Ibrahim's book is postponed so [the U.S. Army Heritage and Education Center] can pair Mr. Ibrahim's military history insights in close proximity with another historical perspective" (DeJesus, 2019).

The Islamophobia Network's work can lastly be grouped under the theme of clouding mainstream and social media with dangerous and false speech. Dangerous speech is used here as described by Benesch et al. (2018) in "Dangerous Speech: A Practical Guide." The authors define it as "any form of expression (e.g., speech, text, or images) that can increase the risk that its audience will condone or commit violence against members of another group" (Benesch et al., 2018, p. 503).

MAINSTREAMING ANTI-MUSLIM MEDIA

The spread of such speech through media often works in conjunction with the other activities conducted by the Network around targeting local communities, abusing the legal system, and disseminating false information in the public sphere. A defining feature of dangerous speech is that it often promotes fear, as much as it expresses or promotes hatred (Benesch et al., 2018).

Research by Stanford and University of California Berkeley professors, published in *Institute for the Future*, found empirical evidence that anti-Muslim hate speech causes deep-rooted harm and enables restrictions of Muslims' civil liberties (Pakzad & Salehim, 2019).

Efforts to track Muslim candidates around the country have led to the proliferation of targeted campaigns against them. For example, the most retweeted post on Twitter related to Muslim and Islam around the 2018 midterm election was retweeted 1,500 times. It read, "#MinnesotaPrimary is tomorrow. There are at least 15 anti @POTUS muslim (sic) candidates running. I hope every single Patriot in #Minnesota votes against these ppl! #NoShariaLaw List of muslims (sic) running in Minnesota Primary here" (Pakzad & Salehim, 2019).

Another example of a false claim was the association of Muslim terrorists with the so-called migrant caravan on the United States' southern border the day before the 2018 midterm elections.

There are numerous examples of dangerous speech littering the social media accounts of anti-Muslim hate groups and Islamophobes. For example, raising the specter of anti-Semitism by employing the trope of Muslims as anti-Jewish, Brigitte Gabriel, president of ACT for America, tweeted, "Plain and simple, if anti-Semites like Ilhan Omar and her Farrakhan fan girl colleague Rashida Tlaib are allowed to remain in Congress, the Democrat party has objectively become the party of anti-Semitism" (Gabriel, 2019).

Even efforts to promote Muslim role models are met by the Islamophobia Network with vitriol. For example, Nike celebrated the athleticism of Muslim female athletes in an ad that depicted seven women in athletic gear and a headscarf. The text read, "Don't change who you are. Change the world" (Toronto, 2019). In return, American Freedom Defense Initiative president Pamela Geller tweeted, "Nike Celebrates Sharia Oppression of Women in New Hijabed Ad. The perfect definition of Islamization of the West. Note the angry hijab'ed faces" (Geller, 2019). In equating Islam with oppression and assuming that the religion is an existential threat to the "West," Geller's response fell squarely within the realms of dangerous speech.

Networks and outlets like Fox News and Breitbart are prime purveyors of such dangerous speech in mainstream media. This is especially concerning because, according to Andrea Prat, Professor of Business and Professor of Economics at Columbia University and CEPR Research Fellow, Fox News is the most powerful media company in America. Prat gauges the power of a media company based on an index that analyzes "how many people receive their political information from news sources owned by that company" (Prat, 2014).

Frank Gaffney, president of the Center for Security Policy, has appeared on Fox News to argue that mosques are Trojan horses used by Muslims to promote sedition. Although mosques, like churches, synagogues, temples, and other places of worship, are constitutionally protected houses of worship in America, Gaffney has argued that mosques are used to promote a seditious program. According to Gaffney, mosques advocate Sharia, which is seditious and should not be a protected religious practice.

Beyond simply inviting anti-Muslim bigots on its shows as guests, Fox News hosts themselves are purveyors of dangerous speech about Islam and Muslims. On Jeanine Pirro's show, "Justice with Judge Jeanine," for example, Pirro railed against Congresswoman Ilhan Omar, the first Muslim Congresswoman in American history who wears a headscarf. "Think about it: Omar wears a hijab, which according to the Quran 33:59, tells women to cover so they will not get molested. Is her adherence to this Islamic doctrine indicative of her adherence to Sharia law, which, in itself, is antithetical to the United States Constitution?" she said (Now This, 2019). Much like Geller, in stating that adherence to Islamic practices and principles is an existential threat to the "West," Pirro's response exemplifies dangerous speech.

The steady increase in Islamophobia Network activity against American Muslims is part of a calculated strategy to demonize. A January 2016 Pew Research Center survey found that 25% of U.S. adults thought half or more of Muslims in the United States were "anti-American," while an additional

24% thought "some" Muslims are anti-American (Pew Research Center, 2016). Pew's April 2017 poll found that half of American adults say Islam is not part of mainstream American society and that the U.S. public is split over whether there is a "natural conflict" between Islam and democracy (Pew Research Center, 2017).

The artificially generated fear of the other is a core element of the process of dehumanization, which in turn justifies, enables, and exacerbates inter-personal and structural violence. It has created a climate where a person feels emboldened to vandalize an existing mosque and hurl verbal and physical abuse at those who appear to be Muslim. As a result, those who are, or appear to be Muslim, suffer direct personal violence. CAIR's civil rights reports, which track hate crimes and anti-Muslim bias incidents annually, have shown a steady uptick in cases since 2014. The number of cases increased; they are also increasingly violent (Islamophobia.org, 2019).

This process of dehumanization has made it possible for a sitting president to, within his first month of office, issue a ban on individuals from several Muslim-majority countries from entering the country. Moreover, it has made it possible for the National Security Strategy released in December 2017 to state, "Jihadist terrorists such as ISIS and al-Qa'ida continue to spread a barbaric ideology. . . These jihadist terrorists attempt to force those under their influence to submit to Sharia law."

Dangerous speech, prejudiced action, and discriminatory policies targeting Muslims have experienced rapid growth in the last decade due to continued multimillion-dollar financing. It is these funding channels of Islamophobia that are examined next.

MAINSTREAM PHILANTHROPY AND THE FUNDING OF HATE

As the previous section has demonstrated, the Islamophobia Network comprises a complex but tightly knit group of actors with allied financial, social, and political interests that intend to orchestrate long-term negative impact on public perceptions about Islam and Muslims. This web of anti-Muslim special interest groups has played both arsonist and fire-fighter by actively spreading and fomenting alarmist and conspiratorial misinformation campaigns and then providing well-financed "solutions" to counter the alleged problem.

Although Islamophobia has deep roots in structural racism in the United States, many argue that anti-Muslim special interest groups moved from the fringes of society into the mainstream during the 2010 midterm elections when the so-called Ground-Zero mosque controversy occurred. This was the case in which an Islamic community center was to be founded by interfaith-oriented Imam Faisal Abdul Rauf near the former World Trade Center in Manhattan. Mainstream journalists and academics also noticed the rise of the Islamophobia Network 2 years prior, when on the eve of the presidential election of 2008, nearly 30 million free copies of the vitriolic video "Obsession" were mailed directly to people's homes in key swing states (Ose, 2017).

To better understand the Islamophobia Network, scholars, journalists, and advocacy groups have tracked the financial and political capacity of the nebulous Islamophobia Network for nearly a decade in order to demonstrate its impact on society and threat to democracy. Through two reports entitled *Fear Inc.* and *Fear Inc. 2.0*, the Center for American Progress was among the first to provide systematic indexing of the groups primarily responsible for promoting anti-Muslim vitriol among the American public (Ali et al., 2011; Duss et al., 2015). CAIR published reports in 2013 (*Legislating Fear*) and 2016 (*Confronting Fear*) documenting the spread of the anti-Sharia legislation movement as well showing the impact of the Islamophobia Network's activities in the political, legal, and media spaces (Islamophobia.org, 2019). Independent and university-based researchers such as Todd Green, Khaled Beydoun, Deepa Kumar, Nathan Lean, and Erik Love have also contributed to a growing body of literature documenting how anti-Muslim special interest groups operate and influence society.

CAIR's 2019 Islamophobia report, *Hijacked by Hate: American Philanthropy and the Islamophobia Network*, uncovered previously unreported aspects of how this network of actors is financed. Namely, *Hijacked by Hate* found that many mainstream American charitable institutions have been used as legal money laundering conduits to anonymize wealthy donors' contributions to the Islamophobia agenda. In total, between 2014 and 2016, 1,096 tax-exempt 501(c)(3) organizations were used to funnel just over $125 million to anti-Muslim special interest groups.

While it is unsurprising that private foundations and ideologically oriented funds play a significant role in this phenomenon, it is also evident that regional community foundations and commercial financial institutions are also implicated in the Islamophobia Network's funding machine. For example, groups like Sheldon Adelson's Adelson Family Foundation and Sear's heiress, Nina Rosenwald's Abstraction Fund, have a long history in promoting far-right and militant Zionist agendas that promote fear of Islam and Muslims. In addition, however, mainstream corporate charities, such as Fidelity and Schwab, and reputable social service–oriented, religious foundations such as the Jewish Communal Fund and the National Christian Charitable Foundation appear as mega-donors of anti-Muslim bigotry (Arain & Barzegar, 2019).

Even more concerning than the sheer volume of funds enabling Islamophobia is the fact that tax-subsidized charitable institutions, which should be dedicated to promoting the public good, are being used to undermine American democracy and polarize society. This section summarizes findings that document the distribution of funds from philanthropic institutions to the Islamophobia Network, highlighting some of the largest donor groups. This review draws from CAIR's 2019 Islamophobia report, *Hijacked by Hate*. We then discuss the role that donor-advised funds (DAFs) play in this process.

AMERICAN PHILANTHROPY AND THE ISLAMOPHOBIA NETWORK

According to CAIR researchers, between 2014 and 2016, a total of $125 million was donated to anti-Muslim organizations by 1,096 family foundations, commercial charities, community foundations, religious foundations, DAFs, or a combination thereof. The donors responsible for this pattern of giving varied from dedicated propaganda networks, whose sole purpose is to advocate for "national security" by spreading fear about Muslims and Islam, to others who belong to mainstream conservative rather than fringe or far-right groups. Others still, however, belong to politically neutral institutions.

It is to be expected that ideologically committed foundations will donate to efforts that support their political goals. However, when scrutinized, such activity clearly skirts the legal boundaries of what constitutes appropriate behavior for a 501(c)(3) tax-exempt entity. Moreover, it raises the ethical question of tax-subsidized dollars being used for xenophobic activity. A particularly demonstrative example of this problem is the family foundation, Christians Advocates Serving Evangelism (CASE). CASE is directed by Jay Sekulow, most widely known as President Trump's lawyer, during the Special Counsel's investigation of possible collusion between the Trump campaign and Russian state actors. Long before he became a household name, Sekulow was a Washington, DC–based political figure and talk radio host who served as chief counsel at the American Center for Law and Justice. The ACLJ, which positions itself as a conservative counterweight to the American Civil Liberties Union (ACLU), was founded by televangelist Pat Robertson and is directed by Jordan Sekulow, Jay Sekulow's son. Sekulow also serves as president of the Law and Justice Institute, which reports no employees according to Charity Watch.

Between 2014 and 2016, CASE donated $32 million to the ACLJ. The ACLJ's anti-Muslim agenda is well documented and notably aggressive—it submitted amicus briefs in support of the Muslim ban, and it has promoted anti-Sharia legislation across the country. It proudly defends its leading role in the Park 51, "Ground-Zero mosque" controversy, that many point to as the moment when Islamophobia became a normalized feature of conservative politics (ACLJ, 2011). CASE also serves as a tax-free holding company for Sekulow and his family's political activities and interests. In 2017, investigations concerning the financial and legal practices of CASE, its subsidiaries, and family interests were opened by the Attorney Generals of North Carolina and New York. The allegations asserted that CASE directed tens of millions in properties and salaries to the Sekulow family network (Swaine, 2017).

Other foundations that promote anti-Muslim interest activity under cover of 501(c)(3) status include the Adelson Family Foundation and the Abstraction Fund. The former belongs to Sheldon Adelson, the well-known casino and property owner who donated over $24 million to the Trump campaign. Adelson is a well-known supporter of Benjamin Netanyahu and plays a heavy role in the Israeli political arena as one of the chief investors in *Israel Hayom*, the country's largest free newspaper, also known for its right-leaning bias. The Abstraction Fund, directed by Nina Rosenwald, is another example of an anti-Muslim political advocacy group operating under tax-exempt status. Nina Rosenwald is heiress to Julius Rosenwald, the cofounder of Sears, a well-known supporter of African American educational and civic advancement projects such as Booker T. Washington's Tuskegee Institute. However, her philanthropy has gone in a decidedly different direction. Rosenwald is responsible for providing sustained financing to nearly every prominent figure and organization in the Islamophobia Network, such as Daniel Pipes, Frank Gaffney, John Bolton, Brigitte Gabriel, and Geert Van Wilders through the Gatestone Institute, where she serves as president. Like Sheldon Adelson, Rosenwald shares a commitment to supporting far-right Israeli politics and militant Zionist activities, including providing contributions to illegal settlement activity in the Golan Heights and West Bank (Blumenthal, 2019).

In addition to such ideologically focused foundations, mainstream religious foundations also funnel donor money to the Islamophobia Network. Because these organizations represent a broad base of donors who share a common moral and ideological vision grounded in their faith commitment, they tend to be extremely large and capable of mobilizing vast sums of funding. The National Christian Foundation (NCF), for example, boasts of having raised and distributed over $10 billion since its inception in 1982. Most of this money has been raised through the strategic use of DAFs. NCF supports traditional religious charitable causes such as proselytization activities, humanitarian relief, and poverty alleviation domestically and internationally. NCF is also on record as directing funds to mainstream organizations such as the American Cancer Society, Alzheimer's Association, and the American Heart Association. However, it has also allowed its donors to direct funds to Sekulow's ACLJ and the fundamentalist Christian advocacy group, the American Family Association (AFA), founded by Donald E. Wildmon in 1977. Through various organs, the AFA has promoted the idea that Islam is not a religion but a political ideology that should not enjoy First Amendment guarantees. One of AFA's most vocal ideologues, Bryan Fischer, was removed from Facebook for his anti-Muslim hate speech in 2018. Between 2014 and 2016, the NCF granted $3 million to the AFA.

The Jewish Communal Fund of New York (JCFNY) is another example of a broad-based religious organization using DAFs and others means to fund anti-Muslim and Islamophobic activities. While the majority of funds at JCFNY provides support for Jewish communities in New York and abroad, JCFNY resources also impact the public good by supporting nonsectarian organizations such as the Museum of Modern Art, New York Public Radio, and Columbia, Brown, N.Y.U., and other universities (Jewish Communal Fund, 2018). In 2018, JCFNY boasted an asset base of $1.6 billion and a grant distribution total of $435,000 (Jewish Communal Fund, 2018). Unlisted in its public reporting is the fact that JCFNY also supports organizations such as MEMRI, the Gatestone Institute, the Clarion Project, and other ideologically hardened anti-Muslim special interest groups. Between 2014 and 2016, CAIR researchers found that JCFNY donated at least $3.2 million tax-exempt dollars to the Islamophobia Network.

However, the most concerning use of DAF dollars to support the Islamophobia Network comes from commercial financial institutions whose sole purpose is to manage and distribute charitable dollars at the behest of its donors. Unlike the previous examples, which use DAFs to support their values-based charitable missions, these financial institutions operate as neutral platforms and provide donors with a maximum tax benefit and anonymity as to the final destination of their donation. Commercially backed foundations now rank as the largest "charities" in the United States due to their use and mobilization of DAF dollars and their distribution to well-recognized charitable names. Fidelity and Schwab count among industry leaders in this regard, boasting 2018 distributions of $4.5 billion and $2.2 billion, respectively. Fidelity Charitable funneled its largest donations to Doctors Without Borders, the Salvation Army, and the American Red Cross (Fidelity Charitable Giving Report, 2018). Schwab Charitable also provided funding through DAFs to the same organizations, securing its place as a pillar of mainstream American philanthropy (Schwab Charitable.org, 2018). However, both institutions also allowed their platforms to be used by donors to direct funds to anti-Muslim special interest groups such as the David Horowitz Freedom Center, The Lawfare Project, MEMRI, and Camera. In total, Fidelity Charitable was responsible for distributing $1.8 million and Schwab $2.8 million to the Islamophobia Network between 2014 and 2016 (Arain & Barzegar, 2019). When asked about their responsibility in vetting donor decisions to direct funding toward hate groups, both Fidelity and Schwab responded that while they take grantee misuse of charitable dollars seriously, they ultimately rely on IRS designations of 501(c)(3)s and that reports of the misappropriation of funds should be directed there (Fadel, 2019).

While it is to be expected that ideologically hardened networks of organizations and individuals will skirt the letter of the law and blur the ethical boundaries of using tax-exempt dollars for political purposes, recent research reveals the complex ways these patterns of behavior have entered into mainstream philanthropy. Whether through communal funds backed by faith groups or commercially supported charitable institutions, the intermingling of hate speech, xenophobic political work, and charitable giving has created a complex problem for scholars and practitioners to examine. As the next section demonstrates, the use of DAFs as a vehicle for charitable giving has caused great concern among stakeholders in the nonprofit, advocacy, tax-policy, and philanthropy sectors. The problem is far more extensive than simply providing tax-exempt cover for hate speech. Instead, it promises to change the face of philanthropy altogether.

FUNDING ISLAMOPHOBIA: A PUBLIC TAX PROBLEM?

From abusive campaign finance practices to the power of corporate lobbies, the problem of private wealth influencing politics and public life is as perennial as it is pervasive. Thus, it is no surprise that Islamophobia is funded with and enabled through hundreds of millions of tax-subsidized dollars. The financial mechanism that makes this possible is a DAF, a unique form of charitable giving that provides immediate and maximum tax benefits to private donors and inherently delays distributing funds to active charitable causes. It also provides donors with anonymity, a feature that may be attractive to those supporting anti-Muslim activity. Several of the financial and regulatory features of DAFs, reviewed later, ultimately make Islamophobia a public tax problem.

The damaging impact of Islamophobia, anti-Muslim bigotry, and other forms of bias, discrimination, and racism in the public sphere is evident in the steady rise of hate crimes and bias incidents throughout the United States since 9/11. In addition to the personal, political, and cultural price society pays for Islamophobia, there is a financial cost of anti-Muslim bigotry through public tax subsidies. Tax-exempt organizations, such as religious organizations, soup kitchens, and relief agencies, receive a subsidy because they are intended to benefit the public good. The Islamophobia industry, however, exploits the 501(c)(3) status to promote xenophobic ideas and spread misinformation in the public space. The dynamic between the public trust and private donation is summed up by the authors of the report, "Warehousing Wealth" by the Institute for Policy Studies:

> Any tax deduction is a cost to the U.S. taxpayer; it reduces the amount of revenue available each year to spend on public programs. It is, essentially, a subsidy from the public to the person taking the deduction. Therefore, a tax deduction must provide a benefit to society that outweighs its cost to warrant the subsidy. In the case of the charitable deduction, the bargain that was struck with the public was that in exchange for their donors getting a deduction for their gifts, the charity's work would benefit the public as a whole and not any

single individual. When a donor uses the U.S. government-created charitable deduction to reduce their taxes in exchange for a gift, we, as taxpayers, effectively provide matching funds for that gift. For every dollar a billionaire gives to charity, the taxpayer has to supply between 37 and 57 cents to make up for lost tax revenue.

Donors may believe that their donations should not be subject to scrutiny. Nevertheless, it is in the public interest to ensure that revenue claimed for a tax deduction is used for the purposes for which the deduction was intended. This justifies oversight and accountability from both donor and recipient. Of course, if a donor wishes to avoid this oversight, they are free to give donations without claiming deductions. (Collins et al., 2018)

As DAFs are increasingly used to funnel funds to the Islamophobia Network, the taxpaying public should be aware that they indirectly contribute to political, educational, and advocacy activities that damage the public square. In this way, in addition to everything else, Islamophobia is also a tax problem.

Another criticism of DAFs is that they inherently provide donors with anonymity and control over monies that should be surrendered to charitable activity. With standard charities or nonprofits, if a donor provides a financial contribution, that donor understands that they lose control over the way their funding is managed or used. It is also the case that when a donor receives a tax deduction for their financial contribution to a charity, that donor is identified as such in public records. This is the case, again, because the public essentially subsidizes that tax deduction. However, in the case of DAFs, both elements—surrender and transparency—are avoided. Instead, the structure of the DAF creates a scenario in which a donor contributes to an account legally and logistically managed by an external agency, but in practice and reality remains in the donor's control. In this way, a donor can contribute anonymously to a 501(c)(3), but that contribution can remain hidden from public purvey. Thus, the public only sees an untraceable DAF serving as a buffer and intermediary between anonymous donors and 501(c)(3)s.

DAFs also benefit donors at the expense of public interest due to how they structure their taxes and "payout" rates. In a typical scenario, donors receive their tax deduction when a contribution is transferred to an active charity. The immediate tax benefit corresponds to the immediate transfer of wealth or investment into the public sphere. However, DAFs are not active charities—they are funds that are not obligated to be transferred (paid out) to an active charity within a particular time period. Nonetheless, the donor receives an immediate tax benefit at the time of the contribution. It is also the case that complex, non-cash assets which escape objective valuation, such as art or real estate, can be "donated" to a DAF and thus maximize a tax deduction. In this scenario, the DAF is under no compulsion to transfer this contribution to active charity. Taken together, the various aspects of a DAF enable a form of legal, charitable money laundering that protects and maximizes the interests of individual wealthy donors and their families at the expense of public interests.

While DAFs play a key role in the funding of Islamophobia and other forms of xenophobic activity, they also constitute a significant concern for stakeholders in the nonprofit and charity sectors whose funding streams are directly impacted by the diversion of charitable dollars into what are, in essence, legal, charitable tax shelters. In order to remedy this problem, there are several legislative proposals at state and federal levels calling for reform to DAFs that would result in a more equitable distribution of the benefits they provide between individual donors and active charitable causes. For example, in 2019, the California Association for Nonprofits (Calnonprofits), which boasts nearly 10,000 organizations in its membership, backed Bill AB-1712 in the California state legislature, calling for greater transparency and regulation of DAFs (McCambridge, 2019). Specifically, the bill calls for annual reporting that is consistent with the requirements of other charitable vehicles, a fixed annual distribution rate similar to traditional family foundations, and other nonprofit best practices. Calnonprofits supported their legislative advocacy with survey data of nearly 500 nonprofits, most of which receive a considerable amount of funding from DAFs, who supported regulation. The provisions in AB-1712 have precedent in other attempts at legislative appeal at the federal level, but which did not materialize in any substantive action.

In addition to the regulatory measures stakeholders have pursued to reform DAFs, advocacy groups, philanthropy thought leaders, and even commercially backed DAF sponsors (e.g., banks) have called for actions to curb the problem of hate group funding that is concealed through DAFs. At the forefront of this effort was the "Hate Is Not Charitable" campaign formed in 2019 and led by the Amalgamated Foundation, the charitable division of Amalgamated Bank. The campaign called upon stakeholders at the intersection of philanthropy, nonprofit work, and advocacy to demand that DAFs "exercise their legal discretion over grants made by donor-advised funds and reject donor recommendations to organizations engaged in hateful activities" (Amalgamated Foundation, 2019). In 2017, GuideStar, a leading information service provider about nonprofits, briefly experimented with addressing this issue by flagging nonprofits dubbed hate groups by the Southern Poverty Law Center. They were quickly sued in a spurious defamation allegation that resulted in immediate dismissal. However, the risk to GuideStar staff as well as the heated public debate led to the abandonment of the effort. The episode serves as a demonstrative example of the difficulties in providing stakeholders and the public good with resources to curb the problem of tax-exempt hate group funding (Hogan, 2017).

CONCLUSION

Despite continued research and learning, the full extent of the Islamophobia Network's influence on policy, culture, and political life remains to be discovered. As this chapter has demonstrated, it can no longer be assumed that anti-Muslim bigotry is merely a sentiment or attitude, but rather like structural racism, it is a form of discrimination that pervades public and private institutions. While activists and applied research scholars attempt to counter the influence of the Islamophobia Network through coalition building, raising public awareness, and leveraging public pressure, they face a formidable challenge given the Islamophobia Network's powerful and complex use of financial and legal resources. However, it may be the case that the Trump administration's full embrace of anti-Muslim bigotry created an opportunity for greater visibility of the Islamophobia Network. In this way, it could be argued that advocacy networks could advance their counter-Islamophobia campaigns in a new and more receptive environment. The example of removing Raymond Ibrahim as a speaker from the Army War College cited earlier is an apt example of how advocacy coalitions were able to leverage public pressure against a conservative national security institution even during the Trump administration. Moreover, the fact that financial and philanthropic institutions are working to curb the funding of hate speech taking place on their platforms may indicate a new era in American cultural politics. It is unlikely, nor should it be expected, that the Islamophobia Network or anti-Muslim bigotry will disappear from American society in the near future. However, a greater understanding of the dynamics of the Islamophobia Network, its funding sources, and modes of operation will likely lead to greater empowerment of advocacy networks working to curb its influence. Continued research, therefore, becomes of paramount importance.

REFERENCES

Alfonsi, S. (2015, February 11). Truth in Texas textbooks reviews: Pearson World History (high school) 2014. Truth in Texas Textbooks.

Ali, A. H. (2018, June 15). Twitter post. 5:58 p.m. Retrieved from https://twitter.com/Ayaan/status/1007782022226382848

Ali, S. (2017, June 10). A.C.T. for America stages nationwide marches against 'sharia law. CNBC. Retrieved from https://www.cnbc.com/2017/06/10/act-for-america-stages-nationwide-marches-against-sharia-law.html

Ali, W., Clifton, E., Duss, M., Fang, L., Keyes, S., & Shakir, F. (2011, August 26). Fear, Inc.: The roots of the Islamophobia Network in America. Center for American Progress. Retrieved from https://www.americanprogress.org/issues/religion/reports/2011/08/26/10165/fear-inc/;

Amalgamated Foundation. (2019, March 19). Hate is not charitable campaign. Retrieved from http://amalgamatedfoundation.org/hate-is-not-charitable

American Center for Law and Justice (ACLJ). (2011, March 15). ACLJ to New York court: No mosque at Ground Zero. Retrieved from https://aclj.org/ground-zero-mosque/aclj-to-new-york-court-no-mosque-at-ground-zero

Amons, N. (2012, February 14). Group that opposes "Islamic movement" trains deputies. WSMV TV. http://www.wsmv.com/story/16930386/group-that-opposes-islamic-movement-trains-deputies-murfreesboro

Arain, Z., & Barzegar, A. (2019). Hijacked by hate: American philanthropy and the Islamophobia Network. Council on American-Islamic Relations. Retrieved from http://www.islamophobia.org/images/IslamophobiaReport2019/CAIR_Islamophobia_Report_2019_Final_Web.pdf

Ballor, C. (2017, June 10). Sharia law protesters, some toting rifles, gather in front of North Texas Islamic center. *Dallas News*. Retrieved from https://www.dallasnews.com/news/news/2017/06/10/anti-shariah-protesters-gather-front-north-texas-islamic-center

Benesch, S., Buerger, C., Glavinic, T., & Manion, S. (2018, December 31). Dangerous speech: A practical guide. Dangerous Speech Project. Retrieved from https://dangerousspeech.org/guide/

Berglund, T. (2019, January 2). Brigitte Gabriel exposes the truth about Islam, Quran. *Charisma News*. Retrieved from https://www.charismanews.com/us/74637-brigitte-gabriel-exposes-the-truth-about-islam-quran

Blumenthal, M. (2019, July 14). The sugar mama of anti-Muslim hate. *The Nation*. Retrieved from 2019, https://www.thenation.com/article/sugar-mama-anti-muslim-hate/

CAIR. (2019, May 28). Philadelphia to Major General Kem and Provost Dr. Breckenridge. Retrieved from https://pa.cair.com/wp-content/uploads/2019/06/Letter-US-Army-War-College.pdf

Careym, A. (2018, June 26). Classrooms pushing Islamic propaganda. Church Militant—Serving Catholics. Retrieved from https://www.churchmilitant.com/news/article/islamic-indoctrination-in-schools-subverts-constitution.

Collins, C., Flannery, H., & Hoxie, J. (2018). *Warehousing wealth: Donor-advised charity funds sequestering billions in the face of growing inequality*. Institute for Policy Studies.

DeJesus, I. (2019, June 11). Army War College postpones appearance of controversial author with anti-Islam history. PennLive. Retrieved from https://www.pennlive.com/news/2019/06/army-war-college-postpones-appearance-of-controversial-islamic-historian.html

Duss, M., Taeb, Y., Gude, K., & Sofer, K. (2015, February 11). Fear, Inc. 2.0: The Islamophobia Network's efforts to manufacture hate in America. Center for American Progress. Retrieved from https://www.americanprogress.org/issues/religion/reports/2015/02/11/106394/fear-inc-2-0/

Elliot, A., & Yerushalmi, D. (2011, July 30). The man behind the anti-shariah movement. *New York Times*. Retrieved from https://www.nytimes.com/2011/07/31/us/31shariah.html

Fadel, F. (2019, May 7). Mainstream charities are unwittingly funding anti-Muslim hate groups, report says. NPR. Retrieved from https://www.npr.org/2019/05/07/720832680/mainstream-charities-are-unwittingly-funding-anti-muslim-hate-groups-report-says

Fidelity Charitable Giving Report. (2018). Retrieved from https://www.fidelitycharitable.org/content/dam/fc-public/docs/insights/2018-giving-report.pdf

Fischer, B. (2011, March 24). Islam and the First Amendment: Privileges but not rights. Retrieved from http://www.renewamerica.com/columns/fischer/110324

Gabriel, B. (2008). *They must be stopped: Why we must defeat radical Islam and how we can do it.* St. Martin's Press.

Gabriel, B. (2011). Education or indoctrination? The treatment of Islam in 6th through 12th grade American textbooks. A.C.T. for America Education.

Gabriel, B. (2019, February 18). Twitter post. 1:04 pm. Retrieved from https://twitter.com/ACTBrigitte/status/1097602673468153856

Geller, P. (2019, May 15). "Religious hatred": 5 Christian children and teacher killed in Sunday School in Ramadan terror attack in Syria. Geller Report. Retrieved from https://gellerreport.com/2019/05/ramadan-terror-christian-chilren-school.html/?utm_source=dlvr.it&utm_medium=twitter

Geller, P. (2019, June 4). Twitter post. 6:03 pm. Retrieved from https://twitter.com/PamelaGeller/status/1135894746474242048.

Goodstein, L. (2011, March 7). Brigitte Gabriel draws crowds with anti-Islam message. *New York Times.* Retrieved from https://www.nytimes.com/2011/03/08/us/08gabriel.html

Grantham, C. (2010, September 27). Murfreesboro mosque opponents appear in Chancery Court. *Murfreesboro Post.* Retrieved from https://www.murfreesboropost.com/news/murfreesboro-mosque-opponents-appear-in-chancery-court/article_1ad791ff-d868-50e6-a7fb-c04396bd3848.html

Hogan, S. (2017, June 26). After conservative backlash, charity tracker GuideStar removes "hate group" labels. *The Washington Post.* Retrieved from https://www.washingtonpost.com/news/morning-mix/wp/2017/06/26/after-conservative-backlash-charity-tracker-guidestar-removes-hate-group-labels/?utm_term=.912f949e88d1

Hooper, I. (2019, June 6). CAIR-Philadelphia, partners call on U.S. Army War College to drop Islamophobic speaker. Council on American-Islamic Relations. Retrieved from https://www.cair.com/cair_philadelphia_partners_call_on_us_army_war_college_to_drop_islamophobic_speaker

Horowitz, D. (2011). Speech at Brooklyn College. Southern Poverty Law Center. Retrieved from https://www.splcenter.org/fighting-hate/extremist-files/individual/david-horowitz

Ibrahim, R. (2018, May 28). Sword and scimitar. Interview by *Frontpage Magazine.* Retrieved from https://www.frontpagemag.com/fpm/270266/sword-and-scimitar-jamie-glazov

Ibrahim, R. (2019). About. Retrieved from https://www.raymondibrahim.com/about/

Islamophobia Research and Documentation Project. (n.d.) U.C. Berkeley Center for Race & Gender. Retrieved from https://www.crg.berkeley.edu/research/islamophobia-research-documentation-project/.

Islamophobia.org. (2019). Reports: Islamophobia. Retrieved from http://www.islamophobia.org/research/reports.html

Jewish Communal Fund, Giving Report. (2018). Giving report. Jewish Communal Fund. Retrieved from https://jcfny.org/app/uploads/2018/12/JCF-2018-Giving-Report.pdf

Kern, S. K. (2018, March 20.). Germany: Migrant rape crisis still sowing terror and destruction. Retrieved from https://www.gatestoneinstitute.org/12066/germany-rape-crisis.

Kurzman, C., Moosa, E., & Schanzer, D. (2010). *Anti-terror lessons of Muslim Americans.* Duke University and University of North Carolina-Chapel Hill.

LaCasse, A. (2015, January 13). How many Muslim extremists are there? Just the facts, please. *The Christian Science Monitor.* Retrieved from https://www.csmonitor.com/World/Security-Watch/terrorism-security/2015/0113/How-many-Muslim-extremists-are-there-Just-the-facts-please

Levinson, M. (2018). Constructing an enemy: Representations of the Middle East and Islam in U.S. textbooks. Unpublished undergraduate thesis.

McCambridge, R. (2019, March 19). California Association of Nonprofits sponsors bill to regulate D.A.F.s. *Nonprofit Quarterly.* Retrieved from https://nonprofitquarterly.org/california-association-of-nonprofits-sponsors-bill-to-regulate-dafs/

Marr, T. (2006). *The cultural roots of American Islamicism.* Cambridge University Press.

Matthews, D. (2016, June 13). Donald Trump's pro-gay Islamophobia is straight out of the European right-wing playbook. *Vox.* https://www.vox.com/2016/6/13/11924826/donald-trump-islamophobia-muslim-lgbtq-europe-wilders

Now This. (2019, March 12). Fox News separates network from Jeanine Pirro's Islamophobic comments on Ilhan Omar. NowThis, Retrieved from https://nowthisnews.com/videos/politics/fox-news-jeanine-pirros-islamophobic-comments-on-ilhan-omar.

Ose, E. (2017, December 6). Pro-McCain group dumping 28 million terror scare DVDs in swing states. *HuffPost.* Retrieved from https://www.huffpost.com/entry/pro-mccain-group-dumping_b_125969

Pakzad, R., & Salehim, N. (2019, May 7). Anti-Muslim Americans computational propaganda in the United States coordinated online attacks during the 2018 U.S. midterm elections. Institute for the Future.

Pew Research Center. (2016, February 3). Republicans prefer blunt talk about Islamic extremism, Democrats favor caution. Retrieved from https://www.pewforum.org/2016/02/03/republicans-prefer-blunt-talk-about-islamic-extremism-democrats-favor-caution/

Pew Research Center. (2017, July 26). How the U.S. general public views Muslims and Islam. Retrieved from https://www.pewforum.org/2017/07/26/how-the-u-s-general-public-views-muslims-and-islam/

Prat, A. (2014, August 22). Can we measure media power? *World Economic Forum.* Retrieved from https://www.weforum.org/agenda/2014/08/measure-power-of-media/

Ricarrdi, N. (2010, October 28). Measure would outlaw Islamic law in Oklahoma—where it doesn't exist. *L.A. Times.* Retrieved from https://www.latimes.com/archives/la-xpm-2010-oct-28-la-na-sharia-oklahoma-20101029-story.html

Schleifer, T. (2016, March 10). Donald Trump: "I think Islam hates us." CNN. Retrieved from https://www.cnn.com/2016/03/09/politics/donald-trump-islam-hates-us/index.html

Schwab Charitable.org. (2018, July 18). Schwab Charitable donors set granting records in fiscal year 2018. Retrieved from https://www.schwabcharitable.org/public/charitable/about_schwab_charitable/news_pr/press_releases/granting_records_fiscal_year_2018.html

Scott, E. (2018, December 13). In farewell, Hatch calls on religious conservatives to find common ground with LGBT community. *The Washington Post*. Retrieved from https://www.washingtonpost.com/politics/2018/12/13/farewell-hatch-calls-religious-conservatives-find-common-ground-with-lgbt-community/

Stalcup, M., & Craze, J. (2011). How we train our cops to fear Islam. *Washington Monthly*, March/April. Retrieved from https://washingtonmonthly.com/magazine/marchapril-2011/how-we-train-our-cops-to-fear-islam/

Swaine, J. (2017, June 27). Authorities to investigate Jay Sekulow nonprofit after "troubling" revelations. *The Guardian*. Retrieved from https://www.theguardian.com/us-news/2017/jun/27/trump-lawyer-jay-sekulow-obamacare-repeal-christian-nonprofit

Thomas B. Fordham Institute. (2004). *The mad, mad world of textbook adoption*. Thomas B. Fordham Institute.

Tomaso, B. (2017, June 10). Anti-Shariah rallies nationwide "intended to manufacture fear." Religious News Service. Retrieved from https://religionnews.com/2017/06/10/anti-sharia-rallies-nationwide-intended-to-manufacture-fear/

Toronto, N. (2019, May 29). Instagram post. Retrieved from https://www.instagram.com/p/ByDjWsoBgCJ/

United States Army. (2019). About the U.S. Army War College. U.S. Army. Retrieved from https://www.armywarcollege.edu/overview.cfm

Usuli Institute. (2018, January 6). Part I: Usuli Institute Second Halaqa, 6 Jan 2018. YouTube video, 1:13:53, Usuli Institute. Retrieved from https://www.youtube.com/watch?v=ND59u6oX5oc

Van-Bakel, R. (2007, October 10). The trouble is the West. Retrieved from http://reason.com/archives/2007/10/10/the-trouble-is-the-west/4.

3

Ripples of Hate

Measuring How Hate Crimes Hurt More

RANDY BLAZAK■

Less than a week after the March 15, 2019, terrorist attack in Christchurch, New Zealand, that left 51 worshipers in two mosques dead, I spoke to a Muslim student of mine who had emigrated from Algeria. "My 11-year-old son told me he doesn't want to leave the house now because they are killing Muslims," she told me, adding, "It is scary to me and my children to go to the mosque in this time. We have Ramadan coming soon where the Muslims gather together in the mosques. It will be very scary. We run from the civil war in our countries to get killed in the country where we think we are safe." Their fears about a mass murder on the other side of the world were not unwarranted. Supporters of the Christchurch shooter, a White nationalist named Brenton Tarrant, heaped praise on the killer on the dark web Tarrant inhabited. On March 24, 2019, a poster on the "Politically Incorrect" page of the 8chan platform wrote:

> Brenton Tarrant did what everyone on this board only dreams about. He took the fight to the enemy and won. He is an inspiration to all the White nations of the world who are enduring the never ending onslaught of brown invaders flooding into their countries at the behest of their own governments. He shows us that we can fight back,

Randy Blazak, *Ripples of Hate* In: *Islamophobia and Acts of Violence*. Edited by: Carolyn Turpin-Petrosino, Oxford University Press. © Oxford University Press 2022. DOI: 10.1093/oso/9780190922313.003.0003 that we can make a difference, and above all that we are not beaten. This is only the beginning. . . . THE FIRE RISES!

That same day a mosque in Escondido, California, was the target of an attempted arson that included graffiti that referenced the slaughter in Christchurch (Hauser, 2019).

Understandably, the New Zealand killings impacted the global community of Muslim people. That is the intention of hate crime.

MEASURING HOW HATE HURTS MORE

Hate crimes are qualitatively different from other types of crime because of their broader impacts on communities. The refrain that "Every crime is a hate crime" falls flat when both the terroristic intent and the terrorizing effects of bias-motivated criminality are revealed (Blazak, 2011). Understanding the broader trauma caused by hate-motivated violence is key to framing these acts as having wide-ranging consequences beyond those associated with more traditional criminal acts. This broader impact is one reason state and federal statutes have singled out hate crimes as distinct offenses (Broad & Jenness, 1997). Hate crime laws recognize that the harm done by a racially motivated assault, for example, is greater than the harm done by a non-bias-motivated assault. Harm is extended to nonvictims (Bell & Perry, 2014). Such laws designate penalty enhancements for specific offenses that have a bias motive toward a protected class.

The first attempt to empirically investigate this wider effect of hate crimes was Paul Iganski's 1999 study of hate crime victims in Boston. Iganski identified the more profound and prolonged effects of hate crime victimization. Others (Bell & Perry, 2014; Lim, 2009; Willams & Tregidga, 2014) have further researched community and psychological impacts of hate crime victimization. This study seeks to map out waves of community impact in the wake of one bias-motivated incident, the brutal knife attack on a Portland, Oregon, commuter train in 2017 that left two people dead and one severely injured. While the immediate victims were White men, the attack started as an anti-Muslim, anti-immigrant attack on two teenage girls of color. It was perpetrated by a White man with a history of racial harassment in the city of Portland.

This study utilizes interviews with various populations, including local Muslim and immigrant community members, to chart collective trauma across demographic space and time. The interviews revealed that the 2017 attack brought out the trauma associated with it and emotional memories of a similar attack in 1988 in which racist skinheads murdered an Ethiopian immigrant in Portland.

WAVES OF HATE CRIME TRAUMA

The experience of being a victim of a crime is inherently traumatizing. The body of literature on the long-lasting effects of sexual victimization look at life-long maladies associated with posttraumatic stress disorder (PTSD), including disturbing thoughts, physical distress, attempts to avoid trauma-related cues, depression, and self-harm, including suicide (Kamphius & Emmelkamp, 1998). However, even less grievous offenses can have emotional effects. The understanding now, in the wake of Iganski's pioneering research, is that hate crime victims experience greater stress than the victims of the same crime without a bias motive. However, that effect extends beyond the immediate victim. We can conceptualize six levels of impact that allow us to understand these crimes as acts of terrorism, adding to Iganski's five "waves of harm" created by a hate crime.

For this discussion, we will use the example of being the victim of a violent assault. The first level of impact is on the victim. It should be mentioned that most traditional victims of assault are attacked by someone they know. Bias-motivated assaults are more likely to be committed by attackers not known to the victim. In addition to the physical, emotional, and psychological effects of such assault is the added effect of the bias motive itself. If an individual is attacked because of their race, religion, sexual orientation, or other protected status, their perceived sense of vulnerability increases. Because these are immutable categories, victims are now fully aware that they may be attacked again for the same reason. Hate crime victims have been shown to have deeper psychological distress, like depression, over a longer time than similar non-bias-motivated victims (Garcia et al., 1999). In addition, these victims are more likely to change their behavior patterns, including withdrawing from their communities. For example, a woman who is the victim of an anti-lesbian assault may focus on her vulnerability to future homophobic violence and decide to be less visible as a lesbian.

The second level of impact is within the victim's target communities. Since hate crimes are message crimes, victims are more likely to be randomly selected. A hatemonger wishing to strike out against African Americans in general, for example, is likely to find a suitable target when the opportunity presents itself. Any Black person serves the purpose of terrorizing the group as a whole. Therefore, other members of the Black community experience distress and heightened anxiety. After the September 11, 2001, attacks, hate crimes against Arabs and Muslims skyrocketed over the following months. Muslims across the United States feared that their family members or community members would become victims (Perry, 2003).

Gay bashings have been shown to impact local communities as a whole, including increasing anxiety in the local gay community and decreasing involvement in gay community activities after attacks (Bell & Perry, 2015). Iganski divides this level into two separate waves, the targeted community living in the neighborhood of the crime and that community living outside of the neighborhood, highlighting the importance of proximity to trauma and perceived vulnerability.

The third level is the impact among other marginalized communities. Since hate criminals often misidentify their targets, there is a wider impact field. The targets of anti-Muslim and anti-Arab hate crimes are often neither. For example, Sikhs are often the victims of anti-Muslim animus and are killed as part of the acts motivated by Islamophobic hate mongers. In 2012 a White supremacist attacked a Sikh temple in Wisconsin, killing six worshipers. The surviving victims widely believed that the shooter mistook them for Muslims (Yaccino et al., 2012). In addition, the occurrence of a bias-motivated attack is a "reminder" that violent hate "still occurs in this day and age," which, for marginalized groups who have a history of victimization, brings historical trauma back to the surface. The anxiety over "who will be the next victim" spreads across groups. An anti-lesbian attack has a psychological impact on the transgender community. An anti-Somali attack creates waves of fear among Ethiopian immigrants, the larger East African community, and even larger communities of African immigrants and African Americans.

Hate crimes can also impact the broader community outside of targeted groups. Tensions can increase as residents feel forced to choose sides on divisive issues. Levin and McDevitt (1993) have written about how distrust among community members can increase when a hate crime occurs, and the fabric of neighborhoods can be damaged. They highlight racial crimes in New York neighborhoods like Bensonhurst (1989) and Crown Heights (1991). Tensions between local groups, for example Blacks and Jews, can spill over into other violence and even riots. Levin and McDevitt write:

> one of the most difficult issues for victims of hate crimes is wondering how widespread the bigotry is. How many other people on the block want them to leave the neighborhood? . . . Victims often want to believe that the hate crime against them was the deviant behavior of a few "screwed up kids," a small number of bigots, but they also fear that these actions reflect the sentiments of the masses. (Levin & McDevitt, 1993, p. 220)

This ties into Ignaski's fifth wave, representing the impact of hate crimes on societal norms and values. His research in Boston found that respondents felt that bias-related crimes offended a collective moral code, stating, "It polarizes communities, it pulls us apart" (Iganski, 2001, p. 134).

Finally, the place where the hate crime happened can become stigmatized by the crime itself. It is hard to mention Laramie, Wyoming, or Jasper, Texas, without considering the 1998 murders of Matthew Shepard or James Byrd, Jr. Before 2018, the Squirrel Hill suburb in Pittsburgh, Pennsylvania, was best known as the actual neighborhood of TV's Mr. Rogers. Now it is synonymous with the violent anti-Semitic attack on the Temple of Life synagogue that left eleven Jewish worshipers dead. From Charleston to Charlottesville, place names become tagged as the places of hate, despite all the positive characteristics they may hold. Portland, Oregon, is linked with the brutal hate crimes that occurred there in 1988 and 2017.

RESEARCH ON TRAUMA AND CRIME

There is a vast body of research on the traumatic impacts of crime victimization, ranging from the psychological effects of terrorism (Frederick, 1987) to bank robberies (Kamphuis & Emmelkamp, 1998). The bulk of this research has been on the effects of sexual violence on victims, linking findings to the physical, emotional, and cognitive disruptions to the experiences of returning veterans under the broad diagnosis of PTSD.

The pioneering work of trauma and sexual victimization was by Ann Burgess and Lynda Lytle Holmstrom in 1974. Burgess and Holmstrom followed and interviewed 146 rape victims admitted to an emergency room (Burgess & Holmstrom, 1974). They utilized victim experiences to develop rape trauma syndrome (RTS) diagnosis that observed rape survivors move through three stages of recovery. First, the acute stage occurs in the days and weeks after the assault and is characterized by numerous behavioral impacts, including diminished alertness and paralyzing anxiety. Second, the outward adjustment stage occurs when the survivor attempts to resume a normal lifestyle but exhibits maladaptive coping mechanisms, including moving to a new city and the development of phobias. Finally, in the renormalization stage, survivors begin to integrate the assault into their lives instead of it being the primary focus of their lives. Subsequent research has reinforced the initial findings on the effects of RTS, including on male victims of sexual assaults (Tewksbury, 2007).

Research on sexual violence trauma has included exploring the secondary effects on others, including on sexual assault trauma counselors and other mental health professionals (Campbell & Raja, 1999; Ghahramanlou

& Brodbeck, 2000). Secondary traumatization has also been documented among the wives and children of veterans suffering from PTSD (Dinshtein et al., 2011; Waysman et al., 1993). The research on secondary trauma has paved the way for the Secondary Trauma Self-Efficacy (STSE) Scale that allows individuals who deal with others experiencing trauma, like first responders, to measure their ability to cope with the ripple effects of traumatic events. This work will be useful in addressing the trauma-related needs of nonvictims of hate crimes.

The general understanding of trauma is that it occurs in response to an acute event that overwhelms the individual's capacity to manage the experience, such as rape or exposure to the violence of war. However, trauma has also been linked to chronic conditions, including poverty and racism. The intergenerational trauma of racism was uncovered by the research in Joy DeGruy's critical text, *Post* Traumatic Slave Syndrome (2017). DeGruy outlines the psychological and behavioral impacts of the legacy of dehumanizing African Americans, including "vacant esteem," "ever-present anger," and racist socialization, in which negative societal attitudes toward Blackness become internalized. Society presents numerous triggers, according to DeGruy, which bring maladaptive coping strategies to the surface.

Understanding the impact of chronic trauma helps to frame the impact of hate crimes on communities who are already traumatized by social circumstances, including previous acute trauma, for example, among refugees from war zones, as well as from the experience of chronic trauma, including from poverty (Collins et al., 2010) and racism (DeGruy, 2017). In addition, research has shown that those most likely to suffer from PTSD have experienced earlier trauma (Regeher et al., 2007).

The research on bias crime victims has found elevated trauma among crime targets. McDevitt and colleagues' 2001 study surveyed bias-motivated assault victims in Boston and a random sample of non-bias-assault victims in the city. They found that, on all measures, bias crime victims suffered more psychological distress than the control group, including being more nervous, more depressed, and having more trouble not thinking about the attack (McDevitt et al., 2001). Focused studies have also identified secondary trauma among nonvictims of hate crimes. For example, Lim's 2009 study of the Asian American community found that anti-Asian attacks made the larger community feel more unsafe and negatively impacted relations with other communities (Lim, 2009). Bell and Perry's 2009 study of the impact of hate crimes on the lesbian, gay, and bisexual (LGB, no transgender people participated in the study) community found similar secondary trauma. They utilized focus group research to gauge the effects of bias-motivated violence within a community. They found similar psychological effects, including depression, anxiety, pain, anger, and feelings of low self-worth, as well as behavior changes, like dressing differently to conceal their sexual orientation better. In addition, Bell and Perry found that some LGB community members engaged in victim-blaming to distance themselves from the crime as a way to manage their fear (Bell & Perry, 2014).

THE PORTLAND MAX ATTACK

By the early 1990s, Portland, Oregon, had earned the nickname "Skinhead City." The tag referred not only to the running battles between racist skinheads and anti-racist skinheads (also known as SHARPs, Skinheads Against Racial Prejudice) but for a violent crime in which members of a racist skinhead gang known as East Side White Pride murdered an Ethiopian immigrant named Mulugeta Seraw. Seraw was attacked by bat-wielding skinheads the night of November 12, 1988. His murder drew national attention to Portland. Furthermore, the subsequent 1990 civil trial against the White Aryan Resistance for instigating the attack extended the media attention on the city. In the late 1990s, Portland became the headquarters of an international skinhead organization known as Volksfront. Vollsfront skinheads were convicted of a 2003 murder in Tacoma, Washington.

On May 26, 2017, memories of the Seraw killing were rekindled when a self-avowed White Nationalist named Jeremy Christian instigated a violent attack on a Portland commuter train. That spring Christian had appeared at an alt-right rally, shouting "Die Muslims!" while wrapped in an American flag and giving a Nazi salute. He had also made anti-Semitic posts on his Facebook page as well as praise for the Oklahoma City bomber, Timothy McVeigh. In the days leading up to the attack, Christian had been harassing minorities on Portland's commuter train, the Max, including throwing a bottle at a Black woman.

On the Friday afternoon of May 26, as commuters were heading home, Christian boarded a crowded Max train and immediately noticed two African American teenage girls, one wearing a Muslim hijab. He began screaming at them, repeating "Muslims should die" and "Get out of my country," along with other racist taunts. Three male commuters attempted to get Christian to calm down while the girls moved to the other end of the train car. Instead, Christian drew a knife and stabbed all three in the neck, killing Ricky Best, 53, Taliesin Namkai-Meche, 23, and gravely injuring Micah Fletcher, 21. Best died on the platform of the Hollywood Max station, as Christian escaped into a nearby neighborhood. Namkai-Meche and Fletcher were transported to a nearby hospital, where Namkai-Meche succumbed to his injuries. Portland Police quickly arrested Christian, who had been pursued by passengers on the train, allegedly saying upon his apprehension, "I just stabbed a bunch of motherfuckers in the neck . . . I can die in prison a happy man."

The Hollywood Max station where the attack unfolded quickly became a crime scene and then a gathering place for mourners. The station was soon enveloped in flowers, candles, and scrawled messages protesting hate and celebrating the three men who stood up to hate. Within a few days, the station's walls were covered entirely with colorful graffiti, including "Remember Mulugeta Seraw," marking the brutal 1988 murder of an Ethiopian student by racist skinheads, which occurred very near the Max station. "Tell everyone on this train that I love them," the last words of Namkai-Meche as he lay bleeding to death on the train, were also written on the walls. Two days after the attack, residents of the neighborhood held a vigil at the station. The assembled gathering included many members of the local Muslim community, Portland's mayor, a city commissioner, and U.S. Senator Jeff Merkley.

The May 26, 2017, attack placed Portland firmly in the global news cycle. The city had earned a reputation as a liberal stronghold, characterized by the TV show *Portlandia*, not a haven of hate-motivated violence. So the world's media descended on the city, trying to understand "how this could happen in Portland." Many residents knew of the dark history of the region's racism which included the 1988 Seraw murder and the dominance of the Ku Klux Klan in the state in the 1920s. For many (mostly White) residents, the attack was shocking. However, for many people of color, the triple stabbing was part of a wider pattern of traumatic events that have marginalized minority communities, from police profiling to gentrifica-tion patterns that have pushed ethnic minorities out of the city.

In the weeks and months that followed the attack, a discussion emerged of the "two Portlands," the white liberal "Portlandia," and a version of the city experienced by People of Color. TriMet, the public agency that operates the Max train lines, decided to commemorate the community response to the attack by selecting a local Egyptian American artist to transform the station into a permanent marker of the crime and subse-quent healing process. Sarah Farahat completed a massive mural in time for the event's first anniversary in 2018, coinciding with a series of public workshops on hate crimes.

METHODOLOGY

The purpose of this project is to understand the waves of effects of hate crime as outlined in Ignaski's original research article, "Hate Crimes Hurt More." This research was conducted with various communities that could be impacted by an attack motivated by anti-Muslim animus. The five communities in this study are local Muslims, local Ethiopians, local first-generation (Latinx) immigrants, local People of Color, and the larger White Portland community. Christian's tirade on the Portland commuter train was targeted at the two girls based on his perception of them as Muslims and immigrants. Therefore, members of the local Ethiopian community, who are mostly Christian, were included in the interviews because of the temporal trauma linking that group to the 1988 Seraw murder.

Because there was a risk that discussing the triple stabbings may be (re) traumatizing to the interview participants, subjects were informed that they could end the interview at any time and that self-care was encouraged. Additionally, the interviewer informed the subjects of the availability of psychological support resources if needed. Finally, all subjects were informed that their information would be kept confidential, and recordings and emails would be deleted.

The interviews took place in coffee shops, community centers, police precinct meeting rooms, and local mosques. In addition, some interviews had email follow-ups to clarify responses. Interviews were conducted as guided conversations and focused on five questions:

1. How did you perceive the climate of racial and religious tolerance in Portland before the 2017 Max attack?
2. How did you first hear about the attack?
3. What was your initial reaction to the attack?
4. Did the attack have any impact on you? This includes emotional or behavioral impacts.
5. How do you feel about the future of tolerance in Portland?

Two test interviews were conducted to assess the logical order of the question and informal prompts to guide conversations to research themes. Most interviews were recorded on a voice app on the researcher's cellphone and transcribed, and then deleted. The transcriptions were then analyzed for common themes and patterns.

FINDINGS

A total of 25 residents of Portland were interviewed for this project, five from each subpopulation. While it might be expected that those closest to the victims of the crime (local Muslims and immigrants) would have been less forthcoming in reactions due to trauma associated with the attack, the opposite was true. Those interviewees saw the conversations as an opportunity to share at length what they felt was not appropriate to discuss outside of their communities. However, White residents were more reserved in their comments, reflecting the passing noteworthy nature of the attack. The interviews with minority residents tended to last well beyond the allotted time, including several that were happy to spend two hours addressing the questions, while interviews with White residents tended to be brief and follow a straight "Q & A" format.

The first question asked about the perception of race relations in the city before the 2017 attack. Minority residents generally sensed an escalation in tensions following the 2016 election of Donald Trump.

> My tension had been up since the Muslim ban (January 27, 2017). People are pretty progressive here in Portland, but you could just feel a shift. I felt plenty of support, but I was also getting more second looks at my scarf. It might have been people showing concern for me, but some of it felt hostile. Like here we go again. (Muslim respondent)

> It's always hard in America. Things seemed better before the election, and then they seemed worse with all the "Build a Wall" talk. But just the usual assumption that you're not here legally. There's always a low-grade bias. (Latinx respondent)

> You know, it just seemed like Portlandia as usual. Hipsters shopping at New Seasons and complaining about traffic. (White respondent)

Respondents generally heard about the attack through social media, but minority residents were more likely to be contacted directly about the attack from a family member or fellow community member.

> I got a text that afternoon from my brother, who told me to be careful. I was supposed to take the Max home, but I asked him to come and get me from work. (Muslim respondent)

I saw it on the news that night. At first, I was confused about what actually happened, but when they showed the pictures of the guy who did it wrapped in an American flag and sieg heiling, I knew exactly what happened. I started getting a million texts about what should we (local Muslims) do. I had no idea. I think I was in shock. (Muslim respondent)

Someone posted something on my Facebook page about it. I immediately got a sick feeling in my stomach. (Ethiopian respondent)

Initial responses from minority respondents immediately went into a "things have changed for us" narrative for the most part.

It burst my "Muslim bubble." Suddenly I felt like we were under attack. Of course, I felt sorrow for the men who were killed. They are heroes and will be blessed by Allah. But I just felt that things were different now. I think it was like how most Americans felt after 9/11. That nobody was safe. (Muslim respondent)

Then when the attack happened, and word got out that it was two Muslim girls who were the target, I wanted to throw up. It felt like this was the beginning of the end of religious freedom in America. Nazis were now ready to kill to push us out of the country. I was sad for the girls and the men. I was just sad that this was our world now. (Muslim respondent)

It was just a flashback to "skinhead city" [a nickname for Portland after the 1988 murder of Mulugeta Seraw]. Like we're never going to get out of this ugly place. It was a big reminder that this city is not a safe place if you're not white. (African American respondent)

I couldn't believe it. I mean, in the middle of the afternoon? I ride that train, too. There's always homeless people on it. I guess no one is safe. (White respondent)

The most voluminous responses regarded changes following the attack.
For minority respondents, especially Muslims and Ethiopians, these were
deeply emotional but also rational in terms of recognizing the need to
reevaluate personal safety strategies.

> I stopped riding the Max and busses for almost a year. I was just
> asking everyone for rides. I couldn't even think about being on the
> train. This guy wasn't the only one like that. I seriously thought about
> not wearing my hijab anymore. I think I just stayed in and watched
> more TV. Again, some folks were really nice but my faith was now
> an issue. I was depressed and cried some, especially when it was on
> the news. The one-year anniversary felt like it was one day. It's al-
> ways been hard to be a Muslim in Portland, but Trump and then the
> murders just has added this huge weight. My religion is just a small
> part of me but now it seems like it's been made all of me. I'm nothing
> else. Just a Muslim. (Muslim respondent)

> I just think it was an emotional change. Before we were like, oh, we're
> in Portland, everything is fine here. Other parts of the country are
> dangerous but not here. I know we had skinheads and stuff in the
> past but now it was just "Portlandia," you know? So I stopped as-
> suming I was safe. I started looking for people harassing Muslim sis-
> ters. I guess you could say I started taking a more defensive position.
> I always had my phone handy in case I had to record an attack or
> something. The Max thing is never far from my mind. Even if I just
> see a TriMet bus. There's a part of me wondering if there is a racist on
> it harassing somebody. (Muslim respondent)

> Withdrawal. That was the word. I think it helped tighten the
> Ethiopian community, but there was this feeling of just withdrawing
> from Portland in general. It felt like we had gone back in time. At least
> back then you sort of knew who the skinheads were. Now it could be
> anybody. I guess that means it is even worse. Yeah, it was really hard.
> It is really hard. Portland is not safe. (Ethiopian respondent)

I think I was done riding Trimet. I also wanted to stay out of downtown. It felt like there was just a cloud over all brown people. I wondered if those White men would have stood up for me. I think it was just a general depression. (Latinx respondent)

I really want to trust people and assume the best, but, God, how many reminders do I need that this city is racist at its core. Another police shooting? Another racist stabbing people? Another Nazi march? It made me rethink living here, and if I had a chance to move, I would. I give up on Portland. But while I'm here, I've got eyes in the back of my head just in case. (African American resident)

I went to the one-year anniversary memorial at the station and cried a lot. I knew Ricky [Best, one of the victims]. He worked in the floor below me. I think about him a lot. You have to carry on, but I think it changed the city. (White respondent)

The final question addressed the prospects for the future of tolerance in the city of Portland. White respondents seemed more optimistic for the hope of racial reconciliation, while minorities interviewed seemed to link the attack to the current political climate as evidence of a backward slide from true social equity. Muslims in the sample were increasingly resigned to the level of social terror being the new normal.

There's not much reason for hope. Maybe I'm just tired of telling people what Islam is not. My social media life is constant battle. I keep trying to tell people that we're not terrorists. That they don't understand Sharia (law). I probably go looking for the fight. I wasn't like that before. (Muslim respondent)

This city loves to fly the diversity flag, but we're really just so they can claim "inclusion." We're not going anywhere, but I'm spending my energy these days on my own community. (Muslim respondent)

We're still committed to building bridges, but things are very polarized right now. White people have to step up. They are probably more willing to do the work in Portland than other cities, but it still falls on us, and it's tiring. How many of these horrible things have to happen before they will admit that White Supremacy is still a problem? (Ethiopian respondent)

Our community is strong, and Portland cares about inclusion. I worry about the country. I feel pretty shielded here, but if I need to travel to some other areas, and I'm not talking about Alabama, I mean southern Oregon, I think I need to be overly careful. This country is so divided, and it feels like half of it wants to kill me and my family. (Latinx respondent)

It's all connected for me; Trump, Jeremy Christian, gentrification, police killing Black people. They've never wanted us here. If it had been three Black men killed on that train, nobody would have said anything. Where was the outrage when they killed Larnell Bruce? [Bruce was a 19-year-old African American who was murdered by a member of the racist European Kindred gang in suburban Portland in 2016.] Black people know what's up in Portland. (African American respondent)

I hope it was a wake-up call for Portland. The city has poured a lot of resources into fighting hate crime. I think it's a pretty safe city, but it's definitely another black mark. But some good seems to be coming from it. Awareness and all that. (White respondent)

ANALYSIS

Local Portland Muslims, those who could be viewed as closest to the 2017 attack, displayed the clearest evidence of secondary trauma. First, there was the psychological distress caused by an elevated level of anxiety, magnified by the current political climate. Respondents repeatedly expressed concern for their children's safety and the perception that "things had changed" after the attack. In addition, there were clear behavior modifications, including more time spent within the Muslim community, for example, in mosques and education centers, and less time in public settings, like mass transit. These changes reflect Levin and McDevitt's (1993) and Lim's (2001) findings concerning the tendency of hate crimes to erode community fabric through the withdrawal into respective ethnic enclaves. Unlike the LGB subjects in Bell and Perry's (2014) study, local Muslims did not engage in victim blaming but showed concern for the place of Muslims within Portland's culture that outwardly claims to celebrate ethnic diversity.

Like those experiencing PTSD, local Muslims expressed a desire to avoid triggers, three mentioning they have stopped watching the news since the attack. Other trauma-related symptoms that emerged in the interviews included nightmares, flashbacks, and fatigue around having to "defend" their religion. I spoke to two interviewees at a vigil in a local mosque after the 2019 Christchurch attack. Both said the murders in New Zealand immediately took them back to their emotional state after the 2017 Max attack.

The Ethiopians interviewed expressed a feeling of depression concerning how little had changed in the city between the 1988 murder of Mulugeta Seraw and the 2017 Max attack. The stabbings were a reminder of their outsider status in a very White state and vulnerability in a city with a long history of harboring White supremacists. The crime magnified the constant otherness they felt as Black immigrants. Similarly, first-generation Latinx immigrants saw the crime as an extension of the widespread support for Donald Trump and xenophobic political narratives. As one Latinx man told me, "I have to always watch my back these days. It could be some Nazi or ICE coming for me. It's all the same." African Americans were more likely to express anger about the attack and a desire to confront racists. This reflects what DeGruy (2017) describes as the ever-present anger associated with Black trauma.

White respondents had a much more sanguine response to the attack. There was an initial shock and sense of sadness that such a crime could happen in "their city" but also a feeling that the incident provided a "wake-up call" and an opportunity for the city to move beyond its dark past. Any trauma experienced seems to be confined to the immediate time period around the stabbings. No White respondents discussed fear of riding mass transit, feelings of increased vulnerability, or any change in behavior whatsoever. Trimet, to honor the victims, stopped all Portland busses and trains for 1 minute the Friday following the attack. I was on board the Green Line near the Hollywood station where the incident unfolded. I noticed minority riders fall silent while most White riders continued to chat and appear unmoved by the moment. The privilege of White Portland residents allowed them to experience the crime as a news event and perhaps a brief opportunity to engage in the underlying issues and then resume life as usual. In contrast, the non-White respondents in this study experienced the attack as an act of terrorism with lingering traumatic effects.

This research not only reinforces the notion of a broader impact field of hate crimes but a more profound impact over time. The metaphor would be the difference between throwing a rock into a pond and throwing a cinderblock into a pond. Not only are the splash and subsequent waves bigger, but the disturbance lasts longer. This was in evidence after Jeremy Christian was sentenced to life in prison on June 24, 2020, for the Portland murders. I checked in with a Muslim community leader about the sentencing, in which Christian had to be removed from the courtroom for making threats to the survivors of his attacks (Green, 2020). "I could not watch it on the television," he told me. "I am hoping for closure, but I feel like the end of this chapter will just lead to another similar chapter." Research on veterans and child abuse victims has found that lifelong trauma impacts cognitive functioning (Van der Kolk, 2015). We can see similar adaptations for hate crime victims and the members of their communities.

LIMITATIONS

The generalizability of these findings faces certain challenges. Aside from the relatively small sample size (25 interviewees), Portland is demographically atypical. According to the 2010 Census, the city is 77.4% White and only 5.7% Black. (For comparison, Birmingham, Alabama, is 71.3% Black and 21.1% White.) It could be argued that the relatively small size of minority groups in Portland would add to feelings of trauma for three reasons. First, the small size of various communities, including Muslims and Latinx immigrant groups, reduces the ability of those communities to provide a healing balance when hate crimes and incidents occur. As a result, minorities in Portland often reflect on feeling "alone" in a White city. Secondly, the small size of minority communities reduces their political capacity to respond to hate crimes and the antecedent conditions that create climates of fear. This disadvantage extends to limited opportunities to recruit non-White officers into municipal police departments. The third observation is the normalization of White perspectives, adding to the othering of non-WASP experiences. To walk through Portland in a minority body is to be constantly reminded of the legacy of White supremacy and cultural marginalization.

Another cautionary aspect of this study is the traumatizing nature of the interviews themselves. While there is no barometer to measure PTSD, many of the respondents were clearly uncomfortable revisiting their thoughts around the 2017 Portland attack. This was most evident when Muslim respondents considered the safety of their children (especially their daughters) after the attack. One Muslim male stopped the interview to choke back the tears before saying, "I'm sorry, I just want my kids to be safe, and I suddenly realized that there's probably no place in the world where they can be. Not even here." This secondary trauma might have been reduced if the interviewer was racially and ethnically matched to the subjects. Instead, the ascriptive characteristics of the interview (White male) may have been an additional source of trauma and effected the responses of the subject.

Future research should explore experiences of post–hate crime trauma in cities with minority-White populations and work to match interviewers and subjects (e.g., Muslim interviewers and Muslim subjects).

THE CHALLENGE OF HEALING FROM HATE

Approaching the second anniversary of the Max train attack, I had the opportunity to sit down with Micah Fletcher, the lone survivor of Jeremy Christian's violent rampage. We met in a Portland coffeehouse and discussed the present tensions in the city between the constantly rallying alt-right and anti-fascist activists. Since Fetcher was quite literally at the center of the crime that has continued to ripple through both demographic space and time, I asked him about how he has fared in the time since the attack.

> It made me kind of extreme. I grew up around a lot of different people, but I'm defensive now. I don't feel safe around homeless people (Christian had been homeless). There are White supremacists all over the country that know my name. I took boxing classes after that. I'm not going to let them do that to me again. I know the odds are completely against it, but why should I take the chance?

The trial of Jeremy Christian began in the summer of 2019, and the Muslim and immigrant communities (and Micah Fletcher himself) discussed an expectation of retraumatization from the media coverage and return to the 2017 attack to the top of the local news cycle. Portland, Oregon, envisions itself as a responsive city and has responded in the wake of this attack. The city formalized support for a local coalition through City Hall called Portland United Against Hate (PUAH) and released $400,000 in community grants for local organizations to build their capacity to respond to and report hate crimes and incidents. The local chapter of the YWCA also sponsored numerous workshops on interrupting hate, empathy, and responding to trauma. Thus, despite the continuation of racial microaggressions, occasional alt-right rallies, hate crimes signaled by swastika drawings, and the rise in anti-Asian bias incidents, Portland is probably better positioned than many cities to respond to the ongoing trauma connected to bias crime.

The waves of hurt outlined by Ignaski's original study were evident in more significant detail among the respondents in this research. This secondary trauma was witnessed beyond the primary target population, Muslim residents, representing the fact that hate crimes can trigger trauma in a wide variety of groups who are the potential targets of hatemongers. It is assumed that if members of the local LGBT, Jewish, or disability communities had been included in the sample of interviewees, similar levels of PTSD symptoms would have been witnessed. These interview data also demonstrate that impacts expand across demographic spaces and across time as members of the Portland Ethiopian community experienced the 2017 attack as a retraumatizing event because of its similarity to the 1988 Portland homicide of an Ethiopian immigrant. In addition, these crimes have served to advertise the unwelcoming violence of the city itself. By understanding these waves of trauma, cities and communities can institute more mindful strategies in response to hate crimes that foster healing instead of extending the hurt.

REFERENCES

Bell, J. G., & Perry, B. (2015). Outside looking in: The community impacts of anti-lesbian, gay, and bisexual hate crime. *Journal of Homosexuality*, 62, 98–215.

Blazak, R. (2011). Isn't every crime a hate crime? The case for hate crime laws. *Sociology Compass*, 4, 244–255.

Broad, K., & Jenness, V. (1997). *Hate crimes: New social movements and the politics of violence*. Routledge.

Burgess, A. W., & Holmström, L. L. (1974). Rape trauma syndrome. *American Journal of Psychiatry*, 131, 982–986.

Campbell, R., & Raja, S. (1999). Secondary victimization of rape victims: Insights from mental health professionals who treat survivors of violence. *Violence and Victims*, 14, 261–275.

Collins. K, Conners, K., Davis, S., Donohue, A., Gardner, S., Goldblatt, E., Hayward, A., Kiser, L., Streider, F., & Thompson, E. (2010). *Understanding the impact of trauma and urban poverty on family systems: Risks, resilience, and interventions*. Family Informed Treatment Center.

DeGruy, J. (2017). *Post traumatic slave syndrome: America's legacy of enduring injury and healing*. Degruy.

Dinshtein, Y., Dekel, R., & Polliack, M. (2011). Secondary traumatization among adult children of PTSD veterans: The role of mother–child relationships. *Journal of Family Social Work, 14*, 109–124.

Frederick, C. J. (1987). Psychic trauma in victims of crime and terrorism. In G. R. VandenBos & B. K. Bryant (Eds.), *Master lectures series. Cataclysms, crises, and catastrophes: Psychology in action*, 55–108. American Psychological Association.

Garcia, L., McDevitt, J., Gu, J., & Balboni, J. (1999). The psychological and behavioral effects of bias and non-bias motivated assault. US Department of Justice, National Institute of Justice.

Ghahramanlou, M., & Brodbeck, C. (2002). Predictors of secondary trauma in sexual assault trauma counselors. *International Journal of Emergency Mental Health, 2*, 229–240.

Green, A. (2020, June 24). Judge sentences MAX train murderer Jeremy Christian to "true life": He should never be released from prison. *The Oregonian*.

Hauser, K. (2019, March 26). Graffiti citing New Zealand attack is found after mosque fire in California. *New York Times*.

Iganski, P. (2001). Hate crimes hurt more. *American Behavioralist, 45*, 627–638.

Kamphuis, J. H., & Emmelkamp, P. (1998). Crime-related trauma: Psychological distress in victims of bank robbery. *Journal of Anxiety Disorders, 12*, 199–208.

Levin, J., & McDevitt, J. (1993). *Hate crimes*. Plenum.

Lim, H. A. (2009). Beyond the immediate victim: Understanding hate crimes as message crimes. In B. Perry & P. Ignaski (Eds.), *Hate crimes: The consequences of hate crime* (pp. 107–222). Praeger.

McDevitt, J., Balboni, L., Garcia, L., & Gu, J. (2001). Consequences for victims: A comparison of bias- and non-bias motivated assaults. *American Behavioral Scientist, 45*, 697–711.

Perry, B. (2003). Anti-Muslim retaliatory violence following the 9/11 terrorist attacks. In B. Perry (Ed.), *Hate and bias crime: A reader* (pp. 183–201). Routledge.

Perry, B. (2014). Exploring the community impacts of hate crime. In N. Hall, A. Corb, P. Giannasi, & J. Grieve (Eds.), *The Routledge international handbook on hate crime* (pp. 47–57). Routledge.

Regehr, C., LeBlanc, V., Jelley, R. B., Barath, I., & Daciuk, J. (2007). Previous trauma exposure and PTSD symptoms as predictors of subjective and biological response to stress. *Canadian Journal of Psychiatry, 52*, 675–683.

Tewksbury, R. (2007). Effects of sexual assaults on men: Physical, mental and sexual consequences. *International Journal of Men's Health, 6*, 22–35.

Van der Kolk, B. (2015). *The body keeps the score: Brain, mind, and body in the healing of trauma*. Penguin.

Waysman, M., Mikulincer, M., Solomon, Z., & Weisenberg, M. (1993). Secondary traumatization among wives of posttraumatic combat veterans: A family typology. *Journal of Family Psychology, 7*, 104–118.

Willams, M. L., & Tregidga, J. (2014). Hate crime victimization in Wales: Psychological and physical impacts across seven hate crime victim types. *The British Journal of Criminology, 54,* 946–967.

Yaccino, S., Schwartz, M., & Santora, M. (2012, August 5). Gunman kills 6 at a Sikh temple near Milwaukee. *New York Times.*

4

Attacking Muslims in North America

An Empirical Analysis of Terrorist Attacks and Plots from 1970 to 2016

BRIAN NUSSBAUM AND ANDREW VITEK■

This chapter looks at a serious problem related to, but in some ways different from, hate crime targeting Muslims and Islamic institutions in North America. While hate crime includes both violent and nonviolent acts and random and planned violence, this chapter narrows the scope of analysis to the planned, organized, and systematically targeted political violence of terrorism aimed at Muslims and Muslim communities. It is mainly focused on attempts at high-intensity violence, attempts to cause multiple or mass casualties, or attempts to wage continuous campaigns of planned violence. Such acts are distinct from many hate crimes, ranging from property damage, intimidation, or spontaneous violence to things that look a lot like terrorism. These distinctions may help to disentangle significant crime characteristics and to identify those traits, such as what threat actors are involved and their motives, and how these differences impact the impact and consequences from these differences.

Brian Nussbaum and Andrew Vitek, *Attacking Muslims in North America* In: *Islamophobia and Acts of Violence*. Edited by: Carolyn Turpin-Petrosino, Oxford University Press. © Oxford University Press 2022. DOI: 10.1093/oso/9780190922313.003.0004

The goal of this analysis is threefold. First, it hopes to lay out an existing empirical case looking at others who have studied terrorist attacks on religious facilities and on Islamic communities and targets within North America to assess a state of the current knowledge of the problem. Second, through analysis of incident-level terrorism data from the Global Terrorism Database (GTD) from 1970 to 2016, it will create a new descriptive empirical case about the nature, and changes, of terrorist targeting of Muslims in North America. Third and most significantly, it will add to these two understandings an analysis of some case studies of foiled plots and successful attacks that provide additional descriptive information about the changing nature of the threat—and threat actors targeting Muslims and Islamic communities in North America. Finally, by using these three sets of data and information, the analysis will attempt to briefly synthesize findings about the nature of anti-Islamic terrorism in North America and critical areas that need further research.

HATE CRIME, TERRORISM, AND POLITICAL VIOLENCE

There is a long history of studying both hate crime and terrorism independently, as well as a long literature linking the two (Hamm, 1998; Ronczkowsk, 2017). Researchers have generally studied terrorism in relation to crime (LaFree & Dugan, 2004) to hate crime in particular (Deloughery et al., 2012). Hate crime and terrorism have been treated so similarly as to require similar investigative techniques (Ronczkowsk, 2017). They have been described as "close cousins" (Krueger & Maleckova, 2003) and treated as part of a spectrum of ideological crime that has included both violent and nonviolent charges (McGarell et al., 2007). The relationship between the two has not been static. Convergence in recent decades is noted. In fact, the convergence between hate crime and domestic terrorism, in the U.S. context, has led them to be called "indistinguishable" (Petrosino, 1999) or that ideologically motivated violence meets "most definitions of terrorism" (McGarell et al., 2007). Both involve political or ideological motives, violence, and attempts to communicate or intimidate an audience in the service of changing social or political relations or arrangements (if only by instilling fear, but more often tied to policy goals).

Domestic terrorism is a widely studied phenomenon (Enders et al., 2011; Sanchez-Cuenca & De La Calle, 2009). There have been waves of domestic terrorism that have been inspired by ideologies of the Left—like anarchist and labor-related terrorism in the early 20th century (Jensen, 2013) as well as revolutionary leftist terrorism like that of the Weather Underground and other violent New Left groups in the 1970s (Varon, 2004). There have also been historical outbreaks of violence and terrorism tied to right-wing politics, like the wave that birthed the violent racist organization the Order (Hewitt, 2000) and many anti-government militias in the 1980s and early 1990s (Michael, 2003). There are questions about the increase in violence and domestic terrorism by groups affiliated with the extreme Right in the United States since 2008 (Piazza, 2017). There has been a move toward studying these issues more empirically in the United States (Piazza, 2017) and Western Europe (Ravndal, 2016).

Scholars have studied this violent domestic political activity in the context of ideologically inspired crime more generally:

The movement has been linked to many crimes that range from acts of domestic terrorism and violent hate crimes to gun charges. Some of these crimes (e.g., the 1995 Oklahoma City bombing) meet most definitions of terrorism. However, other crimes (e.g., non-violent tax refusal cases) do not. It is important to note that it is empirically determined that in the United States, domestic terrorism attacks outnumber international ones 7 to 1. Among domestic groups, far-right-wing groups are especially dangerous (LaFree, Dugan, Fogg, & Scott, 2006). There is also evidence that the number of attacks committed by the far-right has increased with time. Some scholars conclude that far-right extremists, especially groups motivated by religious ideology, are strong candidates to commit future acts using weapons of mass destruction (Gurr & Cole, 2002; Tucker, 2000). It is not surprising that local and state law enforcement agencies have concluded that the domestic far-right poses a major threat to public safety (Carlson 1995; FBI, 1999; Riley, Treverton, Wilson, & Davis, 2005). (McGarell et al., 2007, pp. 147–148)

It is worth noting that while definitional questions remain, these definitions have changed over time. Actors often engage in various types of criminal activity depending on how those phenomena are understood and measured, and hate crime and terrorism definitions are often not mutually exclusive. Some have speculated that hate groups might work in conjunction with traditional criminal groups and influence future trajectories of terrorism (Jensen, 2015). Even the most economically self-interested criminals have engaged in activity that could be described as hate crime or terrorism. For example, during the Boston busing debates of the 1970s, arch-criminal Whitey Bulger engaged in firebombing and arson of a school (Murphy, 2001) to intimidate various audiences, including a local judge who had ruled on the busing controversy. Because of their racial and public policy motivations, these activities would be considered hate crimes and acts of domestic terrorism today. This point suggests that meeting the definition of one type of activity—terrorism, hate crime, bias crime, or others—does not mean an event might not also meet the definition of another category.

TERRORIST TARGETING, RELIGIOUS TARGETS, AND ATTACKS ON ISLAMIC TARGETS

Like terrorism in general, there is an extensive and well-regarded literature on terrorist targeting (Brandt & Sandler, 2010; Hoffman, 1993; Libicki et al., 2007). From choosing particular sectors, like aviation (Crenshaw, 1988) or transportation (Jenkins, 2004), to the selection of soft targets (Asal et al., 2009) or critical infrastructure—there has been much time spent analyzing how and why terrorists select the targets they do. Focus on rational choice models of understanding terrorists are common (Gruenewald et al., 2015; Newman & Hsu, 2012). However, there are many variations on the theme, including analysis of the symbolic nature of targets, familiarity with the targets (Becker, 2014), and the role of the perpetrators' unique characteristics influencing target selection (Hemmingby & Bjørgo, 2015).

Whether targets are selected for rational reasons, convenience or location, or because of personal idiosyncrasies of the targeter, many studies suggest that symbolic issues and issues tied to ideology play an important (if not always definitive) role (Asal et al., 2009; Drake, 1998). This means that the selection of religious institutions for terrorist targets often has communicative insight into the attackers' thinking and goals. However, there is limited literature looking at the targeting of religious institutions in terrorist attacks. Here the literature overlaps with the religious hate crime targeting literature as well.

When it comes to the targeting of Muslims and Islamic religious facilities, the terrorism literature is relatively sparse. Hate crime literature has more to offer (Kaplan, 2006; Welch, 2006) but is still underdeveloped. Moreover, what literature does exist is often localized (Copsey et al., 2013; Githens-Mazer & Lambert, 2010), very time-bound to particular periods like the post–September 11th era (Kaplan, 2006; Welch, 2006), or less systematic than would be ideal.

THE EXISTING EMPIRICAL CASE

There are, however, some good empirical insights into the targeting of religious institutions (START, 2018) and the targeting of Muslims in hate crimes in the United States (Kishi, 2017). However, these have not yet been fully ingested and inculcated—theoretically speaking—into the scholarly literature of terrorism or terrorism target selection. The collection and analysis of some of this data were event-driven.

Following the 27 October, 2018 shooting at a Jewish Synagogue in Pittsburgh, Pennsylvania, START researchers compiled background information, from the United States Extremist Crime Database (ECDB) on ideologically motivated fatal far-right violence in the United States, generally, and far-right extremist homicides and plots related to religion and religious institutions, specifically. (START, 2018)

The data suggest that while members of the extreme right who commit ideologically motivated homicides (which is not the same as terrorism or hate crime per se, but with some similarities) have done so more often for "White supremacist" reasons than religious ones (START, 2018). While most religious targeting in this dataset was focused upon Jewish institutions or individuals, there were several attacks on Islamic targets. Additionally, and importantly for illustrating that successful plots are not the only way to measure the threat of violence against a group or set of targets, there were also many foiled plots.

> From 1990 to 2014, there were approximately 15 ideologically motivated plots against Muslim individuals or Islamic targets by far-right extremists or groups of far-right extremists. In nearly 75 percent of those plots, the far-right extremists had identified a specific individual or location to attack. Law enforcement foiled more than 85 percent of these anti-Islamic plots. (START, 2018)

In the world of hate crime data, which is notoriously challenging, there is evidence of growing and consistent targeting of Muslims and Islamic symbols. For example, in 2017, Pew issued a piece entitled "Assaults against Muslims in the U.S. surpass 2001 level" that detailed increased levels of violence targeting Muslims in the United States. These data are not to be confused with general hate crime data, which often conflate nonviolent crimes like graffiti and property damage with violent hate crimes. Instead, the Pew data show an increase in actual attacks on Muslims in the United States.

Pew reports: "In 2016, there were 127 reported victims of aggravated or simple assault, compared with 91 the year before and 93 in 2001" (Kishi, 2017). While this is a substantial change, what is unclear about this change over the previous decade is the nature of anti-Islamic violence. Between

2002 and 2010, there were 358 assaults on Muslims, an average of about 40 per year. Between 2010 and 2016, there were 505 such assaults, or an average of about 72 a year (Kishi, 2017). That is almost a doubling of anti-Islamic violence. (Note: Even if you add in the attacks from 2001, an outlier year in which there were 93 assaults on American Muslims where the increase is often attributed to the presence of the September 11, 2001, attacks, the average number of these assaults for the first decade of the 21st century was still only 45 per year, only 63% of the 72 average in the following decade.)

Assault is not the only kind of hate crime American Muslims face. To better catalog the scope of the problem, Pew also documented more traditional hate crime activity and how it has risen. According to Pew:

> There were 307 incidents of anti-Muslim hate crimes in 2016, marking a 19% increase from the previous year. This rise in hate crime builds on an even sharper increase the year before, when the total number of anti-Muslim incidents rose 67%, from 154 in 2014 to 257 in 2015. (Kishi, 2017)

These data suggest that violence against Muslims—both attempted plots that have failed or foiled, as well as actual violence that is occurring—is a serious and growing threat. Thus, there is clear empirical evidence that there has existed some threat to American Muslims and their religious and cultural institutions over time. Moreover, there is some compelling evidence that this threat is growing. Combining attack and incident data and analysis of failed or foiled plots enable the rigorous analysis of a real and growing problem.

UPDATING THE EMPIRICAL UNDERSTANDING OF ANTI-ISLAMIC TERRORISM IN NORTH AMERICA

One essential purpose of this chapter's analysis is to supplement and broaden the existing empirical picture of terrorism targeting Islamic communities and targets in North America.

While the term "North America" is used throughout our writing, and it is how data were sought and sorted, historically, this is a predominantly American phenomenon. There are several events recorded in the GTD that took place in Canada. More importantly, evidence might suggest that this, too, is changing. For example, the January 2017 mass shooting at the Islamic Cultural Center of Quebec City that killed six and injured more than a dozen fits within the "high-intensity" nature of more recent anti-Islamic violence. The intent is to combine quantitative event data from the Global Terrorism Database and qualitative data from foiled, disrupted, or other recent plots to better understand the phenomenon and note how it is changing and what trajectories it might follow.

GLOBAL TERRORISM DATABASE—DATA DESCRIPTION AND INCIDENT SELECTION

The data presented here are drawn from the GTD, developed and maintained by The National Consortium for the Study of Terrorism and Responses to Terrorism or START. The GTD is an open-source database that includes comprehensive data on domestic and transnational terrorism events dating back to 1970. A range of data is collected for each distinct incident, namely "the date and location of the incident, the weapons used and nature of the target, the number of casualties, and—when identifi-able—the group or individual responsible" (START, 2018). These data are drawn from a range of open-source and publicly available sources, such as news and media reports, books and journals, and outstanding and existing databases, as well as court filings and other legal documents. To date, the GTD has coded over 180,000 distinct events based on over 4 million documents and is made freely available to both analysts and researchers.

Regarding the inclusion criteria for events, the GTD sets several parameters. To merit inclusion, an event must first be characterized as "an intentional act of violence or threat of violence by a non-state actor." In addition to this, two of the following three criteria must be met: "(1) The violent act was aimed at attaining a political, economic, religious, or social goal; (2) The violent act included evidence of an intention to coerce, intimidate, or convey some other message to a larger audience (or audiences) other than the immediate victims; and (3) The violent act was outside the precepts of International Humanitarian Law" (START, 2018). Additional information addressing collection, coding, and integration of prior versions of the data is found on the GTD website. While the GTD captures data on dozens of event-level variables, the analysis presented here is primarily concerned with the target of the attack, the perpetrator of the attack, weapons used, and the overall distribution of attacks within the given timescale.

GLOBAL TERRORISM DATABASE—INSIGHTS INTO THE NATURE OF NORTH AMERICAN TERRORISM AGAINST ISLAMIC TARGETS

The GTD has recorded 50 attacks against Islamic targets from 1970 to 2016 in North America. Four of the 50 were in Canada, with the remaining 46 taking place in the United States. These attacks primarily focused on places of worship, community facilities (such as cultural centers and schools), and a few targeted individuals.

These 50 attacks were found by searching for incidents where the target or targets included relevant terms like "mosque," "masjid," "Islamic center," "Islamic school," "imam," "cleric," and several others. They were checked and expanded to include targets like museums, cultural centers, community centers, and the like that were focused on Islam or Islamic communities. In a few cases, the targets were prominent individuals in local Muslim communities or otherwise tied to Islamic institutions. In this sense, it took a relatively broad perspective on what was considered an "Islamic" target.

These attacks have been overwhelmingly concentrated within the past 6 years. For example, the yearly average number of anti-Islamic attacks from 1970 to 2010 came in at 0.425, while the 2010–2016 period experienced a tenfold increase with a yearly average of 4.85 anti-Islamic attacks. Conducting the same analysis, of average attacks per year, by decade shows the same pattern—an average of less than one attack per year on average until the past decade. Thus, there has been a rapid and very recent increase in terrorist attacks targeting Muslims in North America. Between 1970 and 2010, only 11 years of the total 40 experienced any anti-Islamic attacks at all, and only 4 years (1982, 1983, 1990, and 1994) had more than one attack. Furthermore, this period was marked by significant stretches where no attacks occurred, the longest of which was 9 years (1995–2004). This distinguishes between the definitions and operationalizations of hate crimes and terrorism. In the period immediately after the September 11 attacks of 2001, there was an increase in anti-Muslim hate crime in the United States However, there does not seem to have been a similar spike in terrorist events.

These data indicate that anti-Islamic terror attacks are largely a recent phenomenon. Additionally, these data cast doubt on the hypothesis that anti-Islamic violence is purely reactionary, coming in response to attacks by jihadist organizations. The immediate years following the September 11 attacks of 2001 did not produce a single instance of anti-Islamic terrorism (again, as opposed to hate crimes). These attacks are also characterized by a significant degree of geographic clustering, with 21 of the 33 attacks in the post-2010 period occurring in only three states and upward of 20% of the total attacks were in New York City alone.

Concerning targeting trends, the overwhelming majority of anti-Islamic terror attacks have targeted Mosques/places of Islamic worship (35 attacks) or Islamic-affiliated institutions (10 attacks)—such as the 2016 attack on the College Preparatory School of America, an Islamic school in Lombard, Illinois. However, the GTD data record only five attacks that targeted private citizens or property, of which only two occurred at personal residences while the remaining three took place in public. These trends illustrate the perceived linkages between jihadist terrorism and Islamic places of worship on the part of the perpetrators of anti-Islamic terrorism, which helps to characterize these attacks as, in some way, retaliatory. It must be noted, however, while existing analysis has established cases of terrorist organizations using Mosques or Islamic schools (madrasas), these actions were almost exclusively outside North America and predominantly in active conflict zones or ungoverned spaces (Blanchard, 2007).

The perpetrators of these attacks share a key characteristic worth noting: out of 50 anti-Islamic attacks recorded, only seven featured any claim of responsibility, with the overwhelming majority of attacks being unattributed. Furthermore, the only attribution recorded in the data stems from individuals; no organization or group has claimed responsibility for an anti-Islamic terrorist attack in this data. That is, historically, terrorist attacks on Islamic targets in North America have tended to be conducted by individuals and small groups without larger institutional affiliations—something that may be changing. Consequently, any meaningful analysis of the demographic or personal characteristics of the perpetrators of anti-Islamic terrorism is highly problematic. In many ways, we simply do not know who they are. Thus, while a degree of extrapolation can be made via data on the perpetrators of anti-Islamic hate crimes, the lack of data in this regard represents a severe limitation in building a reliable analysis of anti-Islamic terrorism.

This trend of nonattribution suggests that the character of the anti-Islamic attacks observed in this period is distinct from the greater body of terrorist activity. Terrorism is sometimes understood as a signaling process between the terrorist organizations themselves and governments and requires attribution, so governments obtain a clearer understanding of what the signals represent. These trends suggest that anti-Islamic terrorism is less concerned with signaling the state to produce policy changes and more with terrorizing or punishing what they see as factions representing transnational Islamic terrorist organizations or Islamic culture in general. This hypothesis is further supported when taken in conjunction with the targeting trends described earlier, as these attacks are not only unattributed but also overwhelmingly target Islamic cultural touchstones such as mosques and educational centers. Additionally, the rare instances of attribution present in the data often featured language associating the victims with the activities of transnational Islamic groups, such as the assailant in Toronto referring to his victim as a "terrorist" in 2015, or an attacker in New York shouting "ISIS, ISIS" at their victim in 2016.

The types of weaponry used in these attacks are mainly consistent with the trends described earlier. The overwhelming majority of recorded attacks (39 of 50) utilized either incendiary or explosive devices, usually crude homemade fire or pipe bombs (in a 2012 incident, the devices simply fizzled out before igniting), and in rarer cases, arson via chemical accelerants. Only six attacks recorded the use of firearms, with the remaining five cases featuring unarmed attackers, the use of knives, or no data on weapons were available. In most cases, devices were simply thrown through the windows or onto the roofs of target buildings or simply placed outside or adjacent to them. Even most of the comparatively rare firearm attacks saw assailants open fire from the exterior rather than inside targeted buildings. Such occurrences are consistent with the earlier hypothesis that attacks of this nature are primarily aimed at terrorizing or punishing domestic Islamic populations rather than coercing policy concessions from any level of government.

PLOTS AND FOILED PLOTS AS ADDITIONAL DATA POINTS FOR CONSIDERATION

While the GTD contains arguably the best terrorist event data available, it is worth noting that there are events that would not be included in its database. Nevertheless, these nonincluded events may offer important insights into the targeting, tactical choices, and other characteristics of terrorism in general—and those plots targeting Islamic sites and communities in particular. So, for example, plots foiled in their early stages will typically not be included in terrorist event datasets because the terrorist attack that qualifies an event never happened. In this regard, some recent events offer additional data points to understand better target selection, tactical choice, or attacker type. However, these incidents also offer some insight into the potential scale of attempted violence undertaken to target Muslims in North America. In addition to foiled plots, some of the more granular details of recent plots offer additional information that could inform threat assessment and appraisals of the goals and decision-making of anti-Islamic threat actors.

While attacks against Islamic targets remain fewer in number than those aimed at Jewish ones, and that motives for both include White supremacy or even jihadist ideology, the fact that there are fewer anti-Islamic attacks is less important than that such attacks seem to be increasing in numbers and intensity. The GTD data clearly depict growth in the numbers over time. A combination of the GTD data and analysis of foiled plots suggests that there are also more attempts at more spectacular violence and attempts to create, at least in some cases, mass casualties. While tactics—the use of explosives and firearms—seem common between foiled or disrupted plots and those carried out in the GTD data, some plots suggest things that might not be clear from the GTD data. In a bizarre case in upstate New York, perpetrators attempted a mass-casualty attack on a Somali community in Kansas by using radiation as a weapon. In their targeting of Muslim communities in Kansas and Indiana, these self-styled militias display plans to achieve better organized and deadlier attacks.

These self-styled militias represent a different model than what is often termed "lone wolf" or "leaderless" resistance plotting commonplace in White supremacist and related movements. The upstate New York case also had organizational connections beyond the individuals, if largely imagined ones—the plotters included a self-proclaimed member of the Klu Klux Klan. They believed they were receiving funding from the Klan (DoJ, 2015). These tactical and organizational differences suggest a more serious story than the mere growth in the number of attacks, but rather that at least some of the attacks and plots have grown in the potential intensity of violence, aims, or actor capabilities.

The purpose of these case descriptions is not to provide a broad empirical survey of the tactics and targeting of Islamic communities in North America—that is better done with the GTD data. Instead, the purpose of these mini case studies is to illustrate some unique and changing dynamics, some distinctions from hate crimes and other less organized violence, and—importantly—to point out the complexity and context from which a distinct anti-Islamic terrorism milieu has arisen.

THE UPSTATE NEW YORK RADIATION DEVICE CASE

In a bizarre case in 2013, two men were arrested in upstate New York for a plot that involved creating "a radiation particle weapon" (R.T., 2013). The weapon, designed by plotter Glendon Scott Crawford—an industrial at General Electric—was designed to be "placed in the back of a van to covertly emit ionizing radiation strong enough to bring about radiation sickness or death against Crawford's enemies" (R.T., 2013). The Department of Justice described the unusual device as "an industrial-grade radiation device intended to be used to kill Muslims in the Albany, New York area" (DoJ, 2015). Oddly, given his self-professed allegiance to the KKK (DoJ, 2015), Crawford approached several upstate New York synagogues to discuss the potential use of the weapon against Muslim communities, which he described as "Israel's enemies" (R.T., 2013). Regarding the sentencing of the other plotter, Eric Feight, in 2015, Assistant Attorney General John Carlin said that he "aided Glendon Scott Crawford in altering a dispersal device to target unsuspecting Muslim Americans with lethal doses of radiation" (DoJ, 2015).

In videotape presented at the trial, Crawford discussed potential targets, including those associated with the Muslim community and others. For example, according to the Associated Press, "Crawford mentioned an Albany storefront mosque and the New York governor's mansion" (A.P., 2015). In this sense, Crawford's prejudice and anger at Muslims was potentially part of a broader constellation of angry and violent ideologies.

> "Mr. Crawford hated Muslims, and other politically liberal people," [the prosecutor] told the jurors. He replayed earlier Friday the first secretly taped conversation of Crawford with another FBI informant in which Crawford said, "I think Islam is an opportunist infection of DNA" and "Radiation poisoning is a beautiful thing." (A.P., 2015)

Crawford was convicted in 2015 of "conspiring to use a weapon of mass destruction and distributing information about weapons of mass destruction"

(A.P., 2015) and sentenced to 30 years in prison in December 2015 (NBC, 2016). Co-plotter Feight was convicted in December 2015 for "providing material support to terrorists" and sentenced to serve 97 months (DoJ, 2015). While this case was very unusual, the potential use of radiological material—specifically by someone with engineering training—in a plot targeting American Muslims is very concerning. The combination of anti-Islamic ideology as part of a constellation of political and religious ideologies and the tactical choice to pursue unconventional weapons like radiation makes this plot stand out as significant.

THE KANSAS SOMALI COMMUNITY PLOT

One of the most significant plots targeting Muslims in North America in recent years was foiled in Kansas in 2016. The plotters, self-styled militia called "The Crusaders" (A.P., 2018a), plotted a series of "bombings that they hoped would inspire a wave of attacks on Muslims throughout the U.S." (A.P., 2018). The plotters Patrick Stein, Gavin Wright, and Curtis Allen were charged with "conspiracy to use a weapon of mass destruction and conspiracy against civil rights" (A.P., 2018). They, and a fourth man—a government informant—had recorded discussions in which they assessed potential bombing targets in 2016. The three men were convicted in April 2018 (DoJ, 2018a) of "one count of conspiracy to use a weapon of mass destruction and one count of conspiracy to violate the housing rights of their intended victims. Both conspiracies stemmed from the defendants' plot to blow up the apartment complex to kill the Somali Muslim immigrants who lived there" (DoJ, 2018a).

According to the prosecution, the militia intended to conduct a very deadly attack. Purportedly, "on the day after Election Day, they hoped to detonate four car bombs outside of a mosque and an apartment complex that was home to Somali refugees" (A.P., 2018a) in Garden City, Kansas. Garden City is a meatpacking town 60 miles from where the plotters were based, ironically in a town named Liberal, Kansas. They were arrested several weeks before the election (Smith, 2018). The plot was developed enough that authorities discovered "aerial photographs in one vehicle depicting what appear to be apartment complexes marked with large x's, as well as an aerial photo of a church and a Burmese mosque" (A.P., 2018a).

This plot was not mere talk or speculation; the plotters took concrete steps to further an attack.

> According to prosecutors, Stein was recorded discussing the type of fuel and fertilizer bomb that Timothy McVeigh used in the 1995 Oklahoma City bombing, killing 168 people. Stein was arrested when he delivered 300 pounds (135 kilograms) of fertilizer to undercover FBI agents to make explosives.
>
> Prosecutors also allege that Wright and Allen made an explosive in the kitchen of Wright's business and used it to successfully test a blasting cap, to use it to cause a much larger explosion at the apartment complex. (A.P., 2018)

This militia was not disorganized or careless. In fact, according to the Associated Press, in their planning session, "the four men took precautions to avoid getting caught, putting their cellphones in a separate room and locking the door to prevent anyone from walking in on them" (A.P., 2018). This kind of operational security could indeed be effective if there was no informant in the organization. The informant was not, in any sense, an agent provocateur. He was a group member who went to law enforcement "after becoming alarmed by the escalating talk of violence and later agreed to wear a wire as a paid informant" (A.P., 2018).

Again, the anti-Islamic ideology and violent impulses here were part of a broader constellation of ideologies and sociopolitical goals, including anger at immigration. According to prosecutors, the men "planned to bomb the Somali apartments only after considering other attacks—on elected officials, churches that helped refugees and landlords who rented to immigrants" (Smith, 2018). Garden City, a meatpacking town that is home to Tyson foods facilities, has a large immigrant community by the area's standards (A.P., 2018).

TENNESSEE MINISTER PLOT

Among a series of strange and bizarre plots, the following does not deviate from the oddness. In June 2017, a Reuters news report began with an alarming line: "A former Congressional candidate from Tennessee has been sentenced to nearly 20 years in prison for plotting to burn down a mosque, a school and a cafeteria in upstate New York" (Ghianni, 2017). Robert Doggart (65 years old at the time of his conviction) was both a former candidate for Congress (Ghianni, 2017) as well as a Christian minister (Guardian, 2018). He was arrested after plotting an attack on an Islamic community in central New York, including "plotting to burn down a mosque, a school, and a cafeteria" (Ghianni, 2017). Doggart did not plan to act alone; in fact, he was "recruiting people online to carry out an armed attack," according to the Department of Justice (DoJ, 2017). In his trial, the prosecution played recordings of Doggart saying, "I don't want to have to kill children, but there's always collateral damage" (DoJ, 2017).

Doggart was subsequently convicted of "solicitation to commit a civil rights violation and solicitation to commit arson" and sentenced to "235 months in prison"—or almost 20 years, as well as three years of supervised release afterwards" (Torrez, 2017). This occurred after a plea agreement he attempted to enter into was rejected by the judge (Peterson, 2018). There remain questions about whether the sentence will be revisited in appeal (Peterson, 2018).

BLOOMINGTON, MINNESOTA, PIPE BOMB ATTACK

In August 2017, an attack was conducted on a mosque in Bloomington, Minnesota. The attack, consisting of a pipe bomb thrown through the window of the mosque, did not kill or injure any of the five people inside but did cause extensive property damage (DoJ, 2018b). The bomb, made of PVC pipe (Department of Justice, 2018b) and "fuel and black powder" (Sepic, 2018), caused a fire in the Islamic Center, but the center's fire suppression system was able to put it out (Montemayor, 2018). The three arrested men—Michael McWhorter (29), Joe Morris (22), and Michael B. Hari (47) (DoJ, 2018b)—"allegedly carried out their August 5, 2017, attack under the banner of a militia they called the "White Rabbits 3 Percent Illinois Patriot Freedom Fighters" (Montemayor, 2018). A fourth man, Ellis Mack (18), was indicted with the other three on weapons charges stemming from possessing a machine gun (DoJ, 2018c).

According to the Department of Justice, the intent of the attackers to target Muslims was clear.

> The charges allege that the defendants targeted the mosque with intent to damage the mosque because of its religious character and with intent to obstruct Muslims from worshipping there. DAF serves as a religious center as well as a religious school for children. As described in the complaint previously filed with the Court, McWhorter said in reference to the DAF explosion that the defendants did not intend to kill anyone, but they wanted to "scare [Muslims] out of the country" and to "show them hey, you're not welcome here. (DoJ, 2018d)

Despite the obviousness of the targeting of the Muslim community, this militia group, like the Kansas one, seems to have included anti-Islamic hate among a constellation of other grievances and motivating ideological impulses. "Prosecutors say the militia members tried bombing a women's clinic in Champaign, Ill. They also allegedly robbed or tried to rob Walmart stores and a drug dealer, tried extorting money from a railroad by putting bombs on train tracks, and planted explosives in the yard of another Clarence resident with whom Hari had a disagreement about loose dogs" (Sepic, 2018). Its attacks on non-Islamic targets again suggest that anti-Muslim anger is increasingly tied to other ideological grievances as well, and in this case, perhaps even criminal and personal grudges. In this sense, the militia involved here seems to have had aspects of a criminal organization in addition to its violent political aims.

THE QUEBEC CITY MASS SHOOTING

On January 29, 2017, Alexandre Bissonette (28) attacked an Islamic cultural center in Quebec City, using two firearms—a 9mm pistol and a .223 Czech Small Arms rifle (Page, 2018). While the rifle jammed, Bissonette was still horribly effective with the pistol. Using the Glock pistol, he conducted a mass shooting that injured 19 and killed 6 (Bilefsky, 2018). This attack was one of the deadliest mass killings in "recent Canadian history" (A.P., 2018b).

Bissonette's rampage was sparked by anger over a news item that he watched suggesting that immigrants who would be denied entry to the United States by President Trump might be allowed to instead immigrate to Canada (Bilefsky, 2018). So from the very beginning, it was relatively clear that the ideological reasoning behind the attack was more complicated than merely anti-Islamic xenophobia. However, subsequent information released in court proceedings and reporting suggest that Bissonette, far from a narrowly focus anti-Muslim bigot, was mired in a bouillabaisse of online media that depicted immigrants, Muslims, mainstream politicians, and various others as enemies.

Prosecutors presented a 45-page document outlining Bissonette's online activities before the shooting (Coletta, 2018). The document described a young man who:

> spent hours in front of his computer screen reading about mass shooters and scouring the Twitter accounts of right-wing commentators, alt-right figures, conspiracy theorists and President Trump, according to evidence presented at his sentencing hearing. (Coletta, 2018)

This mix of ideological currents is similar to other recent cases of anti-Islamic violence. Rather than a commitment to attacks on a specific religious faith or group, there appears to be a constellation of ideological components underpinning this violence.

PLOTS AND ATTACKS ILLUSTRATE AN EMERGING
ANTI-ISLAMIC TERRORISM MILIEU

It is easy to overread anecdotal evidence or draw conclusions from in-complete information. Inferring too much in the cases described here is inadvisable. That said, there are some commonalities worthy of further discussion and analysis illustrated in Table 4.1. The fact that numerous attackers were willing to accept, and especially to pursue, mass casualty attacks seems—in general—at odds with much of the historical targeting of Islamic facilities described by the GTD data. The fact that the pace of attacks has increased in recent years is disturbing, but perhaps even less so than the increase in desired violence and carnage. Researchers need to dig deeper into both this increase in frequency but also the increase in intensity.

As the GTD data suggest, many historical attacks on Islamic targets in North America were conducted by individuals, or in many cases, unattrib-uted. In this sense, it seemed to reflect traditional hate crime—micro-level violence designed to scare and intimidate, but without the kind of organ-izational drivers that often underpinned violence like White supremacist violence. While sometimes treated as a series of discreet and unconnected acts, White supremacist violence in the United States often draws on a set of organizations and networks for tactical and ideological support, as outlined in Kathleen Belew's book, *Bring the War Home: The White Power Movement and Paramilitary America* (Belew, 2018). The seemingly recent rise of plots and attacks that feature organizational connections or or-ganizations—even if self-described militias or relatively unsophisticated ones—is a disturbing possible emerging trend. Organizational character-istics like size and age are vital explanatory variables for thinking about terrorist lethality (Asal & Rethemeyer, 2008).

The fact that many of these plotters connected their anti-Islamic ide-ology to various other perceived grievances—from anger at liberals to anger at women's reproductive rights to criminal intent and even to var-ious personal grudges—suggests that understanding the decision-making

Table 4.1 COMMONALITIES IN DOMESTIC TERRORIST PLOTS

Incident/Plot	Tactical Innovation?	Organizational Connection?	Ideology? (Solely Anti-Islamic?)	Consistent with Previous (GTD) Trends?
Upstate New York Radiation Plot (2013)	Yes—Use of radioactive/ unconventional weapons	Perceived Klu Klux Klan support	No	Potentially more serious
Kansas Militia Plot (2016)	Yes—Mass casualty intent, VBIEDs	"The Crusaders"	No	Potentially more serious
Tennessee Minister Plot (201)	Not really—Arson	None	Yes	Generally similar
Bloomington, Minnesota, Mosque Bombing (2017)	Not really— Pipe bomb	"White Rabbits 3 Percent Illinois Patriot Freedom Fighters"	No	Potentially more serious
Quebec City Mosque Mass Shooting (2018)	Maybe— Ideologically inspired mass shooting	None	Yes	More serious

VBIEDs, vehicle-borne improvised explosive devices.

and plotting of such individuals is not simple. Instead, authorities and researchers will need to focus heavily on the various ideological currents— from the "anti-Jihad" movement to more militant forms of White supremacy, misogynist activism, and others.

Related to the ideological currents used to intellectually sanction such violence, the role of media and particularly the role of the Internet in facilitating radicalization and operational capabilities must also be examined in light of the changing nature of anti-Islamic terrorism. In at least one case—that of Robert Doggart—the Internet was explicitly used to attempt to recruit attackers with capabilities or skills the planner did not have. According to some, the role of mass media, particularly cable news coverage, may have played a role in the radicalization process of these actors. This was described regarding Robert Doggart (Guardian, 2018) by journalists and even suggested by the defense attorneys for one of the Kansas militia plotters (Farzan, 2018), who suggested lenience in sentencing due in part to "President Trump's inflammatory rhetoric" (Farzan, 2018). The Internet and social media, and their darker corners of conspiracy theory and hatred, seem to have played a significant role in Alexandre Bissonette's radicalization toward political violence—though the details of how remain unclear.

Finally, the most disturbing part of this phenomenon is the apparent change in willingness to cause mass casualties. The scope of the attack planned by the Kansas militia plotters, the callousness of Robert Doggart's discussion of children as collateral damage, and the embrace of radiological weaponry by the upstate New York plotter all fit a disturbing pattern of more willingness to engage in political violence in new and unusually shocking ways. When this trend is combined with the January 2017 mass shooting in Quebec, which caused almost 20 injuries and 6 fatalities (Murphy, 2018), the intensity of violent threats posed by anti-Islamic terrorists is growing concurrently with its frequency. This is even more important and concerning in light of the March 2019 massacres at the Al Noor Mosque and Linwood Islamic Center in Christchurch, New Zealand.

Ultimately, it is important to rigorously assess the empirical picture of any dangerous phenomenon, of which anti-Islamic terrorism is undoubtedly one. What such an assessment suggests, at the moment, is an environment of comparatively low threat (when compared historically and numerically with white supremacist or jihadist terrorism), but an environment of rapid change, and not for the better. Historically, this has been a terrible but largely fringe and unusual phenomenon. However, the numbers in recent years and the characteristics of foiled plots offer some evidence that this could be changing moving forward. This kind of targeting is very much underexplored, is currently not very well understood, but unfortunately may well become a more salient issue moving forward.

It is important to remember that such assessment and analysis can have important policy implications. For example, in June 2018, Vice News ran a headline that said, "CSIS Stopped Monitoring Right-Wing Extremism Ahead of Mosque Massacre" (Lamoreux, 2018). The story describes how the CSIS (Canada's Security Intelligence Service) had ceased monitoring right-wing extremism about a year before the Quebec mosque shooting. In this case, the CSIS deemed the threat posed by right-wing extremism a "public order" threat rather than a "national security" threat (SIRC, 2018) to be addressed by law enforcement rather than intelligence agencies.

According to the Security Intelligence Review Committee (SIRC):

> As a result of a CSIS internal review, which found that the majority of right-wing extremism activities consisted of, or were "near to," lawful protest, advocacy, and dissent . . . CSIS determined that the current threat environment no longer met the threshold of a CSIS investigation. In addition, CSIS also determined that the public order threat (versus the national security threat) was being appropriately addressed by law enforcement and questioned the value-added of its efforts. CSIS ended its investigation of right-wing extremism in March 2016. (SIRC, 2018)

This position changed quickly in the wake of the attack in 2017:

> As a result of the attack on the Grande Mosquée de Québec in January 2017, CSIS reopened its investigation of domestic extremism. Following the attack, SIRC has seen CSIS engage more extensively and frequently with the Royal Canadian Mounted Police (RCMP) and other law enforcement partners to understand better the threat posed by right-wing extremism that would fall under CSIS's mandate. (SIRC, 2018)

The question of whether anti-Islamic terrorism in particular, and some broader constellation of what CSIS termed "right-wing" threats in general, are national security problems or public order problems should rest—at least in part—on a rigorous assessment of the threat posed by such actors. This analysis is intended to be an initial building block to understand this threat landscape better. However, like all attempts at analysis and scholarship, it illustrates as many unanswered questions as it does answered ones.

This emerging and seemingly worsening milieu of anti-Islamic terrorism needs much further study. Analyses of how these phenomena—both in North America and in Europe and elsewhere—relate to broader political developments will be essential. Questions around connections with perceptions of demographic change, immigration, the rise of far-right populist parties and leaders, and other ideological currents ranging from "eco-fascism" to growing misogynistic currents will be important to explore in case studies and comparative analysis. Another set of questions that are initially touched on here are tactical questions. Do anti-Islamic terrorists and plots feature the same, or different, tactical and targeting decision-making as other, better-understood varieties of terrorism and political violence? These questions are important both for law enforcement in direct tactical terms and broader questions of resource deployment, preparedness, and countermessaging; and answers must be vigorously sought. While it would be beneficial to frame anti-Islamic violence and terrorism in the broader context of political violence or sociopolitical discrimination and abuse, a clearer understanding of these still unfolding parameters must first be achieved.

REFERENCES

Asal, V., & Rethemeyer, R. K. (2008). The nature of the beast: Organizational structures and the lethality of terrorist attacks. *Journal of Politics, 70*(2), 437–449.

Asal, V. H., Rethemeyer, R. K., Anderson, I., Stein, A., Rizzo, J., & Rozea, M. (2009). The softest of targets: A study on terrorist target selection. *Journal of Applied Security Research, 4*(3), 258–278.

Associated Press (A.P.). (2015, August 15). Upstate NY man convicted in plot to target Muslims with X-ray weapon. Retrieved from https://www.syracuse.com/state/index.

ssf/2015/08/upstate_ny_man_convicted_in_plot_to_target_muslims_with_x-ray_weapon.html

Associated Press (A.P.). (2018a, March 17). Militia members accused of targeting Somalis to stand trial. Retrieved from https://apnews.com/877c68bc70094913b72d5ab9e5447465

Associated Press (A.P.). (2018b, April 24). Deadliest mass killings in recent Canadian history. Retrieved from https://www.apnews.com/0e0fa24ab580404b8c9997454cca1472

Becker, M. (2014). Explaining lone wolf target selection in the United States. *Studies in Conflict & Terrorism, 37*(11), 959–978.

Belew, K. (2018). *Bring the war home: The white power movement and paramilitary America.* Harvard University Press.

Bilefsky, M. (2018, May 5). Quebec mosque shooter was consumed by refugees, Trump and far right. New York Times. Retrieved from https://www.nytimes.com/2018/05/05/world/canada/quebec-mosque-attack-alexandre-bissonnette.html

Blanchard, C. M. (2007). Islamic religious schools, madrasas: Background. Congressional Research Service (CRS). Library of Congress. Retrieved from https://apps.dtic.mil/dtic/tr/fulltext/u2/a463792.pdf

Brandt, P. T., & Sandler, T. (2010). What do transnational terrorists target? Has it changed? Are we safer? *Journal of Conflict Resolution, 54*(2), 214–236.

Colletta, A. (2018, April 18). Quebec City mosque shooter scoured Twitter for Trump, right-wing figures before attack. *Washington Post.* Retrieved from https://www.washingtonpost.com/news/worldviews/wp/2018/04/18/quebec-city-mosque-shooter-scoured-twitter-for-trump-right-wing-figures-before-attack/

Copsey, N., Dack, J., Littler, M., & Feldman, M. (2013). Anti-Muslim hate crime and the Far Right.

Crenshaw, W. A. (1988). Civil aviation: Target for terrorism. *The Annals of the American Academy of Political and Social Science, 498*(1), 60–69.

Deloughery, K., King, R. D., & Asal, V. (2012). Close cousins or distant relatives? The relationship between terrorism and hate crime. *Crime & Delinquency, 58*(5), 663–688.

Department of Justice (DoJ). (2015). Upstate New York man sentenced for providing material support to terrorists: Conspired to modify lethal radiation device to be used to kill Muslims in New York State. Retrieved from https://www.justice.gov/usao-ndny/pr/upstate-new-york-man-sentenced-providing-material-support-terrorists

Department of Justice (DoJ). (2017). Chattanooga man sentenced for solicitation to burn down a mosque in Islamberg, New York. Retrieved from https://www.justice.gov/opa/pr/chattanooga-man-sentenced-solicitation-burn-down-mosque-islamberg-new-york

Department of Justice (DoJ). (2018a). Three Southwest Kansas men convicted of plotting to bomb Somali Immigrants in Garden City. Retrieved from https://www.justice.gov/opa/pr/three-southwest-kansas-men-convicted-plotting-bomb-somali-immigrants-garden-city

Department of Justice (DoJ). (2018b). Three Illinois men charged in the bombing of Bloomington, Minnesota Islamic Center. Retrieved from https://www.justice.gov/usao-mn/pr/three-illinois-men-charged-bombing-bloomington-minnesota-islamic-center

Department of Justice (DoJ). (2018c). Four East Central Illinois men arrested, charged by complaint with possession of machine gun: Complaint affidavit alleges criminal activity related to bombing in Minnesota; Attempted bombing of Champaign, Ill., women's clinic, and other violence. Retrieved from https://www.justice.gov/usao-cdil/pr/four-east-central-illinois-men-arrested-charged-complaint-possession-machine-gun

Department of Justice (DoJ). (2018d). Three Illinois men indicted on federal civil rights and hate crimes charges in the bombing of Bloomington, Minnesota, Islamic Center. Retrieved from https://www.justice.gov/opa/pr/three-illinois-men-indicted-federal-civil-rights-and-hate-crimes-charges-bombing-bloomington

Drake, C. J. (1998). The role of ideology in terrorists' target selection. *Terrorism and Political Violence, 10*(2), 53–85.

Enders, W., Sandler, T., & Gaibulloev, K. (2011). Domestic versus transnational terrorism: Data, decomposition, and dynamics. *Journal of Peace Research, 48*(3), 319–337.

Farzan, A. (2018, October 30). Pointing to Trump's rhetoric, attorneys for Kansas militiaman convicted of mosque bomb plot ask for a more lenient sentence. *Washington Post.* Retrieved from https://www.washingtonpost.com/nation/2018/10/30/pointing-trumps-rhetoric-attorneys-kansas-militiaman-convicted-mosque-bomb-plot-ask-more-lenient-sentence/?utm_term=.ad64e4cc4b0e

Gerges, F. A. (2003). Islam and Muslims in the mind of America. *The Annals of the American Academy of Political and Social Science, 588*(1), 73–89.

Ghianni, T. (2017, June 15). Tennessee man sentenced over plot to attack Muslim community. *Reuters.* Retrieved from https://www.reuters.com/article/us-tennessee-muslim-crime/tennessee-man-sentenced-over-plot-to-attack-muslim-community-idUSKBN1962R7

Githens-Mazer, J., & Lambert, R. (2010). Islamophobia and anti-Muslim hate crime: A London case study. http://hdl.handle.net/20.500.12389/20715

Gruenewald, J., Allison-Gruenewald, K., & Klein, B. R. (2015). Assessing the attractiveness and vulnerability of eco-terrorism targets: A situational crime prevention approach. *Studies in Conflict & Terrorism, 38*(6), 433–455.

Guardian. (2018, July 20). White fright. Retrieved from https://www.theguardian.com/world/ng-interactive/2018/jul/20/white-fright-the-plot-to-attack-muslims-that-the-us-media-ignored

Hamm, M. S. (1998). Terrorism, hate crime, and anti-government violence: A review of the research. In H. W. Kushner (Ed.), *The future of terrorism: Violence in the new millennium* (pp. 59–96). Sage.

Hemmingby, C., & Bjørgo, T. (2015). *The dynamics of a terrorist targeting process: Anders B. Breivik and the 22 July attacks in Norway.* Springer.

Hewitt, C. (2000). Patterns of American terrorism 1955–1998: An historical perspective on terrorism-related fatalities. *Terrorism and Political Violence, 12*(1), 1–14.

Hoffman, B. (1993). Terrorist targeting: Tactics, trends, and potentialities. *Terrorism and Political Violence, 5*(2), 12–29.

Jenkins, B. M. (2004). Terrorism and the security of public surface transportation (No. CT-226). RAND Corp. Retrieved from https://www.rand.org/content/dam/rand/pubs/testimonies/2004/RAND_CT226.pdf

Jensen III, C. J. (2015). Potential drivers of terrorism out to the year 2020. *American Behavioral Scientist, 59*(13), 1698–1714.

Jensen, R. B. (2013). *The battle against anarchist terrorism: An international history, 1878–1934.* Cambridge University Press.

Kaplan, J. (2006). Islamophobia in America?: 11 September and Islamophobic hate crime. *Terrorism and Political Violence, 18*(1), 1–33.

Kishi, K. (2017). Assaults against Muslims in U.S. surpass 2001 level. Pew Research Foundation. Retrieved from http://www.pewresearch.org/fact-tank/2017/11/15/assaults-against-muslims-in-u-s-surpass-2001- level/

Krueger, A. B., & Malečková, J. (2003). Education, poverty and terrorism: Is there a causal connection? *Journal of Economic Perspectives, 17*(4), 119–144.

LaFree, G., & Dugan, L. (2004). How does studying terrorism compare to studying crime? In Mathieu Deflem (Ed.), *Terrorism and counter-terrorism* (pp. 53–74). Emerald Group.

Lamoreaux, M. (2018). Police Charge Canadian Teenager With Terrorism in Alleged Incel Murder. Vice news. Retrieved at: https://www.vice.com/en/article/wxq8n4/police-charge-canadian-teenager-with-terrorism-in-alleged-incel-murder

Libicki, M. C., Chalk, P., & Sisson, M. (2007). *Exploring terrorist targeting preferences* (Vol. 483). Rand Corporation.

McGarrell, E. F., Freilich, J. D., & Chermak, S. (2007). Intelligence-led policing as a framework for responding to terrorism. *Journal of Contemporary Criminal Justice, 23*(2), 142–158.

Michael, G. (2003). *Confronting right wing extremism and terrorism in the USA.* Routledge.

Montemayor, S. (2018, December 12). At least 2 Illinois militia members accused in Bloomington mosque bombing to be tried in Minnesota. *Star Tribune.* Retrieved from http://www.startribune.com/illinois-militia-members-allegedly-behind-mosque-bombing-now-in-minnesota-to-face-charges/502501171/

Murphy, J. (2018, January 29). Quebec mosque shooting: A year on Muslims face "new reality." BBC. Retrieved from https://www.bbc.com/news/world-us-canada-42782097

Murphy, S. (2001, April 22). Bulger linked to '70s antibusing attacks. *The Boston Globe.* Retrieved from http://archive.boston.com/news/local/massachusetts/articles/2001/04/22/bulger_linked_to_70s_antibusing_attacks/

NBC. (2016, December 19). New York man gets 30 years in prison for plot to target Muslims with x-ray gun. Retrieved from https://www.nbcnewyork.com/news/local/NY-Man-Sentenced-Plotting-to-Target-Muslims-With-X-Ray-Gun-407397825.html

Newman, G. R., & Hsu, H. Y. (2012). Rational choice and terrorist target selection. In Updesh Kumar & Manas K. Mandal (Eds.), *Countering terrorism: Psychosocial strategies* (pp. 227–249). Sage.

Page, J. (2018, May 22). Survivors of Quebec mass shootings plead for ban on assault weapons. CBC. Retrieved from https://www.cbc.ca/news/canada/montreal/survivors-of-quebec-mass-shootings-plead-for-ban-on-assault-weapons-1.4673386

Peterson, Z. (2018, October 24). Man sentenced for threatening Muslims could be getting out of prison sooner than expected. Times Free Press. Retrieved from https://

www.timesfreepress.com/news/local/story/2018/oct/24/msentenced-threatening-muslims-could-be-getti/481735/

Petrosino, C. (1999). Connecting the past to the future: Hate crime in America. *Journal of Contemporary Criminal Justice, 15*(1), 22–47.

Piazza, J. A. (2017). The determinants of domestic right-wing terrorism in the USA: Economic grievance, societal change and political resentment. *Conflict Management and Peace Science, 34*(1), 52–80.

Ravndal, J. A. (2016). Right-wing terrorism and violence in Western Europe: Introducing the RTV dataset. *Perspectives on Terrorism, 10*(3), 2–15.

Ronczkowski, M. R. (2017). *Terrorism and organized hate crime: Intelligence gathering, analysis and investigations.* CRC Press.

Russia Today (R.T.). (2013, June 20). Feds unravel plot to build, sell x-ray weapon in Upstate New York. Retrieved from https://www.rt.com/usa/terrorism-radiation-weapon-plot-uncovered-966/

Sánchez-Cuenca, I., & De la Calle, L. (2009). Domestic terrorism: The hidden side of political violence. *Annual Review of Political Science, 12*, 31–49.

Security Intelligence Review Committee (SIRC). (2018). Building for tomorrow: The future of security intelligence accountability in Canada. Retrieved from http://www.sirc-csars.gc.ca/pdfs/ar_2017-2018-eng.pdf

Sepic, M. (2018, December 11). Alleged Bloomington mosque bomber pleads not guilty. MPR News. Retrieved from https://www.mprnews.org/story/2018/12/11/bloomington-mosque-bomber-suspect-morris-plea-notguilty

Smith, M. (April 18, 2018). Kansas Trio convicted in plot to bomb Somali immigrants. *New York Times.* Retrieved from https://www.nytimes.com/2018/04/18/us/kansas-militia-somali-trial-verdict.html

START. (2018). Far-right fatal ideological violence against religious institutions and individuals in the United States: 1990–2018. University of Maryland. Retrieved from https://www.start.umd.edu/sites/default/files/publications/local_attachments/START_ECDB_FarRightFatalIdeologicalViolenceAgainstReligiousTargets1990-2018_Oct2018.pdf

Torrez, J. (2017, June 14). Signal Mountain man sentenced to 19 years in prison over terrorism charges. News Channel 9. Retrieved from https://newschannel9.com/news/local/signal-mountain-man-sentenced-to-19-years-in-prison-over-terrorism-charges

Tunnell, K. D. (Ed.). (1993). *Political crime in contemporary America: A critical approach.* Garland.

Varon, J. P. (2004). *Bringing the war home: The Weather Underground, the Red Army Faction, and revolutionary violence in the sixties and seventies.* University of California Press.

Welch, M. (2006). *Scapegoats of 11 September: Hate crimes and state crimes in the war on terror.* Rutgers University Press.

5

The Victimization of Muslim American Women and the Challenges of Imperial Feminism in Comparative Context

ENGY ABDELKADER■

INTRODUCTION

The Breadwinner, a critically acclaimed animated film with a world pre-miere at the 2017 Toronto International Film Festival, dramatically portrays Muslim women's lived experiences under Taliban rule immedi-ately prior to the 2001 U.S. invasion of Afghanistan. Nominated for Best Animated Feature by the Academy Awards and Golden Globe Awards, the film focuses on the experiences of Parvana, the girl child protagonist, as she struggles with, adapts to, and challenges the ultraconservative group's extreme interpretation of Islamic law. In this way, *The Breadwinner* both reinforces and complicates a familiar Orientalist narrative about Muslim women and girls that this chapter explores in greater detail in a compar-ative context.

Initially, *The Breadwinner* portrays Muslim women and girls as *victims* (Mutua, 2001). After the Taliban imprisons Parvana's father, the family

Engy Abdelkader, *The Victimization of Muslim American Women and the Challenges of Imperial Feminism in Comparative Context* In: *Islamophobia and Acts of Violence*. Edited by: Carolyn Turpin-Petrosino, Oxford University Press. © Oxford University Press 2022. DOI: 10.1093/oso/9780190922313.003.0005 languishes without its breadwinning patriarch. In response, 11-year-old Parvana resolves to assume her father's position at the local marketplace. In order to negotiate her social, political, and economic rights in the public sphere, Parvana acquires a male gender identity. She alters her name, hair, attire, and demeanor to fulfill normative gender expectations in a repressive society in which the Taliban has erased women's visibility. Parvana is now *Aatish*, a male name that means "fire or explosive." As viewers follow Parvana/Aatish's struggles and observe another similarly situated girl child masquerading as a boy in the public sphere, the film exposes the fire: myriad human rights violations. In fact, these abuses are now popularly associated with Muslims and Islam more broadly.

From mandatory burkas and forced marriages to restrictions on women's freedom of movement and state-sanctioned gendered violence, *The Breadwinner* confirms the Taliban's *savagery* (Mutua, 2001). Relying on rights-restrictive interpretations of Islamic law, the Taliban mandated wearing the burka—a head-to-toe flowing gown with a small mesh screen for vision. Taliban militiamen physically beat women found in public without it, *The Breadwinner* reminds its viewers. The ultraconservative group also imposed debilitating restrictions on women's freedom of movement, culminating in their enforced seclusion. Women were only permitted to venture outside the home if accompanied by a male relative and otherwise risked public beatings. The group also prohibited women from gainful employment and banned girls from securing an education. Indeed, *The Breadwinner*'s faithful portrayal of country conditions in Taliban-controlled Afghanistan (U.S. State Department, 2001) contextualizes the protagonist's bifurcated gender identity.

As American military jets later fly overhead, viewers recognize (even if subconsciously or implicitly) that Muslim women do need considerable saving (Abu-Lugod, 2013). Furthermore, the United States is the appropriate *savior* (Mutua, 2001) to extinguish the fire. Then First Lady of the United States Laura Bush advised us as much approximately 1 month following *Operation Enduring Freedom*, the U.S.-led military strike in Afghanistan intended to vanquish al-Qaida and Taliban forces in the immediate aftermath of the September 11 terrorist attacks. In November

2001, in a radio address to the nation, the First Lady announced "a world-wide effort to focus on the brutality against women and children by the al-Qaida terrorist network and the regime it supports in Afghanistan, the Taliban" (Bush Center, 2001). Connecting the U.S.-led military invasion to the liberation of Muslim women, she further explained:

> The brutal oppression of women is a central goal of the terrorists. Long before the current war began, the Taliban and its terrorist allies were making the lives of children and women in Afghanistan miserable. . . . Women cannot work outside the home or even leave their homes by themselves. The severe repression and brutality against women in Afghanistan is (sic) not a matter of legitimate religious practice. Muslims around the world have condemned the brutal degradation of women and children by the Taliban regime. The poverty, poor health, and illiteracy that the terrorists and the Taliban have imposed on women in Afghanistan do not conform with the treatment of women in most of the Islamic world, where women make important contributions in their societies. Only the terrorists and the Taliban forbid education for women. Only the terrorists and the
>
> Taliban threaten to pull out women's fingernails for wearing nail polish. The plight of women and children in Afghanistan is a matter of deliberate human cruelty carried out by those who seek to intimidate and control. Civilized people throughout the world are speaking out in horror—not only because our hearts break for the women and children in Afghanistan, but also because in Afghanistan we see the world the terrorists would like to impose on the rest of us. . . . Join our family in working to ensure that dignity and opportunity will be secured for all the women and children of Afghanistan. (Bush Center, 2001)

Set against this backdrop, *The Breadwinner* reinforces an Orientalist narrative and advances imperial feminism insofar as Muslim women are portrayed as *victims*, the Taliban as *savages*, and U.S. military forces as *saviors.* While the Taliban oppressed, tyrannized, and tormented many Muslim women, did the U.S. military invasion save them?

In response, related government statements and reports published at *Operation Enduring Freedom*'s conclusion may prove instructive. On December 29, 2014, for instance, U.S. President Barack Obama declared an end to the combat mission explaining, "We are safer, and our nation is more secure" (The White House, 2014). He made no mention of Muslim women, however. In addition, Secretary of Defense Chuck Hagel also issued a related statement regarding the war's conclusion (Department of Defense, 2014). In his remarks, Secretary Hagel made no reference to Muslim women either. Given their collective silence on the issue, the U.S. State Department's official data on country conditions in Afghanistan, particularly the status of women, prove useful.

According to the U.S. State Department's Afghanistan Country Report on Human Rights Practices for 2014, "domestic and international gender experts considered the country very dangerous for women" (U.S. State Department, 2014). Notwithstanding laws criminalizing such abuses, rape, so-called honor killing, forced marriage, and domestic violence persisted at the war's end due to lack of implementation and enforcement. Regarding other human rights violations previously highlighted, the official data reveal that "[c]ultural prohibitions on free travel and leaving home unaccompanied, prevented many women from working outside the home and reduced their access to education, health care, police protection, and other social services." Regarding education, specifically, the report notes that the situation remains one of "grave concern," where girls are besieged with formidable obstacles such as "poverty, early and forced marriage, insecurity, lack of family support, lack of female teachers, and the long distance to school." In addition, female students are subject to "violent attacks." Such data expose the imperial feminist narrative advanced in the 2001 national radio address and subtly incorporated in *The Breadwinner* for global consumption. Thus, as the U.S. combat mission ended, freedom and equality remained elusive for Afghan women and girls.

This chapter explores the status of American Muslim women in comparative context to further interrogate the imperial feminist agenda.

The next section identifies several prominent anti-Muslim stereotypes, canards, and tropes manifesting in contemporary Orientalism, to contextualize the inquiry. The following two sections examine human rights themes previously highlighted: the right to education and employment. A related discussion regarding imperial feminism follows separately.

ANTI-MUSLIM STEREOTYPES, CANARDS, AND TROPES

Imperial feminism perpetuates Orientalist stereotypes to advance an agenda of Empire. Orientalism refers to a system of representations of the East that exaggerates differences with and emphasizes the superiority of the West in furtherance of the accumulation of people and territories (Said, 1979). For instance, Orientalist stereotypes that pervade popular culture—films, television, video games—include depictions of Muslims, Arabs, and South Asians as "backward," "uncivilized," "primitive," and "barbaric" (Shaheen, 2003). In addition, Orientalism manifests in news media discourse as the overrepresentation of Muslims as "terrorists" and the Islamic faith tradition as a constant source of peril (Abdelkader, 2018; Kearn, 2019). Significantly, the dehumanization of inhabitants of the East facilitates its invasion, occupation, and re-creation—Orientalism's ultimate objective—as in Afghanistan and Iraq.

It is important to note that Orientalist understandings of Muslims and Islam have also culminated in a spectrum of canards and tropes that undermine the minority faith community's reputational and dignitary interests. According to research from the Public Religion Research Institute, many Americans lack a strong understanding of Islam or consistent contact with religious adherents (Cox, 2011). A small minority, approximately 14%, claim to know a lot about Muslim beliefs and practices, and 40% report they have not engaged in conversation with a Muslim in the last year. This creates fertile ground for misconceptions to flourish. Several of the most relevant stereotypes, myths, rumors, and conspiracy theories are identified here:

Patriarchal Oppression: Muslim Americans are often subject to claims that their social, cultural, and religious beliefs and practices are misogynistic. This may translate in a solitary focus on Muslims as perpetrators of unlawful practices deemed "primitive" and "uncivilized" such as so-called honor killings, domestic violence, female genital mutilation, and forced marriages while ignoring evidence that gender-based violence transcends religion, culture, race, and national boundaries. It may also appear as claims that the headscarf transmits a patriarchal worldview.

Lack of National Loyalty: Muslim Americans are frequently maligned that they conspire to shape public policy for Islamic interests or that their patriotism is less than that of their compatriots. This manifests as claims that Muslim Americans are disloyal to the United States. To be accepted as loyal Americans, they are sometimes asked to disavow their belief in "Sharia" or Islamic law, a source of moral guidance and a key aspect of identity for some. This is particularly so for individuals, including Muslim American women, who desire a role in American public life, such as elected political positions.

Global Domination: This conspiracy theory claims that Muslims are conspiring to take over the world in a bid to establish Islamic political rule for their own interests. In this context, the hypothetical threat of Islamic world domination to women, religious minorities, and others is distorted, magnified, and exaggerated.

Militant Indoctrination: Muslim Americans are often perceived as hapless subjects of indoctrination. This may appear as claims that mosques are bastions of radical extremism that promote extrajudicial violence. It may also manifest as allegations that women who wear a headscarf have been manipulated rather than exercising personal freedom and choice as others who choose nonreligious attire. The headscarf then becomes a symbol of militancy, not a manifestation of spiritual belief and devotion.

Creeping Sharia: This conspiracy theory asserts that Islamic law is becoming increasingly influential in the American legal system to the detriment of women. It may inform oppositional movements to mosque construction and expansion projects. It also manifests claims that American Muslims are surreptitiously working to supplant federal, state, and local laws with Sharia. Since 2010, the conspiracy theory has given life to more than 200 bills in state legislatures prohibiting judges from considering Islamic or "foreign" law in the adjudication of cases. The U.S. Constitution protects the legal system from such hypothetical plots.

Taqiyya: Muslim Americans are often subject to claims that they, as individuals or as a community, are engaged in intentionally deceptive practices for their own gain. This may translate as suspicion and distrust toward members of the minority faith community who are presumed to be lying about a spectrum of issues in order to "conquer the infidels." Orthodox Islamic teachings prioritize the importance of honesty.

Although not an exhaustive compilation, this list is intended to reveal several significant elements of Islamophobic discourse. Anti-Muslim stereotypes, canards, and tropes breed fear, distrust, and suspicion, further contributing to Muslims' social, political, and economic marginalization as individuals and as a community. Specifically, such modern representations of Orientalist thought may culminate in discriminatory practices, policies, and laws that construct formidable barriers to Muslim women and girls' education and employment.

EDUCATION

The Right to Education

The right to education is a fundamental human right recognized in myriad international documents and treaties. Significantly, the right is set forth in the Universal Declaration of Human Rights (UDHR), an international document that enumerates the fundamental rights and freedoms inherent to all human beings, irrespective of race, ethnicity, nationality, religion, gender, place of residence, or any other status (UDHR, 1948). In addition, particular gendered protections are located in the UN Convention on the Elimination of All Forms of Discrimination Against Women (CEDAW), the only international agreement that addresses women's rights in the political, civil, cultural, economic, and social spheres (CEDAW, 1979). Further, the UN Convention on the Rights of the Child (CRC), an international treaty setting out the civil, political, economic, social, and cultural rights of every child, also recognizes and protects this right (CRC, 1989).

To fully realize a woman's right to education, education is required to be *available, accessible, acceptable,* and *adaptable* (Rudolf, 2012, pp. 255–256). Accessibility requires a prohibition against discrimination and encompasses both a physical and economic component (Rudolf, 2012, p. 256). For instance, education is inaccessible where school registration fees are cost prohibitive or classrooms are not wheelchair accessible. Acceptability refers to the quality of the curriculum and instruction, while adaptability considers that education must be responsive to a society's needs (Rudolf, 2012, p. 256). For example, a classroom where the teacher-to-student ratio is 1:100, and the curricula are taught in a language incomprehensible to students, is unacceptable. Taken together, these principles are intended to prevent discrimination and promote gender equality in education.

Interestingly, public, political, and news discourse often focuses on direct discrimination against Muslim women related to social, religious, and cultural factors in South Asia, Africa, and the Middle East. Direct discrimination arises when women and girls are treated differently because of their gender identity (Rudolf, 2012, p. 273). For instance, in *The Breadwinner*, education is *inaccessible* and *unavailable* because girls are barred from attending school and face reprisal if found doing so. Such abuses are attributed to the Taliban's rights-restrictive (mis)interpretation of religious law; these discriminatory practices are now associated with Muslims and Islam more broadly.

However, indirect discrimination against Muslim women in education has not received parity in treatment, although its effects are equally pernicious. Here, seemingly neutral laws and policies have a discriminatory effect on female students (Rudolf, 2012, p. 273). For instance, a blanket prohibition on all headgear or religious symbols in public schools may have a disparate impact on Muslim women and girls who wear a headscarf. Related legal controversies have arisen domestically and internationally but with distinct results.

The Case of Nashala Hearn

The case of Nashala Hearn illustrates the indirect discrimination that compromises the right to education. In 2003, Nashala was an 11-year-old (like Parvana) student enrolled in the 6th grade at the Ben Franklin Science Academy in Muskogee, Oklahoma (Hearn, 2004). Since 1997, to prevent gang-related activity, the public school adhered to a neutral dress code (CNN, 2003). Specifically, the policy provided that "[s]tudents shall not wear ... hats, caps, bandannas, plastic caps, or hoods on jackets inside the building" (DOJ Brief, 2004). However, the principal enjoyed discretion in excepting students on a case-by-case basis.

Rather than stem gang-related activity, however, school officials employed the dress code to coerce Nashala into removing her headscarf on the second anniversary of 9/11. In related testimony to the U.S. Congress, Nashala explained:

> But my problems started on September 11, 2003. I was in the breakfast line when my teacher came up to me and said that after I was done eating to call my parents because my hijab looks like a bandanna or a handkerchief and that I was not allowed to wear it. So after I was finished, I went to the office. Mrs. Walker had already called my parents. When my parents got there, they were very upset. The principal said it was a bandana and I had to change it or go home.

And this is how the battle of being obedient to God by wearing my hijab to be modest in Islam versus the school dress code policy began. I continued to wear my hijab—because it would be against my religion not to. So—like I said before, I was suspended from school on October 1 for 3 days. When I came back to school on October 7—I was suspended again. This time it was for 5 days. (Hearn, 2004)

Apparently, school officials expanded the dress code's original intent to encompass all criminal activity, thus reducing an 11-year-old girl child to a "terrorist other." Significantly, following Nashala's two suspensions, the school's legal counsel alleged that federal law did not allow for special accommodations on account of her bona fide religious practices (CNN, 2003). Further, the school district argued that it prohibited Nashala from wearing her headscarf to enhance "school safety," maintain a "religion-free zone" in schools, and to avoid "unnecessary disruption" (DOJ Brief, 2004). In response, in November 2003, Nashala's parents filed a related lawsuit against the school officials claiming the policy violated her First Amendment rights to free speech and free exercise of religion under the U.S. Constitution (Rutherford Institute, 2003). The family's lawsuit demanded that school officials amend its dress code to accommodate religious attire such as Nashala's headscarf.

In March 2004, the U.S. Department of Justice (DOJ) intervened in the case on Nashala's behalf. In its legal filing, the DOJ alleged unconstitutional religious discrimination and insisted, "No student should be forced to choose between following her faith and enjoying the benefits of a public education." Specifically, the DOJ argued that Muslim women and girls wear headscarves as "a demonstration of modesty" in public for bona fide religious reasons (DOJ Brief, 2004). Further, the school district did not apply the dress code equally since it prohibited the headscarf but exempted students on secular grounds (e.g., those undergoing chemotherapy treatments were permitted headwear). The DOJ explained that the school dress code was not neutral but used to discriminate against Nashala.

Shortly thereafter, the parties settled the matter. As a result, the school district revised its policy to permit exceptions for religious accommodations and Nashala returned to school observing her head-scarf (DOJ Settlement, 2004). The school also implemented a relevant training program for educators and publicized the amended dress code. Additionally, in September 2004, the U.S. Department of Education issued a related "Dear Colleague" letter to elementary, secondary, and postsecondary school officials across the nation (Dept. of Ed., 2004). Reaffirming the federal government's commitment to upholding constitutional principles in education, the correspondence focused on cases in which religious discrimination against Arab, Muslim, Sikh, and Jewish students intersect with racial, ethnic, and gender discrimination (Dept. of Ed., 2004).

According to intersectionality theory, two or more dimensions of one's identity may result in multiple layers of discrimination (Crenshaw, 1989). Intersectionality theory considers how gender, ethnicity, religion, disability, marital and immigration status, and other facets of social identity are interconnected. Significantly, the interconnected dimensions of one's identity produce unique experiences with oppression. For instance, the Oklahoma school dress policy detrimentally affected Nashala not merely because she is Muslim but also due to her gender. It is important to recognize that Nashala would not have experienced discrimination but for her gender status. While the dress code was originally devoid of discriminatory intent, its application resulted in indirect discrimination because Nashala was denied *access* to education. At the intersection of religion and gender, the school's actions undermined Nashala's fundamental human right to an education.

The case of Nashala Hearn diverges from the international community's common understanding of a Muslim woman's right to education. Here, as in *The Breadwinner*, the girl child is still the *victim*. The *savages* who undermined her fundamental rights, however, are school officials employed in public service. But who is Nashala's *savior*? First, Nashala demonstrated agency. Initially, she refused to remove her headscarf. She later returned to class while adhering to her religious belief practices. Nashala subsequently testified before the U.S. Congress about her experience, exhibiting strength, courage, and character. More recently, the Obama White House recognized Nashala's struggle for equality. Indeed, Nashala Hearn challenges the "Muslim woman as a helpless victim" stereotype. Second, Nashala's parents supported her right to education when they instituted a lawsuit against those undermining it. This, too, is significant. Unsupportive family members are frequently depicted as social and cultural obstacles to Muslim women's *access* to education. Third, in this specific instance, the federal government's commitment to constitutional principles also helped ensure Nashala's unfettered *access* to education. To be sure, the case of Nashala Hearn complicates the Savages-Victims-Saviors paradigm (Mutua, 2001) in potentially provocative ways. It reveals the indirect discrimination that undermines Muslim women's right to education in a Western liberal democracy.

The Comparative Context

In contradistinction, related international developments have proven much more restrictive to Muslim women's right to education. In 2004, France proposed its law prohibiting headscarves and other conspicuous "religious symbols" demonstrating a student's faith beliefs in public schools. The measure's proponents argued that it was necessary to protect the separation of church and state in public education. As a settlement agreement was announced in favor of Nashala in the United States, France implemented its new law. Unsurprisingly, it disproportionately impacts Muslim women whose headscarves are perceived as a sign of militancy and political Islam (Vaisse, 2004, p. 4). Unlike the United States, which has signed but not ratified CEDAW, France is a state party to CEDAW but has apparently stripped Muslim female students of their status as women.

The French law may appear insignificant except to the local Muslim community. In the intervening 15 years since its passage, however, similar measures have infected nations in all corners of the world. In 2015, for instance, Belgian officials prohibited headscarves at some public schools (Daily Sabah, 2018). The following year, in 2016, a high school in Spain demanded a student remove her headscarf before pursuing academic studies; the decision was later overturned (Khaleej Times, 2016). In 2017, Kazakhstan—a Muslim-majority country in Central Asia—similarly prohibited the headscarf in public education (Urnaliev, 2017). More recently, in January 2019, Kenya's highest court upheld a prohibition on headscarves in educational institutions while permitting each school to determine its dress code (Al Jazeera, 2019). Most recently, in May 2019, Austria approved a dress code prohibiting headscarves in primary education. Notably, the Austrian measure prohibits any "ideologically or religiously influenced clothing which is associated with the covering of the head" (Olterman, 2019). Significantly, Belgium, Spain, Kazakhstan, Kenya, and Austria have all signed and ratified CEDAW.

While such laws, practices, and policies are routinely viewed through the solitary lens of religious freedom, each detrimentally affects Muslim women's fundamental rights on a disproportionate basis. Recall, to fully realize a woman's right to education, education is required to be *available*, *accessible*, *acceptable*, and *adaptable* (Rudolf, 2012, pp. 255–256). Yet, from Belgium to Kazakhstan to Kenya, education is *unavailable* and *inaccessible* to Muslim women and girls who choose attire disfavored by the state. If these students are forced to pursue academic studies in private institutions with insufficient resources, curricula, and instruction, then education is more likely to be *unacceptable*. In certain European contexts, this also demonstrates an inability to *adapt* to an increasingly multicultural society. The UN Human Rights Committee has previously found such state action to violate human rights; offenders flout the UN decision without legal repercussions (UN, 2011). In doing so, they undermine women's personal freedoms and choices and create fertile ground for additional rights violations. Who, then, will save *these* Muslim women?

EMPLOYMENT

The Right to Employment

The right to work and freely choose employment is grounded in the UDHR with gendered protections found in CEDAW (Rudolf, 2012, p. 282). Viewed as "essential for realizing other human rights," this includes a prohibition against discrimination in hiring, training, and compensation (Rudolf, 2012, pp. 282, 285). Moreover, this requires government officials to enact and enforce laws and policies that prevent discriminatory exclusion of women from the labor market (Rudolf, 2012, p. 285). In the United States, for instance, Title VII of the Civil Rights Act of 1964 prohibits employment discrimination on account of sex, race, color, national origin, and religion.

The religious, social, and cultural attitudes that impede Muslim women's equal participation in the labor market, particularly in South Asia, Africa, and the Middle East, have been heavily scrutinized by activists, artists, journalists, scholars, and policymakers, among others. For instance, in *The Breadwinner*, Parvana assumed a male gender identity (Aatish) to earn an income outside the home to support her family financially. She is a victim of direct discrimination because the difference in treatment is explicitly due to her status as a girl. The direct discrimination against Afghan women and girls in employment arises from the Taliban's rights-restrictive approach to interpreting Islamic law; this restrictive stance has since been erroneously imputed to Muslims and Islam more generally.

Analogous to education, however, indirect discrimination against Muslim women in employment has not always attracted as much attention despite its similarly deleterious effects. Specifically, Muslim women are excluded from the labor market due to neutral laws and policies that have a discriminatory effect on female job applicants. For instance, an employer's generally applicable dress code prohibiting all headgear during working hours may have a disparate impact on women who observe modest attire on account of bona fide religious beliefs. Related legal controversies have emerged both domestically and internationally.

The Case of Samantha Elauf

In the United States, the case of Samantha Elauf is instructive. In 2008, Samantha was 17 years old when she applied for a position with an Abercrombie store located in a local mall in Tulsa, Oklahoma (Abercrombie III, 2015). After an employment interview, a manager determined Samantha was qualified for the position. She was concerned, however, that Samantha's headscarf violated the store's "Look Policy" that included a neutral dress code prohibiting "caps" (Abercrombie III, 2015). Samantha wore the headscarf when in public or in the presence of male strangers in accordance with her sincerely held faith beliefs. Ultimately, the manager refused to hire Samantha for this reason. In response, the young woman filed a legal complaint with the Equal Employment Opportunity Commission (EEOC), the federal government agency that enforces laws against discrimination in employment. The EEOC chose to sue Abercrombie on Samantha's behalf.

In 2009, the EEOC filed its lawsuit pursuant to Title VII of the Civil Rights Act of 1964 alleging religious discrimination (Abercrombie I, 2011). Title VII makes it unlawful for an employer to discriminate against a job applicant based on religion, including faith practices. To this end, an employer is required to "reasonably accommodate" religious observance— such as the headscarf—unless it can demonstrate an undue hardship to its business. The EEOC argued that Samantha observed hijab pursuant to a bona fide religious belief that conflicted with Abercrombie's dress code. It further argued that that the store knew this and refused to hire her on that basis.

In response, Abercrombie presented several counterarguments. First, citing expert testimony that women wear headscarves for myriad reasons, Abercrombie insisted that Samantha observed the hijab for cultural—rather than religious—reasons. However, the court found that Samantha had previously asserted the religious underpinnings informing her choice to wear the headscarf. Notably, legal protections will likely not extend to those who adopt the headscarf due to political or cultural motivations.

Second, Abercrombie questioned the sincerity of Samantha's religious beliefs. Samantha did not perform all her daily ritual prayers, Abercrombie argued. Nor did she know the address for her local mosque. However, the court found that it must focus on the sincerity of Samantha's belief about hijab specifically because that belief required accommodation (Abercrombie I, 2011). In its view, Samantha had a bona fide religious belief.

Third, Abercrombie claimed that it lacked adequate notice because Samantha had not requested a reasonable accommodation or exemption from its dress code at the time of her interview. The court deemed this unpersuasive as well. It held that Samantha had met the notice requirement because Abercrombie knew that a conflict existed between its dress code and her religious belief practices.

Lastly, Abercrombie argued that allowing exemptions to the Look Policy compromised its brand and image, creating an undue hardship to its business. However, the court found this argument similarly unconvincing because it lacked empirical data to support its claim. Thus, initially, Samantha was awarded $20,000 in damages (Abercrombie I, 2011).

When Abercrombie appealed the decision, the Tenth Circuit Court of Appeals, a federal appellate court, ruled in the retailer's favor. The appellate court dismissed the case, reasoning that Samantha had not informed Abercrombie that she wore the headscarf for religious reasons and required an exemption from the dress code based on bona fide religious beliefs, (Abercrombie II, 2013). As such, the Tenth Circuit reasoned Abercrombie lacked sufficient notice that she required reasonable religious accommodation under Title VII. The EEOC then appealed to the U.S. Supreme Court.

In 2015, the U.S. Supreme Court ruled in Samantha's favor in an 8-1 decision holding that Abercrombie had intentionally discriminated against the young Muslim woman when it refused to hire her on account of its Look Policy. It found that the Tenth Circuit had misinterpreted Title VII's requirements regarding notice to trigger an employer's legal obligation to accommodate a bona fide religious practice. It agreed with the federal district court that Abercrombie had enough information to make it aware that a conflict existed between Samantha's religious attire and the company's dress code. In response to Abercrombie's insistence that its policies are neutral, generally applicable, and nondiscriminatory, the Court explained in relevant part,

> An employer is undoubtedly entitled to have ... a no-head wear policy as an ordinary matter. But when an applicant requires an accommodation
> as an "aspec[t] of religious . . . practice," it is no response that the subsequent "fail[ure] . . . to hire" was due to an otherwise neutral policy. Title VII requires otherwise-neutral policies to give way to the need for an accommodation.

It is important to note that this is the first U.S. Supreme Court case involving the reasonable accommodation of the Islamic headscarf *in any context*. Two months later, Samantha received the monetary damages initially awarded to her in 2011 (Haynes, 2015).

Interestingly, this fact pattern does not necessarily reflect the international community's understanding of a Muslim women's right to employment. The public, news, and political discourse treat such cases strictly in terms of religious freedom value rather than framing such controversies as also implicating women's rights. Similar to the case of Nashala Hearn, many overlook the compelling intersection between religion and gender. It is essential to recognize that Samantha would not have experienced discrimination but for her status as a woman. In fact, during litigation, the evidence demonstrated that Abercrombie had previously hired Jewish men who wore a yarmulke and were exempted from the Look Policy. Samantha's experience in the labor market was adversely impacted because of the choices she made as a woman.

Moreover, the case of Samantha Elf complicates the Savages-Victims-Savior paradigm, (Mutua, 2001). Here, as with Parvana, Samantha is the *victim*. The *savage* undermining her basic human rights is a popular retailer who prioritizes its brand and image over women's economic empowerment. Who is the *savior*? Significantly, this Muslim woman saves herself and countless others. She demonstrates agency. Initially, she filed a legal complaint rather than complacently accepting Abercrombie's unlawful employment decision. Her courage culminates in a U.S. Supreme Court decision that clarified an aspect of employment and labor law and strengthened legal protections for *all* faith groups. Indeed, shortly after the U.S. Supreme Court's ruling in 2015, the Obama White House recognized Samantha's contribution to the nation (Haynes, 2015). In addition, in this case, the federal government's commitment to constitutional principles—such as the free exercise of religion—and civil rights laws also helped preserve the right to employment at the intersection of religion and gender.

The Comparative Context

In contradistinction, related legal developments in the European Union have proven much more restrictive to Muslim women's rights. In 2017, the European Court of Justice—the European Union's highest court—found that a company's dress code prohibiting the wearing of "any political, philosophical or religious sign" was not "direct discrimination" (European Court of Justice, 2017). However, the Court left unresolved whether such a policy constitutes "indirect discrimination." The judgment derives from distinct legal controversies arising in Belgium and France, where Muslim women refused to remove their headscarves pursuant to an employer's directive. The facts of each case are set forth here.

In 2003, Samira Achbita was employed as a receptionist with a private company in Belgium (European Court of Justice, 2017). At that time, there was an allegedly "unwritten rule" prohibiting religious symbols in the workplace. Several years later, in 2006, Samira advised her employer that she had begun to observe hijab. Her manager informed her that this was unacceptable. A few weeks later, the company amended its regulations to read, "Employees are prohibited, in the workplace, from wearing any visible signs of their political, philosophical or religious beliefs or from engaging in any observance of such beliefs" (European Court of Justice, 2017). However, when Samira insisted on wearing the headscarf, she was terminated. She then filed a related lawsuit. The corollary case has its origins in France.

In 2008, Asma Bougnaoui began an internship with a private company in France, (European Court of Justice, 2017). A representative had previously advised her that wearing a headscarf may be problematic. So Asma wore a bandana at first but eventually began working with the headscarf. She received an offer of employment as a design engineer at the end of her internship. However, when a customer complained, the employer asked Asma to remove her headscarf. She refused and was terminated. Like Samira, she sued her former employer.

In response to both cases, the European Court of Justice found no "direct discrimination" where the company has an internal policy prohibiting the wearing of visible signs of political, philosophical, or religious beliefs that is generally applicable to all employees. Instead, it reasoned that such a policy "treats all employees of the undertaking in the same way, notably by requiring them, generally and without any differentiation, to dress neutrally" (European Court of Justice, 2017). Interestingly, the employer adopted the policy following her choice to observe hijab in Samira's case. Furthermore, in Asma's case, she was permitted to wear the headscarf until a customer complained.

However, the Court makes clear that such a policy may give rise to "indirect discrimination." This may be the case where evidence demonstrates, the Court explains, that the policy disadvantages specific groups that adhere to particular belief practices. The Court continues, however, that such differential treatment is "justified by a legitimate aim and if the means of achieving that aim were appropriate and necessary." Finally, eliminating any doubt regarding the legality of the employers' actions, the Court confirms that their commitment to "project[ing] an image of neutrality" politically, philosophically, and religiously is valid.

These cases arose from discrimination by private actors but culminated in a judgment by a public actor responsible for upholding the rule of law. Instead, that judgment institutionalized anti-Muslim prejudice and discrimination across the European Union. Whereas the U.S. Supreme Court found that neutral dress codes must give way to religious accommodations, the European Court of Justice found that faith practices must give way to neutrality. In institutionalizing anti-Muslim prejudice, the European Court of Justice also signaled the degradation of the Muslim woman's right to employment. While all of these cases are routinely viewed through the exclusive lens of religion, each compromises a woman's right to work. Arguably, Asma and Samira would still be working at their respective companies but for their status as women. The Court's judgment deprives them of personal freedom and choice and results in economic disempowerment. Who will save *these* Muslim women?

DISCUSSION: IMPERIAL FEMINISM

Religion, race, and geopolitics, rather than an unwavering commitment to international human rights standards, often influence collective concern regarding the rights of Muslim women and girls. For example, the coerced wearing of the burka in Afghanistan evokes outrage in America and the European Union. Depriving Muslim women and girls the personal freedom to make such choices is simply *barbaric*. In contrast, the coerced wearing of "neutral" attire in Western Europe evokes considerable apathy. Additionally, refusing equal employment opportunities to women in Afghanistan on social, cultural, and political norms is *oppressive*.

Nevertheless, doing so in Belgium or France—arguably for the same pretextual reasons—is *different*. Whereas there is outsized international concern about Muslim women's rights when the "*savages*" is one of "*them*," that same community is relatively silent when the oppressors are from among "*us*." In this way, Western feminism is reduced to a political tool employed to achieve an Orientalist agenda of accumulation.

Imperial feminism or gendered Orientalism negatively affects Muslim women and girls. Significantly, imperial feminism does not speak to the full spectrum of Muslim women's experiences with oppression, marginalization, and discrimination. For instance, imperial feminism prioritizes a Muslim woman's right to education and employment in Africa, South Asia, and the Middle East as important issues. But it renders those rights invisible in a Euro-American context. Imperial feminism may prioritize a Muslim women's right to be free from violence in the private sphere where the oppressor is her husband, brother, or father (e.g., protecting her from the patriarchal Muslim male). But it renders otherwise invisible her right to the same physical security in public spaces susceptible to bias crimes. Indeed, such action and nonaction reflect a hierarchy in political priorities rather than a sincere commitment to Muslim women's social, political, and economic empowerment irrespective of the geopolitical context. It also reflects an Orientalist ideology where Muslim men are the chief perpetrators of women's oppression. There is a double standard.

Additionally, imperial feminism attempts to empower Muslim women and girls from an Orientalist perspective that reinforces anti-Muslim stereotypes, asserts Euro-American superiority over "others," and maintains Empire. In doing so, it exacerbates an intensifying climate of Islamophobia in Europe and the United States. This is because Muslim women's experiences are not understood holistically as influenced by myriad facets of their complex social identity, but rather vis-à-vis a narrow Orientalist framework that problematizes Islam. Ironically, heightened anti-Muslim sentiment in a Euro-American context further contributes to Muslim women's social, political, and economic disempowerment.

For instance, in 2013, academic researchers conducted a field experiment to investigate the extent to which Muslim women wearing a headscarf—a prominent religious marker—encounter discrimination on the labor market (Ghumman & Ryan, 2013). Students (ages 19–22) from diverse ethnic backgrounds sought employment with and without the headscarf at retail stores and restaurants in middle-class cities in the Midwest. The findings revealed that wearing a headscarf had a negative impact in all aspects of the hiring process compared to Muslim women who did not wear a hijab, including the permission to complete employment applications, job availability, callbacks, interview time, and employer's lack of interest. Interestingly, these research findings reflect Samantha Elauf's discriminatory experience with Abercrombie & Fitch in Tulsa, Oklahoma. They also intersect with *The Breadwinner*, where viewers watched with dismay when Parvana altered her physical appearance to support her family financially. Again, there is a double standard.

CONCLUSION

As noted, *The Breadwinner* both reinforces and complicates a familiar Orientalist narrative about Muslim women and girls that this chapter explored in greater detail in comparative context. Similar to Nashala and Samantha, the fictional Parvana demonstrated agency in response to adversity. She challenged gendered norms, assumed the role of breadwinner, and ultimately secured her father's release from prison. Indeed, Parvana is a cinematic Muslim heroine in full animated glory. Still, as U.S. military jets fly overhead, the conflict between "good and evil" and the "clash of civilizations" implicit in Mrs. Bush's 2001 national radio address becomes apparent. The imperial feminist agenda—reinforcing anti-Muslim stereotypes, asserting Euro-American superiority, and maintaining Empire—is unmistakable. The imperial feminist agenda prioritized Muslim women's rights in Afghanistan in a film that grossed in excess of $4 million worldwide. That same agenda renders those women invisible in Western Europe, however. As such, imperial feminism does not speak to the full spectrum of Muslim women's experiences with oppression, marginalization, and discrimination. It does not support the American Muslim woman's empowerment, politically, economically, and socially. Rather, it upholds a double standard that undermines women's rights, the rule of law, and even, Empire.

REFERENCES

Abdelkader, E. (2018). Humanitarian Islam. 30 *Pace Int'l L. Rev.* 175–277. Retrieved from https://digitalcommons.pace.edu/pilr/vol30/iss2/1.

Abu-Lugod, L. (2013). *Do Muslim women need saving?* Harvard University Press.

Amos, V., & Parmar, P. (1984). Challenging imperial feminism. *Feminist Review, 17*, 3–19.

Convention on the Elimination of All Forms of Discrimination Against Women (CEDAW). (1979, December 18). *United Nations*. Retrieved from https://www.ohchr.org/en/professionalinterest/pages/cedaw.aspx

Court of Justice for the European Union Judgments in Cases C-157 and C-188 (European Court of Justice) (2017, March 13). An internal rule of an undertaking which prohibits the visible wearing of any political, philosophical or religious sign does not constitute direct discrimination. Retrieved from https://curia.europa.eu/jcms/upload/docs/application/pdf/2017-03/cp170030en.pdf

Cox, D., Dionne Jr., E.J. Jones, R. P., & Galston, W. A. (2011, September 6). What it means to be an American: Attitudes towards increasing diversity in America ten years after 9/11. Public Religion Research Institute. Retrieved from https://www.prri.org/research/what-it-means-to-be-american/

Crenshaw, K. (1989). Demarginalizing the intersection of race and sex: A black feminist critique of antidiscrimination doctrine, feminist theory and antiracist politics. *University of Chicago Legal Forum, 1989*(1), Article 8, 139–167. Retrieved from http://chicagounbound.uchicago.edu/uclf/vol1989/iss1/8

Dept. of Justice intervenes in Institute case on behalf of Muslim girl's right to wear "hijab." (2004, March 31). The Rutherford Institute. Retrieved from https://www.rutherford.org/publications_resources/on_the_front_lines/pr484

EEEOC v. Abercrombie & Fitch Stores, Inc. (Abercrombie I). 798 F. Supp. 2d 1272 (ND. Okla. 2011), rev'd and remanded, 731 F.3d 1106 (10th Cir. 2013), rev'd and remanded, 135 S. Ct. 2028, 192 L. Ed. 2d 35 (2015).

EEOC v. Abercrombie & Fitch Stores, Inc. (Abercrombie II). 731 F.3d 1106 (10th Cir. 2013), rev'd and remanded, 135 S. Ct. 2028, 192 L. Ed. 2d 35 (2015).

EEOC v. Abercrombie & Fitch Stores, Inc. (Abercrombie III). 135 S. Ct. 2028 (2015).

Eyvine Hearn and Nashala Hearn v. Muskogee Public School District: US Memorandum of Law. (DOJ Brief) US Department of Justice, May 6, 2004. Retrieved from https://www.justice.gov/sites/default/files/crt/legacy/2010/12/14/hearnokbrief.pdf

Friedan, T. (2004, March 31). US to defend Muslim girl wearing scarf in school. CNN.com. Retrieved from http://www.cnn.com/2004/LAW/03/30/us.school.headscarves/

Ghumman, S., & Ryan, A. M. (2013). Not welcome here: Discrimination towards women who wear the Muslim headscarf. *Human Relations, 66*(5), 671–698.

Haynes, D. (2015). Abercrombie pays $25K in headscarf case settlement. *UPI.* Retrieved from https://www.upi.com/Business_News/2015/07/21/Abercrombie-pays-25K-in-headscarf-case-settlement/7511437510165/

Justice Department reaches settlement agreement with Oklahoma district in Muslim student headscarf case (DOJ Settlement). (2004, May 19). US Department of Justice. Retrieved from https://www.justice.gov/archive/opa/pr/2004/May/04_crt_343.htm

Kearns, E., Betus, A. E., & Lemieux, A. F. (2019). Why do some terrorist attacks receive more media attention than others? *Justice Quarterly, 36*(6), 985–1022.

Kenya's Supreme Court overturns ruling on wearing hijab in schools. (2019, January 24). *Al Jazeera.* Retrieved from https://www.aljazeera.com/news/2019/01/kenya-court-overturns-ruling-wearing-hijab-schools-190124142110267.html

Local court in Belgium rules against headscarf ban at schools. (2018, February 24). *Daily Sabah.* Retrieved from https://www.dailysabah.com/europe/2018/02/24/local-court-in-belgium-rules-against-headscarf-ban-at-schools

Muslim girl suspended for head scarf. (2003, October 11). CNN.com. Retrieved from http://www.cnn.com/2003/EDUCATION/10/11/scarf.reut/.

Muslim students in Spain now allowed to wear hijab in school. (2016, September 26). *Khaleej Times*. Retrieved from https://www.khaleejtimes.com/international/europe/muslim-students-in-spain-now-allowed-to-wear-hijab-in-school

Mutua, M. (2001). Savages, victims, and saviors: The metaphor of human rights. *Harvard International Law Journal, 42*(1), 201–245.

Oltermann, P. (2019, May 16). Austria approves headscarf ban in primary schools. *The Guardian*. Retrieved from https://www.theguardian.com/world/2019/may/16/austria-approves-headscarf-ban-in-primary-schools

Radio address by Mrs. Laura Bush. (2001, November 17). George W. Bush Presidential Center. Retrieved from https://www.bushcenter.org/publications/articles/2013/02/radio-address-by-mrs-laura-w-bush-crawford-tx-november-17-2001.html

Ranjit Singh v. France. UN Human Rights Committee 102nd session 11–29 July 2011, issued September 27, 2011. Retrieved from http://ccprcentre.org/doc/OP1/Decisions/102/1876%202009%20France_en.pdf

Rudolf, B., Freeman, M. A. & Chinkin, M. (2012). *The UN Convention on the Elimination of All Forms of Discrimination against Women: A commentary*. Oxford University Press.

Said, E. (1979). *Orientalism*. Vintage Books.

Shaheen, J. G. (2003). Reel bad Arabs: How Hollywood vilifies a people. *The ANNALS of the American Academy of Political and Social Science, 588*(1), 171–193.

Spanish women denied classes over her hijab. (2016, September 16). *The Local*. Retrieved from https://www.thelocal.es/20160916/spanish-woman-denied-access-to-classes-over-hijab

Statement by the President on the End of the Combat Mission in Afghanistan. (2014, December 28). *The White House*. Retrieved from https://obamawhitehouse.archives.gov/the-press-office/2014/12/28/statement-president-end-combat-mission-afghanistan.

Statement by Secretary of Defense Chuck Hagel on Operation Enduring Freedom and Operation Freedom's Sentinel (DOD). (2014, December 28). US Department of Defense. Retrieved from https://dod.defense.gov/News/News-Releases/News-Release-View/Article/605332/statement-by-secretary-of-defense-chuck-hagel-on-operation-enduring-freedom-and/

Testimony of Ms. Nashala Hearn (Hearn). (2004, June 8). United States Congress: The Subcommittee on the Constitution, Civil Rights and Property Rights. Beyond the Pledge of Allegiance: Hostility to religious expression in the public square. Retrieved from https://www.judiciary.senate.gov/imo/media/doc/hearn_testimony_06_08_04.pdf

Title VI and Title IX Religious Discrimination in Schools and Colleges (Dept. of Ed.) (2004, September 13). US Department of Education. Retrieved from https://www2.ed.gov/about/offices/list/ocr/religious-rights2004.html

Universal Declaration of Human Rights (UDHR) (1948). Retrieved from https://www.un.org/en/universal-declaration-human-rights/

Urnaliev, S. (2017, November 19). Hijab v. Education: Kazakh schoolgirls face dilemma over headscarf ban. *Radio Free Europe*. Retrieved from https://www.rferl.org/a/kazakhstan-schools-head-scarf-ban/28862676.html

U.S. State Department Human Rights Report: Afghanistan. (2001). Retrieved from
  https://20092017.state.gov/j/drl/rls/hrrpt/2001/sa/8222.htm
Vaisse, J. (2004). Veiled meaning: The French law banning religious symbols in public
  schools. The Brookings Institute. Retrieved from https://www.brookings.edu/wp-
  content/uploads/2016/06/vaisse20040229.pdf

6

An Opinion

What the Qur'an Says That Disqualifies the Perspectives of Militant Radical Muslims

JABBAR A. AL-OBAIDI■

A major feature of the evolution of public controversies over Islam in the United States and Europe since 2000 is the trend toward a standardization of anti-Muslim arguments and of the objects around which Western fears and fantasies crystalize.

—NADIA MARZOUKI (2013, *p. 13*)

INTRODUCTION

This chapter offers a theological, historical, cultural, and political analysis as to what is stated in the Qur'an and enforced by the Hadith sayings and practices of the Prophet Muhammad and the shifted interpretations by extremists who pervert traditional teachings and apply them to justify nonpeaceful practices. This chapter also seeks to carefully challenge the misinformation about Islam that the general readers may have developed over the decades. It is, however, not an attempt to strike a debate with

Jabbar A. Al-Obaidi, *An Opinion* In: *Islamophobia and Acts of Violence*. Edited by: Carolyn Turpin-Petrosino, Oxford University Press. © Oxford University Press 2022. DOI: 10.1093/oso/9780190922313.003.0006

Islamic scholars and researchers on the issue of militant radical Muslims and how they skew certain surahs/chapters from the Qur'an.

It is of the utmost necessity to expose erroneous interpretations due to the escalating global reaction of animus, especially in the West, against the Muslim community. This development occurred without others paying attention to the fact that Muslims themselves are also the victims of extremist violence. They have undergone all kinds of suffering, harassment, and killings by terrorists in the name of Islam. Case in point, a recent incident against Muslims occurred on August 18, 2019 (BBC News, 2019). A bomb exploded and killed 63 people at a wedding ceremony in the Afghan capital, Kabul. The so-called Islamic State (I.S., ISIS, or ISIL or Daish in Arabic) claimed responsibility. Militant radical Muslims are in the business of waging war against Muslims and non-Muslims. It is more of an ideology than an Islamic movement, an essential point of distinction, that some media pundits want to call it, which prompts these acts of violence. As for the ideology, organizations such as al-Qaeda and Daish have co-opted traditional Islamic language, and often give the impression of a contradictory values with cultural roots (Halliday, 2003).

These two terrorist organizations, and a few others, claim to address social, political, and economic issues in the Middle East and the world by referencing their acts to Islam. They have directed, for example, their aggression and terror against moderate, progressive, and secular forces in the Middle East, as well as against other nations (Halliday, 2003). Regrettably, such deliberate distorted reference has contributed to discoloring the image and reputation of Islam. However, committing bad things in the name of religion is not confined to Islam. Former President Barak Obama referred to this point when he addressed the National Prayer Breakfast in February 2015 in Washington, DC. He said: "And lest we get on our high horse and think this is unique to some other place, remember that during the Crusades and the Inquisition, people committed terrible deeds in the name of Christ. In our home country, slavery and Jim Crow all too often was justified in the name of Christ." Obama's statement was rejected and criticized by his political critics. Along this line, Todd Green argued that Islam's critics believe the West is leary to criticize Islam and or discuss candidly Islam's relationship with violence (Green, 2019). However, neither the West nor the East, including Muslim leaders, is afraid to criticize wrong deeds committed in the name of Islam.

The terror ideology and the strategy adopted by a small group of militant and radical Muslims are contradictory to the teaching of Islam. According to the Qur'an, Islam disapproves of the killing of a person and forbids all forms of attacks on innocents. Surat/Chapter 32 al Ma'idah says that "whoever kills a person—it is as if he killed the whole of mankind; and whoever saves it, it is as if he saved the whole of mankind" (Sura/Chapter al Ma'idah 5:32). This principle is also deeply grounded in the noble teachings of Islam to preserve life and to forbid violence and destruction. Again, the Qur'an states: "Whoever is guided—is guided for his own good. Moreover, whoever goes astray—goes astray to his detriment. No burdened soul carries the burden of another, nor do we ever punish until we have sent a messenger" (Surat/Chapter al Asra 17:15).

In the West, most generic studies and literature covering Islam tend to impose terminologies such as "radical Islam," "radical Islamism," and "Islamic terror." Besides confusion and inaccuracy, these generic terms are designed to characterize the religion, and not address the radical committers of terror. The argument here is that there is no such thing as radical Islam. The term offends Muslims for sure. Alternatively, the use of a phrase like "radical Muslims" or "radical Islamists" is specific and refers to perpetrators of violence. Those radical individual Muslims represent a narrow minority among the vast Muslim majority who do not condone such radicalism and hatred. This chapter will identify and explicate some of the central ideas where the rationale of radical Muslims departs from the major teachings and principles presented in the Qur'an and other essential sources of Islamic teachings. Within this analysis, the focus is on the broad areas of Islamic theology, the historical presence of Muslims in the West, particularly in the United States, and the cultural aspects of Islamic teachings. The perverted doctrines used by violent extremists likely contribute significantly to Islamophobic attitudes and subsequent hostilities aimed at the Muslim community. It is therefore important for non-Muslims to understand that what Muslim terrorists represent does not in any way reflect Islam. We begin with history.

AMERICAN MUSLIMS' PRESENCE IN AMERICAN HISTORY

In his book *Muslims and the Making of America*, Amir Hussain (2016) claims there has never been an America without Muslims. Despite the 2014 Pew Forum survey in which only 38% of Americans reported to know a Muslim, "the reality is that they all at least know of one, namely, Muhammad Ali, arguably the most famous athlete of all time" (Penner, 2017). Moreover, Hussain highlighted that "significant numbers of African slaves transported to America were Muslims, and that for much of American history, Muslims have come to New York seeking freedom and opportunity" (Hussain, 2016, p. 19). Muslims in Africa, Asia, the Middle East, Latin America, North America, and elsewhere are viewed as Islamic (Loimeier, 2013). They share similar rituals, festivals, values, fasting the month of Ramadan, and teaching traditions that are based on the Qur'an, the compilations of *Sunna* (sayings and practices or credited collection of what the prophet Muhammad had done and said (*Hadith* in Arabic), and a vast number of legal and theological references (Loimeier, 2013, p. 18). The Qur'an says, "This too is a blessed Scripture that We revealed; so, follow it, and be righteous, that you may receive mercy" (Surat/Chapter al An'am 6:155).

Throughout history, the White House has acknowledged the presence of Muslims around the world and in America. According to the Tunisian French scholar Nadia Marzouki, the first instances of the diplomatic recognition of Islam by the United States occurred in 1805 under President Thomas Jefferson, who received at the White House Sidi Sulayman Mellimelli, the envoy of the bey of Tunis (Marzouki, 2013). Marzouki added, "Instead of serving dinner at 3:30 pm, then the customary time, Jefferson asked that the meal be served 'precisely at sunset' to respect the prescribed time for the interruption of fasting during Ramadan" (Marzouki, 2013, pp. 8–9). Furthermore, Washington, DC, welcomed the building of the

Islamic Center in 1952. President Dwight D. Eisenhower attended the dedication ceremony on June 28, 1957. In his speech to the American representatives, he referenced the Islamic world's "traditions of learning and rich culture, which have contributed to the building of civilizations for centuries." President Eisenhower added, "As I stand beneath these graceful arches, surrounded on every side by friends from far and near, I am convinced that our common goals are both right and promising. Faithful to the demands of justice and brotherhood, each working according to the lights of his conscience, our world must advance along the paths of peace" (see www.islamiccenter.us/). Surat/Chapter al An'am emphasizes: "This is My path, straight, so follow it. And do not follow the other paths, lest they divert you from His path. All this He has enjoined upon you, that you may refrain from wrongdoing" (Surat/Chapter al An'am 6:153). Moreover, the fact that Jefferson owned a Qur'an also demonstrates the long history of Islam in the United States (Penner, 2017).

Emphasizing the importance of positive relations with Muslims overseas and in the United States, President Barak Obama on June 22, 2015, said in his remarks to the Muslims attendees during a Ramadan Iftar (breaking the fasting) invitation organized at the White House: "As the Quran teaches, let us answer with Peace." President Obama added:

> We don't simply endure, but we overcome. Together, we can overcome ignorance and prejudice. Together, we will overcome conflict and injustice—not just with words, but with deeds. With what a hero of mine, the civil rights icon John Lewis, calls using our feet—getting out in the real world to organize and to create the change that we seek. That's what so many of you do every single day. And that's what we have to continue to do together, here in America and around the world. As the Quran teaches, let us answer with Peace.

SENSE OF HESITANCY AND CONFUSION

More than two centuries before former President Trump enacted the Muslim ban, "Muslims were statutorily barred from becoming American citizens . . . from 1790 through 1944" (Beydoun, 2018, pp. 46–47). The characterization of Muslim immigrants as less loyal citizens reflects a blemished U.S. immigration policy. Khaled A. Beydoun explained that some of the recent attempts to ban Muslims' entry or restrict Muslim migrants to this country were "driven by the same discourse and stereotypes that prohibited Muslims from becoming U.S. citizens from 1790 through 1944" (p. 47). In addition, "America's first Muslims were also enslaved and reduced to chattel" (Beydoun, 2018, p. 48). Yet it should be noted that there is a general tendency in the West that feeds into a sense of misgiving and suspicion of Islam "that is independent of questions of immigration, social exclusion, and challenges to secularism" (Marzouki, 2013, p. x.). Islam is viewed as "the absolute other whose very presence calls for the rethinking of what makes up the political bond, that's beyond the "social contract and republican integration" (Marzouki, 2013, p. x.). The rejection or even abhorrence of Islam is a collective indication of mis-understanding, ignorance, and mismanagement of secularism and reli-gious affairs within the public sphere. The general sense of hesitancy and confusion comes from three primary sources: lack of knowledge of the religion of Islam, misconceptions of Islamic beliefs and Islamic doctrine, and a fear of future attacks by radical militant Muslims post the terrorist attack on September 11, 2001.

Excluding or including a religious element of any religion is an ex-tremely sensitive matter as it touches on the identity of a person or a group of people. The public sphere is filled with visible religious symbols such as the sign of halal meat, a Muslim woman wearing her hijab or headscarf, a nun in her wimple, a priest in his cassock, or a Sikh in his dastaar or turban. Any attempt to exclude such visible signals or indications calls for an infraction on peoples' rights and choices. The First Amendment protects the rights of people as it states: "Congress shall make no law re-specting an establishment of religion or prohibiting the free exercise thereof; or abridging the freedom of speech, or of the press; or the right of the people to peaceably assemble, and to petition the Government for a redress of grievances."

Some European laws, such as The Law of 1905 in France, were designed to allow an organized religion within the public space (Marzouki, 2013,

p. xii). Therefore, visible references should be recognized as cultural symbols related to freedom of expression, freedom of choice, freedom of religion, or not to have a religion, or to be accepted simply as multiculturalism signifiers.

Western European countries and the United States face immeasurable challenges caused by "post-immigration ethno-religious diversity and that the new Muslim settlement of the last fifty years or so are the center of it" (Modood 2019, p. 1). The U.S. Constitution provides a solid foundation for liberties for all ethnicities, races, and religions. Abraham Lincoln stated, "Don't interfere with anything in the Constitution. It must be maintained, for it is the only safeguard of our liberties" (August 27, 1856, Speech at Kalamazoo, Michigan; www.abrahamlincolnonline.org).

The so-called excluded sphere that the West and the United States thought they had in the past has never been a reality. The nation is made of diverse ethnicities and races. The Native Americans throughout the 16th and 17th centuries, European settlers, and other immigrants, including African Americans and Muslim Americans, were and are part of American history and its social and cultural fabrics. Records from the American Revolutionary War showed that Muslims participated in the war and fought on the American side. Among the documented names of soldiers are Yusuf ben Ali and Bampett Muhamed (ABC News, 2015). Edward Curtis pointed out that 292 Muslims fought in the Civil War (Curtis, 2010). Moses Osman served as captain during the Civil War, and Max Hassan, an African, worked for the military as a porter (Haberman, 2016). The significance of these historical notes illustrates that American Muslims were an integral element of the history of the United States.

THEOLOGICAL PRINCIPLES OF ISLAM AND THE PATHWAYS OF PERVERSION

According to the Pew Research Center, Islam is the religion of an estimated 1.8 billion Muslims worldwide as of 2015. It is about 24% of the global population. Islam is considered the second-largest religious tradition after Christianity. About two thirds (62%) of Muslims reside in the

Asia-Pacific region (Desilver & Masci, 2017; Pew Research Center, 2015). Many people throughout the world, especially in the United States, erroneously think that most Muslims live in the Middle East and North Africa regions. However, Pew Research Center analysis shows that Muslims make up a majority of the people in 49 countries around the globe. Moreover, Pew projects that by 2050 the number of Muslims will reach 2.76 billion (29.7%) of the world's population (www.pewresearch.org).

Islam, in Arabic, means submission to the will of Allah/God. Verse 6 says, "No associate has He. Thus, I am commanded, and I am the first of those who submit" (Surat/Chapter al An'am 6:163). Muslims are commanded to obey, respect, and apply the Qur'anic religious instructions and the sayings and practices of Prophet Mohammad as related to everyday life in a spiritual and peaceful role and application. The Qur'an reminds Muslims of the importance of the Qur'anic revelations and how a Muslim should always strive to be "righteous" and to seek Allah's mercy as "When those come to you who believe in Our verses, say: Peace be upon you. Your Lord has decreed mercy upon Himself" (Surat/Chapter al An'am 6:154).

As lecturer and Middle Eastern scholar William G. Baker points out, "Those who choose to find Qur'anic references to take up arms against their fellow man (*women and children*) can do so by taking the Scriptures out of context and can justify their hateful and murderous acts" (Baker, 2003, p. 137). It is worth noting that one must identify and relate references in the Qur'an that describe situations that the Prophet Mohammad encountered when he was defending, for instance the city of Medina, and other similar situations, to correctly proselytize the religion of Islam in the Arabian Peninsula and beyond to the world.

Muslim convictions and practices include the following beliefs:

1. *Shahada* is the "Declaration of Faith" of Islam, Say He (Allah) is the One.
2. *Salat* is the performing and establishing prayers (five times daily) to "Connect with the Creator/Allah."
3. Fasting is the observation of the Holy Month of Ramadan. It is to "Discipline your lower self." "Ramadan is the month in which the

Quran was revealed. Guidance for humanity, and clear portents of guidance, and the Criterion. Whoever of you witnesses the month, shall fast it. But whoever is sick, or on a journey, then a number of other days. God desires ease for you, and does not desire hardship for you, that you may complete the number, and celebrate God for having guided you, so that you may be thankful" (Surat/Chapter al Baqarah 2:185).

4. *Zakat* is an annual alms tax on certain kinds of properties and cash used for charitable and religious purposes, to help needy people, and to serve humanity at large.

5. *Hajj* is the pilgrimage to Mecca in Saudi Arabia once or more. It is an outward and inward physical, spiritual, and ritual process of intentions.

According to Abdullah Khouj, the director and imam of the mosque in Washington, DC, "The Qur'an, the Muslims' Book of Guidance, calls for a healthy normal human life that is congruent with the natural make-up of the human being to create individuals, societies, and nations. Communication is the key to human relations, especially when it comes to religious values and their effects in our lives" (see www.islamiccenter.us/).

In the wake of tragic events in other locations, such as the Madrid, Spain, bombing in 2004, deeper misunderstandings of Islam by governments and the public on both sides of the Atlantic occurred. Nadia Marzouki highlighted the issue of misconception and mishandling of Islam this way: "A major feature of the evolution of public attitudes regarding Islam in the United States and Europe since 2000 is the trend toward a stand-ardization of anti-Muslim arguments and of the objects around which Western fears and fantasies crystalize" (Marzouki, 2013). The political discourse of invoking fear and suspicion has contaminated the public conversation and the coverage of media. Themes like Islamization in dis-advantaged suburbs; the use of mosques as training camps for jihadists; the oppression of Muslim women by their brothers, husbands, or fathers; stealth jihad; and taqiyya are the standard talking points in the discourse of anti-Muslim groups in the United States and Europe (Marzouki, 2013).

On the other side, some ultraconservative and traditionalist Islamic theologists proposed the concept of the superiority of Islam as a tool to refute the narrative of secularism as foreign and alien (Ismail, 2006). Muhammad Abid al-Jabiri explained that the tensions that instigate the debates concerning Islam's superiority developed "out of the perceived difference between the lived reality and the reality as formed from the model of Islamic resurgence" (Abid al-Jabiri, 1982; Ismail, 2006). According to the Qur'an, Islam's relationship to other divine religions is respectful and complementary. Its message completes and perfects the previous messages of Christianity and Judaism. These divine religions are meant to recognize each other and to coexist harmonically and collaboratively. However, the Salafist Islamic narrative viewed Islam in "a relationship of antinomy with Christianity" and Judaism, for that matter (Ismail, 2006, p. 43). The narrative goes further to indicate that Islam is both (*din wa dunya*) a religion and temporal or secular. Simply said, Islam is seen as both a belief system (religion) and a system of life. Islamic Salafists contest the concept of the separation of religious affairs and the daily life matters (separation of state and religion) and dealings as a product of colonial powers in that they want to control the Islamic world. Colonialism, foreign interference, and economic deprivation continue to be viewed as a cause of the past and present deterioration of relationships between religions and societies of the West and East. Cautions and predictions offered by academic analysts and political commentators speak of the global threats of Islamic fundamentalism to the West and question the compatibility of Islam and Arab culture with democracy and modern lifestyle (Esposito, 1999).

Author and scholar Zulfiqar Ali Shah wrote: "The Qur'anic concept of transcendental (inspirational) monotheism is not evolutionary. It is original and universal. The Qur'an gives this moralistic understanding of monotheism a universal dimension by claiming that this was the same message revealed to all Prophets and nations since the beginning of time" (Shah, 2018). The Qur'an states, "For we assuredly sent amongst every people a Messenger (with the command), "Serve Allah and eschew evil" and "We sent you with the truth; a bearer of good news, and a warner" (Surat/Chapter an Nahl 16:36 and Surat/Chapter Fatir 35:24).

Therefore, "the message is timeless, unchanged and universal" (Shah, 2018). Shah added that "It is significant and worth noting that the Ten Commandments given to Moses were rehearsed by Jesus on the Mount and reiterated by Muhammad in the Qur'an. Moreover, the "*Shalom* of the original Hebrews is the *Salam* and Islam of the Qur'an" (Shah, 2018). Muslims maintain a clear "demarcation line between God and whatever is non-God by holding fast to the concept of His Transcendence, uniqueness, and otherness" (Shah, 2018). Hence, the Islamic declaration in Arabic *Allahu Akbar* (God is Great in English) confesses that God/Allah is omnipotent and highest. Almost every Muslim utters this declaration in the morning and in various circumstances, including joyful or unpleasant situations and unexpected occurrences. Unfortunately, the declaration of *Allahu Akbar* is highjacked by radical Muslims and terrorists as they pronounce the two words prior to or during the execution of their evil terror acts and crimes. They use the words *Allahu Akbar* to justify or instigate acts of brutality and bloodshed. In other words, they say it to confer religious legitimacy on their horrifying actions.

Radical Muslims have consciously and deliberately decided to employ the name Islam and misinterpret selective verses from the Holy Quran to justify their illegal and criminal activities and frame themselves as the defenders and protectors of Islam. However, according to the Council of American-Islamic Relations (CAIR) and the Islamic and the Fiqh Council of North America (FCNA), it is forbidden in Islam to kill the innocent (FNCA, 2005 & CAIR, 2010)). It is also forbidden in Islam to torture people and to attribute evil acts to God (Allah in Arabic) (FNCA, 2005; & CAIR, 2010). Consequently, the image of Islam and Muslims has suffered a great deal since 2001. Leon Wieseltier wrote in a *New York Times Book Review*, in reference to September 11, 2001, that "On September 10, 2001, nobody in America seemed to know anything about Islam" and "On September 12, 2001, everybody seemed to know everything about Islam" (Marzouki, 2013, p. 31; Noah, 2001; Wieseltier, 2011).

RADICAL MUSLIMS AND THE PERVERSION
OF ISLAMIC TEACHINGS

It is important to note that as citizens of a particular country or countries, radical Muslims or insurgents do not have the authority to declare war against a country, a community, ethnicity, or group of people. Further, they are not authorized to commit an act of domestic or international terrorism in the name of Islam, and Muslims and their religious orientations discredit their distorted ideology and theological approaches. This is due to four reasons; first, they do not represent the religion of Islam; second, they lack any legitimate right to act on behalf of the country of their citizenship; and third, they interpret verses from the Qur'an to serve an evil purpose. Islamic scholars and religious leaders contest and challenge the interpretation of any of the Qur'anic verses cited by terrorists, whose purpose is to corroborate their claims as defenders of Islam and Muslims. Finally, most Muslims in Muslim countries and wherever Muslims reside disagree with their interpretation and reject such implications. For example, al-Qaeda committed its crime and aggression on September 11, 2001, which goes totally against section 190 "but do not commit aggression; God does not love the aggressors" (Surat/Chapter al Baqarah 2:190). As for the call for fighting those who chose to fight you, the verse refers to the *state* or the *country*. A state may declare war and enlist its able citizens to join the army establishment and the national guards to defend the homeland. Section 190 states, "And fight in the cause of God those who fight you, but do not commit aggression; God does not love the aggressor" (Surat/Chapter al Baqarah 2:190). Looking for the justifications and moral equivalences offenders claim, result from deliberate misrepresentations intended to sanction and provide authority for such acts. Examples of such acts include attempting to justify or explain the killing of innocent noncombatants by taking out-of-context references to the Qur'an (Badawi, 2012). Regrettably, deranged individuals do wrong things and commit unspeakable acts of violence in the name of a religion, an ideology, or anything else.

THE TRUE MEANING OF JIHAD

Linda Sarsour, a lead organizer of the Women's March January 2021 and one of the most high-profile Muslim activists in the United States, spoke to a predominately Muslim crowd at the annual Islamic Society of North America convention in suburban Chicago and urged her fellow Muslims to speak out against oppression. In her remarks, Sarsour told a story from Islamic history about a man who once asked Prophet Muhammad, "What is the best form of jihad?" The Prophet responded to him, "A word of truth in front of a tyrant ruler or leader, that is the best form of jihad" (Sarsour, 2017). Qasim Rashid, an attorney, author, and national spokesman for the Ahmadiyya Muslim Community U.S.A. wrote a global opinion to the *Washington Post* (2017) that *jihad* appears to have become the scariest word in the world these days. Moreover, "Contrary to what extremists and anti-Muslim personalities claim, the word 'jihad' does not mean 'to wage holy war,' or 'to kill the infidel,' or 'to commit terrorism'" (Rashid, 2017). Rashid added that it is not violence. Not terrorism. Indeed, the only two groups who claim 'jihad = Terrorism' are Islamic State terrorists and Islamophobes with an agenda. Both are ignorant of Islam and serve only one another (Rashid, 2017).

Indeed, one of the most controversial issues debated in the West is the meaning of the word *jihad* in Islam and how it is often associated with extremism and terrorism. The media and some politicians use the expression "Holy War" in reference to jihad. So let us discuss this inaccurate interpretation. To clarify the misinformation surrounding the word *jihad*, William G. Baker wrote:

> We in the West have translated the word Jihad into English to mean Holy War, and today much of the world has come to know the word in this vein. Unfortunately, in an attempt to quickly identify the concept and quantify it in a neat little package, we have mistranslated the concept and now have an incomplete, inadequate, and misleading understanding of the real meaning of Jihad in Islam. (2003, p. 136)

Along the same line, Laura Nader wrote in *Anthropology Today*, "The Arabic word jihad, translated as holy war, has been associated with Islam and is commonly used and misused in contemporary Euro-American society" (Nader, 2015, p. 1). This is to argue that violent extremism does not stem from Islam's sacred texts, the Qur'an, but rather from the interpretation by a small group of Muslim adherents (Ayaan Hiris Ali, www.foreignpolicy.com).

Three points need to be discussed here; first, the word *jihad* is mentioned in the Qur'an. Second, there is no reference anywhere in the Qur'an for the phrase "a Holy War" in the Islamic traditions, in the Qur'an, or in the Prophet's deeds and sayings. Third, the word *jihad* and its derivatives are mentioned in 41 places in the Qur'an. The Arabic word *jihad* means to struggle, strive, work hard, and exert every effort for self-betterment and community service. The Qur'an highlights the word *jihad* with different types of purposes as follows:

(A) *Jihad*, meaning to fight for the sake of Allah, is mentioned in 25 places in the Qur'an, including 14 places that serve as a reminder to take action but not to wage or declare war. (B) In 10 places, the Qur'an mentions *jihad* in the sense of the *mujahideen* (i.e., exerting effort and working hard) and not in the sense of commanding someone who will make mischief and shed blood for the sake of Islam. Islam does not need someone to shed blood . . . instead, it asks its followers to serve humanity. As stated in the Qur'an, "They believe in Allah and the Last Day, and they enjoin what is right and forbid what is wrong and hasten to good deeds. And those are among the righteous (Surat/Chapter al Imran 3:114). (C) A reference to making all kinds of effort and sometimes a fighting effort or even waging war is found in six places in the Qur'an. The Sura/Chapter Pilgrimage 6: 39 indicates: "Permission is given to those who are fought against, and God is Able to give them victory." In addition, Verse 40 directed the attention of followers to speak up and employ every effort to undo any form of injustice, stop an offensive act, and defend their rights. According to Surat al Hajj 6:39 and 6:40, the purpose of *jihad* is to defend and protect one's family, property, and to stop an aggressor, be a person, a group of people, or a nation from invading someone's homeland.

The verse calls for peaceful ways and means, harmony, and friendship as opposed to *demolition*. It is undoubtedly a universal rule, under the constitution, that a nation reserves the right to defend its people, its lands, and its sovereignty in case of war being declared upon them. Islamic nations, as with other nations, have the right to self-defense and the right to live.

However, "insurgents and extremists," whether Muslims or non-Muslims who live in a Muslim or non-Muslim country, are governed by the laws and policies of that particular country. The public, politicians, and legislators are encouraged to view Islam as a faith and a form of spirituality, noting that the uproar and controversies over Sharia or Islamic law should be placed in a proper context. Muslim associations and leaders focus on a simple message: Sharia is not a legal code but a code of ethics that guides the individual's spiritual formation. It is not in competition with the U.S. Constitution or any other constitutions. Moreover, it is not a rejection or a replacement of any other laws and regulations. As a religious code, it may regulate the interior affairs of the Islamic faith without causing friction or conflict with civic and common laws, policies, and regulations.

Anthropologist Laura Nader proposed that the focus on Islamic jihad by the media and politicians in the United States and Europe include invited comparisons of similar jihadists among Christians and Jews. All three religions emanated from an area of the world referred to today as the Middle East, thereby resulting in shared origins and referred to as People of the Book—all three being monotheistic (Nader, 2015). A Muslim is frequently encouraged to constantly do a soul search to become a better person and to do good works for themselves and their respective communities. The effort of in-depth soul searching, working hard, and struggling to provide the legitimate financial means to raise a family is qualified to be described as jihad. Even non-Muslims may pursue similar personal goals. Qasim Rashid explained how the Qur'an describes three types of jihad (struggles), and zero of them mean or permit terrorism. According to Rashid (2017):

These are: the jihad against yourself, the jihad against Satan—which are called the greater jihads—and the jihad against an open enemy— known as the lesser jihad. Prophet Muhammad explained this upon returning from battle: "We are returning from the lesser jihad to the greater jihad." This jihad against yourself manifests in many ways. For example, getting your college education is the greater jihad. Quitting smoking, losing weight, beating cancer, learning a skill, parenting, even "adulting" are all forms of the greater jihad. Thus, the first and greatest form of jihad in Islam is the jihad to improve oneself and to improve all humanity. (Rashid, 2017)

It is worth noting that Islamic scholars may differ on the kinds of jihad in Islam, but they agree on the meaning of jihad that it is not a "destruc- tion" or (terrorism) or "killing innocent people." It is a call on Muslims to struggle for self-betterment and for Islamic communities anywhere in the world to fulfill their obligations as citizens and to support and defend the constitutions and laws of their new countries. Table 6.1 summarizes some of the major kinds of jihad in Islam.

Many Islamic scholars and leaders of Islamic movements rejected and denounced the killing of innocent people on September 11, 2001, "The undersigned, leaders of Islamic movements, are horrified by the events of Tuesday, September 11, 2001, in the United States, which resulted in massive killing, destruction, and attack on innocent lives. We express our deepest sympathies and sorrow. In the strongest terms, we condemn the incidents, which are against all human and Islamic norms. This is grounded in the Noble Laws of Islam which forbid all forms of attacks on innocents." Furthermore, Abdel-Mo'tei Bayyoumi of Al-Azhar's Islamic Research Academy wrote, "for jihad to be legal, it must meet sev- eral conditions. Among them: a Muslim should not provoke aggression; should only fight those who fight him; children, women, and the elderly should be spared. "There is no terrorism or a threat to civilians in jihad" (Al-Ahram Weekly Online, September 20–26, 2001; www.archive.org). The Council of Saudi 'Ulama issued a fatwa (Islamic verdict) in February 2003 describing "the shedding of the innocent blood and the bombing of

Table 6.1 Kinds of Jihad in Islam

Type	Purpose	Verse from Qur'an
Jihad of the soul	Intrapersonal, inertial, and spiritual process. A person should work diligently to purify himself/herself from any illegitimate wanting to inflict harm on oneself or on anyone else within or outside their community	"O believers! Bow down, prostrate yourselves, worship your Lord, and do what is good so that you may be successful" (Surat/Chapter al Hajj 22:77).
Jihad of fancies and strong desires	A strong feeling of wanting to have something or wishing for something to take place at the expense of others. A Muslim is required to struggle against these fancies and desires to sin and commit wrong things.	"O My servants who have transgressed against themselves (by sinning), do not despair of the mercy of Allah. Indeed, Allah forgives all sins. Indeed, it is He who is the Forgiving, the Merciful" (Surat/Chapter az Zumer 39:53854).
Avoiding whispers of Satan/Devil	A psychological process to stop oneself from thinking of committing a sin or even making a poor judgment or to engage in a bad action.	"Indeed, there is for him (Satan) no authority over those who have believed and rely upon their Lord. His authority is only over those who take him as an ally and those who through him associate others with Allah" (Sura/Chapter an Nahl [The Bee] 16:99–100).
Self-purification/ self-sanctification	To struggle to purify the soul and strive against one's own evil inclination	"By the soul and the proportion and order given to it; and its enlightenment as to its wrong and its right; truly he succeeds who purifies it and he fails who corrupts it!" (Surat/Chapter ash Shamas [The Sun] 91:7–10).

(continued)

Table 6.1 CONTINUED

Type	Purpose	Verse from Qur'an
Striving for livelihood	To work and provide for the family and its well-being and care for the family	"Strive for the cause of Allah in the way He deserves, for it is He Who has chosen you and laid upon you no hardship in the religion—the way of your forefather Abraham. It is Allah Who named you 'the ones who submit' in the earlier Scriptures and in this Qur'an, so that the Messenger may be a witness over you, and that you may be witnesses over humanity. So, establish prayer, pay alms-tax, and hold fast to Allah. He alone is your Guardian. What an excellent Guardian, and what an excellent Helper."
Jihad for seeking knowledge	Studying hard, doing research, and traveling domestically or abroad for the purpose of seeking knowledge	"God will exalt those of you who believe, and those who are given knowledge, in high degrees; and Allah is Aware of what you do" (Surat/Chapter al Mujadilah 58:11). "Read in the name of thy Lord who created; created man from a mere clot of blood; read and your Lord is the most generous; the one who taught (them to write) by the pen; taught man what he knew not" (Surat/Chapter al Alaq [The Colt] 96:1–5).

Combat Jihad for the sake of Allah is to defend the homeland and properties	To defend the homeland and properties. The causes of Jihad and all the *defensive* combat when the enemy lurks to undermine the nation is a defense as well, if the information is confirmed that the enemy has prepared their plan and weapons to attack and commit an aggression.	"Fight in the way of Allah those who fight against you but do not transgress. Indeed, Allah does not like transgressors" (Surat/Chapter al Baqarah 2:190).
Jihad of advocacy	Advocate a noble cause, promote peace and justice, and show wisdom and patience.	They are those who, if established in the land by Us, would perform prayer, pay alms-tax, encourage what is good, and forbid what is evil. And with Allah rests the outcome of all affairs" (Surat/Chapter al Hajj [The Pilgrimage] 22:41).

buildings and ships and the destruction of public and private installations is a criminal act against Islam. Those who carry out such acts have deviant beliefs and misleading ideologies and are responsible for the crime. Islam and Muslims should not be held responsible for such actions" (Council of Saudi 'Ulama, 2003).

In the spirit of American citizenship and loyalty to the country, 57 leaders of North American Islamic networks, 77 intellectuals, and several concerned American Muslims released a statement to the media, in which they stressed,

As American Muslims and scholars of Islam, we wish to restate our conviction that peace and justice constitute the basic principles of the Muslim faith. We wish again to state unequivocally that neither the al-Qaeda organization nor Usama bin Laden represents Islam or reflects Muslim beliefs and practices. Rather, groups like al-Qaeda have misused and abused Islam in order to fit their own radical and indeed anti-Islamic agenda. Usama bin Laden and al-Qaeda's actions are criminal, misguided and counter to the true teachings of Islam. (Statement Rejecting Terrorism, September 9, 2002, www.archive.org)

CULTURE MANIFESTATIONS AND POLITICAL RESPONSES

It takes two sides to generate a conflict and a clash of cultures, civilizations, religions, and politics. The rhetoric following September 11, 2001, placed the event and its consequences on all Muslims and in the framework of a conflict between Islam and the West (Halliday, 2003). Hence, the spreading of fear or the idea of an imminent danger of invasion in the United States by Muslims traveled on a fast track. As a religious instruction, Muslims fear His Almighty God and obey His instructions even if someone intended to harm them. Surat/Chapter 28 al-Ma'idah captures this highly applauded code of ethics and states, "If you extend your hand to kill me, I will not extend my hand to kill you; for I fear God, Lord of the Worlds" (Surat/Chapter al Ma'idah 5:28). Abud-Darda reported that Prophet Muhammad said, "Nothing will be heavier on the Day of Resurrection in the scale of the believer than good manners. Allah hates one who utters foul or coarse language" (At-Tirmhdhi, Riyad-us-Salihen, 626). This highly credited saying by the Prophet offers that it is spiritual, healthy, and beneficial to do good by themselves as people of faith and the society. In relation to this approach, Connor Wood explained that Christianity was set apart by its ethos of caring for the sick, which may have produced consequential benefits; e.g., more Christians survived outbreaks of disease than the pagan Romans during the Roman Empire. Islam, too, initially attracted followers by emphasizing honor, humility, and charity, qualities which were not endemic in turbulent 7th Century Arabia (Wood, 2017). Both examples demonstrate the relationship between religious beliefs and how people have navigated individualism and collectivism, even in cross-cultural social environments. Wood further highlighted the significance of sacred values that are often found in several faiths, including: shared goals and standards in institutional religions, the subtle pressure to live according to these standards such as attending services regularly, volunteering, fasting, and tithing. Wood further contends that religious standards are less flexible despite the occasional discomfort felt by members. Indeed, many religious standards are sacred values, shielded from utilitarian second-guessing by an aura of spiritual significance (Wood, 2017).

Though they are a thin minority, radical Muslims strive to put their spin on these "sacred values" and produce their own "religious standards" to achieve their set of goals by applying violence and destruction in the name of religion. It is forbidden to do bad things, act violently, harm someone, or murder a person. The Qur'an states: "Come, let me tell you what your Lord has forbidden you: that you associate nothing with Him;

that you honor your parents; that you do not kill your children because of poverty—We provide for you and for them; that you do not come near indecencies, whether outward or inward; and that you do not kill the soul which God has sanctified—except in the course of justice. All this He has enjoined upon you, so that you may understand" (Surat/Chapter al An'am 6:151).

John L. Esposito, the director of the Center for Muslim-Christian Understanding at Georgetown University, highlighted the critical point that religious extremism remains a threat today as in the past. However, it is not restricted to or inherent in any one religion. A YouGov poll of 2013 showed that 44% of American citizens doubted the loyalty of American Muslims to the United States. Despite condemnation from Muslim nations and Arab countries, and indeed by world leaders, the attack of September 11, 2001, deeply ripped the relationship between American Muslims and the U.S. public in particular, and with the global community in general. Politically, in the immediate reaction, the Bush administration declared war on terrorism, determined to bring Osama bin Laden and al-Qaeda to justice, and vowed to stop the emergence of other terrorist attacks by a strategy of military involvement and economic sanctions. This effort contributed to the destruction of al-Qaeda's networks, diminishing its infrastructures, and to some extent, dried out its financial resources and foundations. This global war strategy on terrorism translated into the most significant American military invasion in modern history and included the overthrow of the Taliban rule in Afghanistan and a forced regime change in Iraq in 2003.

Still, other tragic events in the world, such as the bombings in Madrid in 2004, Sharm El Sheikh, Egypt, and the coordinated London bombings, both in 2005, deepened the public cynicism and misunderstanding of the basic principles of Islamic beliefs. The media coverage of Islam and Muslims and some scholarly writings on Islamist militancy and violence were construed as an affirmation of the clash of civilizations' 'propositions' . . . and the attacks were presented as directed against Western ways of life . . . democracies and the values of freedom and liberty (Ismail, 2006).

MUSLIM AND NON-MUSLIMS
RELATIONS—BUILDING UNDERSTANDING

As'salamu Alaykum in Arabic (peace be with you in English) is the greeting of Muslims around the world. It is a religious salutation that communicates a message of *salam* (peace) to the people a Muslim person meets. From a spiritual angle, it is a call to achieve a state of peace with the other individual or group of people. Attaining peaceful relationships among human beings includes oneself, family, community, society, and humanity. In the context of human relations and connectedness, today's global communities are interdependent and are closer to one another than ever before. The Internet and social media play significant roles in informing and facilitating discussions about global affairs, including religious issues. It is a type of discussion that may challenge general knowledge, raise critical questions, and offer dialogue and engagement in interfaith dialogue. This type of discussion provides opportunities for increased understanding rather than continued ignorance. Generally, Muslims in the world, and Muslim Americans, in particular, strive to establish two critical messages: tWe are citizens with the same rights as you and We are human beings just like you because we have a faith that is equivalent to yours (Marzouki, 2013).

Muslims are also longing for fostering normal relations with neighbors and communities in which they show respect, acceptance, passion, trust, and collaboration. The Qur'an indicates, "O people! We created you from a male and a female, and made you races and tribes that you may know one another. The best among you in the sight of God is the most righteous. God is All-Knowing, Well-Experienced" (Surat/Chapter al Hujurat 49:13). Further, the Qur'an states, "We [Muslims] make no distinction between any of His messengers (i.e., God's messengers)" (Surat/Chapter al Baqarah 2:285).

Moreover, the Qur'an reminds Muslims that "We have inspired you, as We had inspired Noah and the prophets after him. And We inspired Abraham, and Ishmael, and Isaac, and Jacob, and the Patriarchs, and Jesus, and Job, and Jonah, and Aaron, and Solomon. And We gave David the

Psalms" (Surat/Chapter al Nisa 4:163). Still in another verse we read, "He prescribed for you the same religion He enjoined upon Noah, and what We inspired to you, and what We enjoined upon Abraham, and Moses, and Jesus: 'You shall uphold the religion, and be not divided therein.' As for the idolaters, what you call them to is outrageous to them. God chooses to Himself whom He wills, and He guides to Himself whoever repents" (Surat/Chapter ash Shura 42:13). Badawi explained that these Qur'anic texts preclude the notion of narrow partisanship that may lead to hatred or even violence against communities who perceive themselves as followers of other prophets and religions. It is worth repeating part of the Hadith where it says, "Nothing will be heavier on the Day of Resurrection in the scale of the believer than good manners" (Ad-Dimashqi et al., 1999, p. 626). The important principle in this Hadith is that courtesy is an asset, good mannerism is a virtue, and decent language in communication reflects a sound and refined mind that shuns all that is bad and corrupt, including waging terror against innocent people. Islamic teachings emphasize faith as it strengthens pure instinct in self, thus enabling the person to conquer lust and evil desire. It establishes good conduct and proper behavior. Muslim families and communities play a fundamental and highly significant role in the upbringing of young people. They provide the basic elements in the social edifice and offer an imperative layer of protection against crime, deviation of behavior, terrorism, and radicalization.

One of the strategies of terrorist organizations involves recruiting young children to train and brainwash them. These organizations can contribute to the deviation, intellectual and behavioral aberration, and potential toward radicalization, extremism, and terrorism among youth (El-Omairy, 2011). Islam underscores the role of the family in a child's growth. Abu Huraira quoted the Prophet as saying, "Every human being is born with pure instincts. It is his parents who make him/her a Jew, or a Christian, a Magian (or a Muslim)" (Al Bukhari, Vol. 2, p. 198; Muslim, Vol. 4, p. 47).

Understanding the desire of terrorists to recruit, indoctrinate, and radicalize others, the need is great, therefore, to present accurate information about the destructive process of exploitation and radicalization (El-Omairy, 2011). Only qualified scholars and religious institutions such as Al Azhar are entrusted in issuing *Fatwas* (religious opinions). Adhering to the Holy Qur'an and the *Sunnah* of the Prophet promotes the correct understanding of its verses and rejects seducement to extremism and radicalization (El-Omairy, 2011, p. 41). Moreover, it is imperative to unmask "the calls of those who urge terrorism and advocate radicalism and extremism and refute such calls by presenting the right interpretation of the Qur'an and the *Hadith*" (El-Omairy, 2011, p. 26). In addition, the fourth article of the Convention of the Organization of the Islamic Conference of Fighting Terrorism calls for closer cooperation among signatory countries to teach the noble Islamic principles and moral values which prohibit the exercise of terrorism (El-Omairy, 2011). In closing, one of my senior students recapped the importance of intercultural sensitivity as follows: "Learn more about intercultural sensitivity but from what I understand from it, it means that as a person, you have to be sensible and kind to others who are different from you. One must never judge a whole group of people from the same culture just because one person from that group did something wrong. It is important to be sensitive to others." On December 9, 2005, the Organization of the Islamic Conference, Summit Conference issued a statement expressing their determination to fight terrorism: "We are determined to fight terrorism in all its forms. . . . Islam is the religion of moderation. It rejects extremism and isolation. There is a need to confront deviant ideology where it appears, including in school curricula. Islam is the religion of diversity and tolerance" (*Daily Star*, 2005).

INTERFAITH DIALOGUE

Pope Francis of the Catholic Church and Sheikh Ahmed el-Tayeb, Grand Imam of Al-Azhar, signed the Abu Dhabi declaration (agreement), also known as Document on Human Fraternity, on February 4, 2019, in Abu Dhabi, United Arab Emirates. The introduction of the document states, "Faith leads a believer to see in the other a brother or sister to be supported and loved. Through faith in God, who has created the universe, creatures, and all human beings (equal on account of his mercy), are called to express this human fraternity by safeguarding creation and the entire universe and supporting all persons, especially the poorest and those most in need" (Document on Human Fraternity, 2019). The document called "upon intellectuals, philosophers, religious figures, artists, media professionals and men and women of culture in every part of the world, to rediscover the values of peace, justice, goodness, beauty, human fraternity and coexistence in order to confirm the importance of these values as anchors of salvation for all, and to promote them everywhere" (Document on Human Fraternity, 2019). Inciting violence and causing bloodletting for a particular agenda by small groups "result from a political manipulation of religions and from interpretations made by religious groups who, in the course of history, have taken advantage of the power of religious sentiment in the hearts of men and women to make them act in a way that has nothing to do with the truth of religion. This is done to achieve objectives that are political, economic, worldly—and shortsighted" (Document on Human Fraternity, 2019).

The document also calls for ending poverty and injustices to deny radicals from pleading for economic improvements and social and racial justice as a pretext to their criminal acts. It states, "Terrorism is deplorable and threatens the security of people, be they in the East or the West, the North or the South, and disseminates panic, terror and pessimism, but this is not due to religion, even when terrorists instrumentalize it. Rather, it is due to an accumulation of incorrect interpretations of religious texts and policies linked to hunger, poverty, injustice, oppression, and pride. This is why it is necessary to stop supporting terrorist movements fueled by financing, the provision of weapons and strategy, and attempts to justify these movements even using the media. All these must be regarded as international crimes that threaten security and world peace. Such terrorism must be condemned in all its forms and expressions" (Document on Human Fraternity, 2019). In the attempt to mend bridges among Muslims with various sects, Christians, Yazidis, and others, Pope Francis's first papal visit to Iraq on March 5–8, 2021, confirmed the importance of the interfaith dialogue among religions. In one of his short speeches, Pope Francis said: "How cruel it is that this country (referring to Iraq), the cradle of civilization, should have been afflicted by so barbarous a blow, with ancient places of worship destroyed and many thousands of people—Muslims, Christians, Yazidis, and others—forcibly displaced or killed" (www.aljazeera.com).

Pope Francis added, "Today, however, we reaffirm our conviction that fraternity is more durable than fratricide, that hope is more powerful than hatred, that peace more powerful than war" (www.news.un.org/en/story). Reacting to His Holiness Pope Francis to the site of Al Tahera Church, located in the Province of Mosul in Iraq, Noura Al Kaabi, Minister of Culture and Youth of the United Arab Emirates, and Audrey Azoulay, Director-General of the United Nations Educational, Scientific, and Cultural Organization (UNESCO), welcomed the historic visit. They also issued a joint statement which described the historical visit "as sending a clear message to the world that harmony and cohesion between the followers of all religions is the only way for the advancement and progress of humanity and the most effective means by which to address the increasing challenges facing the world" (UNESCO, 2021). The joint message underlined that the Pope's message is once again a call for "peace and fraternity and highlighted the strength and resilience of humanity in countering the divisive message spread by the group responsible for destroying the Al Nouri Mosque, the Al Saa'a and Al Tahera Churches" (www.news.un.org/en/story). It should be noted that ISIS destroyed the historical mosque and the churches in the name of Islam. The reaction of the Islamic world and Muslims to the visit has been positive and uplifting. It provided a "strong impetus to efforts aimed at establishing peace and harmony in Iraq, the region, and the world" (www.news.un.org/en/story).

CONCLUSION

Dear non-Muslim fellow citizens, you may come to understand a critical challenge that Muslims encounter in Western societies (e.g., the United States, Canada, and Europe), "to preserve their religious and cultural identities, and be constructively engaged in the cultural, social, and political life of these societies (Aslan, 2015; Halstead, 2003; Ramadan, 2004; Saada, 2017). The Qur'an requires the faithful always to be conscious of God: "O you who believe! Be conscious of God, and seek the means of approach to Him, and strive in His cause, so that you may succeed" (Surat/Chapter al Ma'idah 5:35). Moreover, the Scripture forewarns that offenders, listeners to misrepresentations, unlawful retributions, and the misguided should be warned and corrected. The Qur'an says, "Listeners to falsehoods, eaters of illicit earnings. If they come to you, judge between them, or turn away from them. If you turn away from them, they will not harm you in the least. However, if you judge, judge between them equitably. God loves the equitable" (Surat/Chapter al Ma'idah 5:42). Additionally, other passages in the Qur'an feature the religious and spiritual importance of the Torah "We have revealed the Torah, wherein is guidance and light" (Surat/Chapter al Ma'idah 5:44). Moreover, the Qur'an recognizes the shared commonalities among Jewish, Christians, and Muslims as follows: "Those who believe, and those who are Jewish, and the Christians, and the Sabeans—any who believe in God and the Last Day, and act righteously—will have their reward with their Lord; they have nothing to fear, nor will they grieve" (Surat/Chapter al Baqarah 2:62). Muslims are commanded to do lawful things in life and among people. "O people! Eat of what is lawful and good on earth, and do not follow the footsteps of Satan. He is to you an open enemy" (Surat/Chapter al Baqarah 2:186).

Muslims in the West and elsewhere need to do more educational work to educate and inform their fellow citizens of their multicultural faith and diverse communities in Islam. Education is key to the golden gate of world peace, prosperity, cooperation, and civility. As stated in this chapter, Islam, like other major religions, has "a set of texts—a holy book, traditions, legal documents, learned writings—that are invoked to justify the actions of Muslims" (Halliday, 2003, p. 114). The variant interpretations of the texts and sayings of the Prophet by those who "seek to justify their actions by reference to a particular traditional authority, this is a choice, not a necessity" (Halliday, 2003, p. 115). The intent of a particular interpretation often conceals the real purpose or the motivation of those who are determined to induce a departure from the texts and their relevant religious, historical, and cultural contexts. Like any other followers and devotees of other regions, Muslims are supposed to adhere to the universal message of peace and solidarity with humanities. The Qur'an stipulates, "O mankind! Lo! We have created you from male and female and have made you nations and tribes that ye may know one another. Lo! The noblest of you, in the sight of God, is the best in conduct. Lo! God is knower, Aware" (Surat/ Chapter al Hujurat 49:13).

Ordinary Muslims, Muslim leaders, and Muslim scholars have publicly (orally in writing) condemned terrorism and have taken measures to change school curriculums. Further, countries with Muslim majorities have outlawed and arrested Muslim extremists, sponsored rehabilitation centers, and rewarded those who repented their wrong and evil actions. As stated earlier, the Abu Dhabi Document on Human Fraternity "may constitute an invitation to reconciliation and fraternity among all believers, indeed among believers and non-believers, and all people of goodwill. This declaration may be an appeal to every upright conscience that rejects deplorable violence and blind extremism; an appeal to those who cherish the values of tolerance and fraternity that are promoted and encouraged by religions" (Document on Human Fraternity, 2019). John L. Esposito cautioned us that "To equate Islam fundamentalism with extremism uncritically is to judge Islam only by those who wreak havoc, a standard not applied to Judaism and Christianity" (Esposito, 1999, p. 286). Indeed, "inciting war, hateful attitudes, violence or the shedding of blood are incompatible with authentic religious teachings" (Pope Francis, March 5, 2021). Therefore, it is expressively critical to acknowledge the humanity of Muslims as human beings proactively engaging with their environment and societies. Or, as Gabriele Marranci wrote, "I wish to suggest that we need to have a paradigm through which the anthropologists of Islam can effectively study Muslims as human beings rather than living symbols of a religion" (Marranci, 2008, p. 100). To my non-Muslim friends and colleagues, this contribution is dedicated to you with unpretentiousness, love, respect, and determination to advance the effort to deconstruct any ethnic, social, and cultural serotypes that may reduce our (all of us) identities to one dimension.

REFERENCES

ABC News. (2015, December 9). *How many Muslims are serving in U.S. military?* ABC News.

Abid al-Jabiri, M. (1982). *Al-Khitab al-Arabi al-Mu'asir* (On Contemporary Arab Discourse). Al-Talia'h.

Ad-Dimashqi, A. Z. Y., & An-Nawawi, B. S. (1999). *Riyad-us-Saliheen.* Vols. 1 and 2. Darussalam.

Al Bukhari—Vol. 2—Online: (99+) (PDF) Sahih al-Bukhari. Volume 2 | MetaksyaGrigoryan—Academia.edu

Al Bukhari—Vol. 4—Online: (99+) (PDF) Sahih Al-Bukhari Volume (4) | Sara Harrachi—Academia.edu

AljazeeraNews.Retrievedfromhttps://www.aljazeera.com/news/2021/3/4/pope-francis-embarks-on-historic-visit-to-iraq

Aslan, E. (2015). *Citizenship* education *and Islam.* In E. Aslan & M. Hermansen (Eds.), *Islam and citizenship education* (pp. 25–45). Springer Fachmedien Wiesbaden.

At-Tirmhdhi, Riyad-us-Salihen, 626—scripture reference in the Book of Miscellany.

Badawi, J. (2012, December 3). *Muslims and non-Muslims relations.* Retrieved from http://fiqhcouncil.org/muslim-nonmuslim-relations/

Baker, G. W. (2003). *Arab, Islam, and the Middle East.* Brown Books.

BBC News. (2019, August 18). Afghanistan: Bomb kills 63 at wedding in Kabul. BBC News.

Beydoun, A. K. (2018). *American Islamophobia: Understanding the roots and rise of fear.* University of California Press.

Council on American-Islamic Relations (CAIR). 2010. CAIR: Who we are—CAIR—Council on American-Islamic Relations.

The Council of Saudi 'Ulama. (2003). Fatwa of February 2003. Retrieved from https://kurzman.unc.edu/islamic-statements-against-terrorism. Infobase Publishing, 2010.

Curtis, E. (2010). *Encyclopedia of Muslim-American history.*

Daily Star (Beirut, Lebanon). (2005, December 9). Retrieved from https://kurzman.unc.edu/islamic-statements-against-terrorism/

Desilver, D., & Masci, D. (2017). *World's Muslim population more widespread than you might think.* Retrieved from https://www.pewresearch.org/fact-tank/2017/01/31/worlds-muslim-population-more-widespread-than-you-might-think/

Document on Human Fraternity for world peace and living together. (2019, February 4). *Abu Dhabi, U.A.E.* Retrieved from https://www.vaticannews.va/en/pope/news/2019-02/pope-francis-uae-declaration-with-al-azhar-grand-imam.html

El-Omairi, M. A. (2011). *Intellectual confrontation of terrorism.* Naif Arab University for Security Sciences.

Esposito, L. J. (1999). *The Islamic threat: Myth or reality.* Oxford University Press.

Fiqh Council of North America (FNCA). (2005). U.S. Muslim religious council issues fatwa against terrorism—IslamiCity. Retrieved from https://www.foreignpolicy.com.

Gouvernement.fr. Observatoire de la laicite. Secularism and religious freedom. Retrieved from https://www.gouvernement.fr/en/secularism-and-religious-freedom

Green, T. (2019). Why Muslims condemn terrorism? Western violence and scapegoating in an age of Islamophobia. Retrieved from https://yaqeeninstitute.org/toddgreen/ why-dont-muslims-condemn-terrorism-western-violence-and-scapegoating-in-an- age-of-islamophobia

Haberman, A., Burns, M., & Parker, A. (2016, July 7). Donald Trump's confrontation with Muslim soldier's parents emerges as unexpected flash point. *The New York Times*.

Halliday, F. (2003). *Islam and the myth of confrontation*. I.B. Tauris.

Halstead, J. (2003). Schooling and cultural maintenance for religious minorities in the liberal state. In K. McDonough & W. Feinberg (Eds.), *Citizenship and* education *in liberal-democratic societies* (pp. 273–299). Oxford University Press.

Hussain, A. (2016). *Muslims and the making of America*. Baylor University Press.

Ismail, S. (2006). *Rethinking Islamist politics: Culture, the state of Islamism*. I. B. Tauris.

Loimeier, R. (2013). *Muslim societies in Africa. A historical anthropology*. Indiana University Press.

Marranci, G. (2008). *The anthropology of Islam*. BERGE.

Marzouki, N. (2013). *Islam: An American religion*. Columbia University Press.

Modood, T. (2019). *Essays on secularism and multiculturalism*. Rowman & Littlefield.

Nader, L. (2015). Three jihads: Islamic, Christian, and Jewish. *Anthropology Today*, *31*(2), 1–2. https://www.wileyonlinelibrary.com/journal/anth.

Noah, T. (2001). The Mullah of Dupont Circle. Retrieved from https://Slate.com/news- and-politics/2001/12

Penner, M. B. (2017). Reviews in religion and theology. Wiley-Blackwell. Retrieved from http://web.b.ebscohost.com.libservprd.bridgew.edu/ehost/pdfviewer/pdfviewer? vid=3&sid=6e8e764b-a04c-43a8-b8e1-535381d182af%40sessionmgr102

Pew Research Center. (2015). https://www.pewresearch.org/fact-tank/2017/01/31/ worlds-muslim-population-more-widespread-than-you-might-think/

Ramadan, T. (2004). *Western Muslims and the future of Islam*. Oxford: Oxford University Press.

Rashid, Q. (2017). Opinion: Jihad is not a dirty word. Washington Post.com. Retrieved at https://www.washingtonpost.com/news/global-opinion/wp/2017/07/08/

Saada, N., & Gross, Z. (2017). Islamic education and the challenge of democratic citizen- ship: A critical perspective studies in the cultural politics of education. *Studies in the Cultural Politics of Education*, *38*(6), 807–822.

Sarsour, L. (2017). Women's march organizer Linda Sarsour spoke of jihad, but she wasn't talking about violence. Time.com. Retrieved from https://time.com/4848454/ linda-sarsour

Shah, Z. A. (2018). *Anthropomorphic depictions of god: The concept of God Judaic, Christian, and Islamic traditions: Representing the unpresentable*. International Institute of Islamic Thought (IIIT).

UNESCO. (2021, July 3). Joint Statement of Their Excellencies Noura Al Kaabi and Audrey Azoulay. https://en.unesco.org/news/joint-statement-their-excellencies-noura-al- kaabi-and-audrey-azoulay

The White House, Office of the Press Secretary. (2015). Remarks by the President at the 2015 Iftar Dinner. Retrieved from https://obamawhitehouse.archives.gov/the-press- office/2015

Wieseltier, L. (2011). What we affirm. Retrieved from https://newrepublic.com/article/94774/leon's-remarks

Wood, C. (2017). Religion and self-regulation: A model (and a trip to Norway). Retrieved from https://www.patheos.com/blogs/scienceonreligion/2017/08/self-regulation-religion-model/

7

Trends and Catalysts of Anti-Muslim Hate Crime and Bigoted Attitudes

A Multidecade Analysis

BRIAN LEVIN■

INTRODUCTION

Over the last few decades, increasingly detailed social science research—and crime data, in particular—has enabled researchers to analyze fluctuations in the targeting of various religious and other groups for stereotyping and aggression over time. Hate crime data enumerate criminal events where the target is selected because of their actual or perceived group status. Cumulatively, these data offer important insight into trends and timing of bigoted aggression. The Federal Bureau of Investigation's (FBI) hate crime definition is "a committed criminal offense motivated in whole or in part by the offender's bias(es) against a race, religion, disability, sexual orientation, ethnicity, gender, and gender identity" (FBI/ UCR: Hate Crime Data Collection Guidelines, 2015).

Muslims, who are among the most diversified and fastest-growing faith communities in the United States, have a presence that predates

Brian Levin, *Trends and Catalysts of Anti-Muslim Hate Crime and Bigoted Attitudes* In: *Islamophobia and Acts of Violence*. Edited by: Carolyn Turpin-Petrosino, Oxford University Press. © Oxford University Press 2022. DOI: 10.1093/oso/9780190922313.003.0007 the nation's founding. Nonetheless, they have faced renewed spasms of bigotry, including hate crime, particularly in the first decades of this century. American Muslims, projected to be slightly more than 1% of the population, are remarkably diverse across numerous demographic variables, including race, birthplace, occupation, expression of practices, and introduction to the faith (Lipka, 2020). Despite the ideals of the U.S. Constitution's Article Six ban on religious tests for office, the First Amendment's prohibition on the establishment or impediment of religion, and the Fourteenth's Amendment guarantee of equal protection, the unequal treatment of American Muslims has from the time of slavery until the present tested these ideals.

In more recent decades, when newer annual tallies of FBI-reported anti-Muslim hate crime became available, several distinct periods emerged where adherents faced cycles of more sustained and widespread prejudice. In the decade before 9/11, national reporting was low and never exceeded a few dozen despite instances of international instability and conflict. This was followed by a record peak immediately around 9/11 (FBI: Hate Crime 1992–2019, 2020). In the years thereafter, an elevated multiyear plateau in anti-Muslim hate crime lasted through 2014—followed by another period of increase, with an elevated "head and shoulders" peak. Since 2001, Muslims have been the second most frequent target for religious motivated hate crimes both numerically and proportionately, after Jews who in 2019 accounted for 13% of all hate crime (FBI: Hate Crime 1992–2019, 2020).

For hate crimes overall, since the start of the FBI national hate crime reporting program in 1992, longer-term, though often "sawtooth" trend patterns were similarly punctuated by spikes correlating to catalytic events and various responses to those events. These spikes occurred above previous plateaus in both overall hate crime and those against particular groups. However, overall hate crime, unlike anti-Muslim offenses, had sustained periods of depressed lower plateaus (FBI: Hate Crime 1992–2019, 2020). In the nearly three decades of FBI collected data, annual overall hate crime totals ranged between 5,000 and 10,000 with shifts in targeted groups and offense types (FBI: Hate Crime 1992–2019, 2020). The most common victims for FBI hate crimes reported to police in 2019 were African Americans, gays, Jews, and Whites, as hate crimes plateaued with a moderate upward tilt but also with a sustained level of violent offenses (FBI: Hate Crime 1992–2019, 2020).

National overall data are limited owing to official underreporting, as only 54% of victims and 12% of police departments submit official reports, and to the fact that supplemental nongovernmental organization (NGO) portals are often not vetted. Still, the thousands of FBI cases collected, along with the findings of other data sets, reveal important consistencies in changes over time, particular a correlation with recent highly charged political or conflictual events (FBI: Hate Crime 1992–2019, 2020; National Crime Victimization Survey, 2019).

FBI enumerated hate crimes overall had a period of decline from a 1996 election year peak, interrupted by a sharp but brief record peak in 2001, followed by another extended lower plateau of 6 years. That plateau eroded into a sustained overall period of decline in 2009 that bottomed in 2014 before rising again into the end of the decade (FBI: Hate Crime 1992–2019, 2020). While hate crimes overall reverted to pre-9/11 levels, the trend was far different for American Muslims experiencing hate crime. Victimizations never reverted to pre-9/11 levels, while over a decade later, anti-Muslim assaults eventually surpassed those of 2001 (FBI: Hate Crime 1992–2019, 2020). (See Chart Array 7.1 and Photo 7.1.)

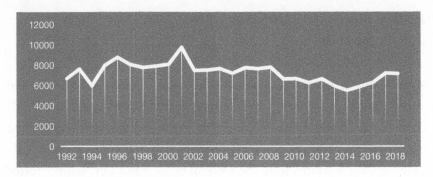

Chart 7.1 FBI: U.S. Hate Crime, 1992–2018
Source: Center for the Study of Hate & Extremism

Photo Array 7.1 American Muslims have been the target of both public derision but also support since the beginning of the new century.
SOURCE: Brian Levin/Center for the Study of Hate & Extremism

NORMALIZING ANTI-MUSLIM STEREOTYPES: TERROR, SHARIA, AND REPLACEMENT

For anti-Muslim hate crime, fluctuations appear around a series of elevated baseline steps with spikes corresponding to catalytic events, like the 9/11 terror attacks, and derisive political statements and media references tied to those events. More recent events where hate crimes contemporaneously spiked against Muslims were the December 2015 San Bernardino Terror attack (Nagourney et al., 2015) and the Muslim ban proposal ("Trump border policy: Who's affected?," 2017), and in 2016, the November election and June's Pulse night club massacre ("What we know about Orlando shooting," 2016).

Increases in expressions of anti-Muslim bigotry crime occur not only around catalytic events like terrorist attacks and international conflicts when fear and stereotyping of Muslims are amplified but in virtual and terrestrial subcultural spaces where a mix of facts, half-truths, and conspiracy theories incubate a mutating narrative of Muslims posing myriad existential threats to American national security and cultural traditions. The post-9/11 sociopolitical landscape catapulted Muslims and Arabs to a new level of scrutiny and bigotry that was increasingly a common bonding point for an array of new far-right enthusiasts across a spectrum of issues. Muslims were increasingly rotated and spotlighted among a new elastic set of connected villains in a post-Soviet political era ("When Islamophobia turns violent," 2016). Bigoted stereotypes, instability in the Middle East, and various terror attacks became lightning rods for a variety of anti-Muslim and anti-Semitic conspiracy theories that ensnare not only these faith groups but also others like leftists who allegedly manipulate America against its own interests toward those of foreign infiltrators. Initially, President George Bush's invocation of the term "New World Order" concerning the international alignment against Iraq for its invasion of Kuwait in 1991 became fodder for a fringe American-born nativist conspiracy theory about a United Nations takeover of America where citizens would be stripped of their rights with the aid of various federal agencies operating black helicopters and concentration camps (Halpern & Levin, 1996).

In the mainstream, however, beginning in 1993 and culminating in his controversial 1996 book, *The Clash of Civilizations and the Remaking of World Order*, American political scientist Samuel P. Huntington posits that population increases in predominantly Muslim nations and rising economies in Asia are a threat to "western" dominance as well as democracy and human rights (Huntington, 1996). However, in the years after 9/11, the fearful "othering" of Muslims and Arabs became a key anchor, not only to fringe neo-Nazi bigots and White supremacists but to an increasingly more mainstream audience of conservatives. While President George

W. Bush spoke of tolerance toward Muslims during the week of the 9/11 attacks, by 2004, his campaign was airing an ad attacking Democrats on national security and counterterrorism by depicting the nation's enemies as wolf packs lying in wait over a narration stating, "Weakness attracts those who are waiting to do America harm" (Historic campaign ad—Bush Cheney '04; Levin & Nakashima, 2019).

By 2007, Act for America, a nationwide anti-Muslim organization was formed. While the group's stated mission seeks to educate "citizens and elected officials to impact policy involving national security and defeating terrorism," the bigoted statements and actions by its leadership and supporters reveal something far more nefarious. That same year its founder, Bridgette Gabriel, who later boasted of her unfettered access to President Trump, lectured the Joint Forces Staff Command College at the Department of Defense, saying a "Practicing Muslim who believes the word of the Koran to be the word of Allah . . . who goes to mosque and prays every Friday, who prays five times a day—this practicing Muslim, who believes in the teachings of the Koran, cannot be a loyal citizen of the United States." Act for America rallies were noteworthy in the breadth of those showing up, but in the 2017 run up to Charlottesville, they were increasingly populated by violent far-right extremist groups like Proud Boys, Oath Keepers, and the neo-Nazi Rise Above movement (ACT for America, Southern Poverty Law Center, n.d.).

As politics, cable news, and social media became increasingly coarse and conspiracy-oriented, anti-Muslim stereotyping became central to discussions, including national security, immigration, religious freedom, and culture. For example, a vicious false rumor that Barack Obama was unfit for the presidency because of his hidden Muslim faith and alleged foreign birth became fodder for various high-profile influencers, including future President Trump. The election cycle ending in Mr. Trump's ascension to the White House was noteworthy for the ubiquity of anti-Muslim statements and policy proposals, including "bans" of Muslim immigration and the pending imposition of "sharia law" ("When Islamophobia turns violent," 2016).

Aided by an increasingly connected international consortium of primarily online far-right extremists, Islam and immigration became a central focus of their evolving invective. While the theme for this new iteration of anti-Muslim bigotry incorporated preexisting fearmongering about Muslims broadly posing stealth terror threats, it has since expanded its reach to include the myriad perceived risks of a looming demographic takeover of Western nations by Muslims, particularly immigrants. "Replacement theory" had a renaissance in 2011 when French author Renaud Camus published "Le grand replacement," which posits that White Europeans will disappear owing to immigration and natural births of non-White Muslims from the Middle East and Africa. A string of fatal mass attacks against Muslims, immigrants, and pro-immigrant White progressives worldwide began with Anders Breivik's mass murder of mostly young White Christian progressives in Norway that same year. Breivik distributed a lengthy online anti-Muslim manifesto that ended up being a template for both anti-Muslim and xenophobic terrorists around the world, who sought to memorialize their violence through online postings and videos (Cai & Landon, 2019; Camus, 2019).

9/11: A NEW REALITY FOLLOWING TERROR, RECORD HATE VICTIMIZATIONS, AND THE BULLY PULPIT

While anti-Muslim violence in the United States had a noteworthy resurgence in the middle of the last decade resulting in a record number of Islamophobic assaults, the period of the 9/11 attacks in 2001 still remains a record year, not only for all Islamophobic hate crimes but for overall hate crime in the United States as well, with 9,730 FBI reported hate crimes (FBI: Hate Crime 1992–2019, 2020). (See Chart 7.2.) The two highest-volume months for overall hate crime ever were September and October 2001, with 1,942 and 1,043, respectively (FBI: Hate Crime 1992–2019, 2020). They were also the only months ever with over 1,000 total hate crimes (FBI: Hate Crime 1992–2019, 2020).

The underlying daily numbers for hate crimes around that time also established records: 9 of the 10 worst days for hate crime overall in the United States came within just 10 days of the 9/11 attack, while 16 of the

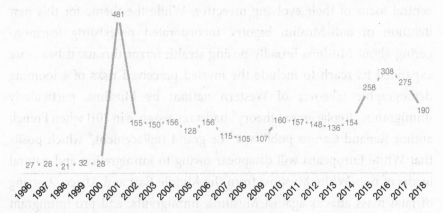

Chart 7.2 FBI: U.S. Anti-Muslim Hate Crime, 1996–2018
Source: Center for the Study of Hate & Extremism

20 worst days ever recorded fell in either September or October 2001 (FBI: Hate Crime 1992–2019, 2020). (See Table 7.1.) Outside of the 9/11 attack period, other days registering the highest numbers of hate crime were around the acquittals of LAPD officers in the Rodney King beating case in 1992 (Sastry & Grigsby Bates, 2017), a violent insurgency during the 2003 Iraq War ("The Iraq War," 2020), the 1995 O. J. Simpson murder acquittal (Dunne, 1995), Israeli/Palestinian violence in 2000, and the 2016 elections (Cook et al., 2020).

Hate crimes overall had a period of decline from a 1996 peak, interrupted by the sharp but brief new record peak in 2001, followed by another lower plateau of 6 years. That plateau eroded into an overall decline in 2009 which bottomed to a record low in 2014, before rising again into the end of the decade (FBI: Hate Crime 1992–2019, 2020). The record-breaking 9/11 spikes, however, were disproportionately directed toward those perceived to be Muslim or Arab (FBI: Hate Crime 1992–2019, 2020). FBI reported anti-Muslim hate crime in September 2001 alone; not only was the highest number ever at 314, but that month was more than the annual total of any entire year before or since. Of 2001's record high 481 anti-Muslim hate crimes, 461 were in the last quarter of the year (FBI: Hate Crime 1992–2019, 2020). Ethnic and national origin crimes more than quadrupled 2000's total, going from 354 to 1,501, driven by a 324% surge in anti-Arab

Table 7.1 WORST DAYS FOR FBI REPORTED HATE
CRIME: UNITED STATES: 1992–2019

1.	2001	0912	181	9/11
2.	2001	0913	154	9/11
3.	2001	0911	148	9/11
4.	2001	0914	139	9/11
5.	2001	0915	125	9/11
6.	2001	0917	121	9/11
7.	2001	0916	105	9/11
8.	2001	0918	104	9/11
9.	1992	0501	87	LAPD Verdict/R. King
10.	2001	0921	86	9/11
11.	2001	0920	75	9/11
12.	1992	0430	73	LAPD Verdict/R. King
13.	2001	0919	69	9/11
14.	2001	0928	68	9/11
15.	1992	0502	67	LAPD Verdict/R. King

hate. In 2001 anti-Arab hate crimes were classified under the more general heading of "non-Hispanic ethnic/nationality" (FBI: Hate Crime 1992–2019, 2020). The increase in these anti-ethnic hate crimes following 9/11 was numerically more than double that of anti-Muslim crimes, which also increased. (See Chart 7.3.) In 2001, anti-Muslim hate crimes alone accounted for over 4.9% of all hate crimes in the United States (FBI: Hate Crime 1992–2019, 2020).

The swift parabolic rise in these targeted hate crimes immediately following 9/11 was dramatically demonstrated by comparisons with the previous week. In the week before the 9/11 terror attacks, there were five anti-Muslim and seven "anti-Ethnic, non-Hispanic crimes" (FBI: Hate Crime 1992–2018, 2018). In the week of the 9/11 attacks, from September 11 through September 17, there were 503 anti-Ethnic, non-Hispanic hate crimes and 197 anti-Muslim ones (FBI: Hate Crime 1992–2019, 2020). Data from this time also show a correlation between political rhetoric

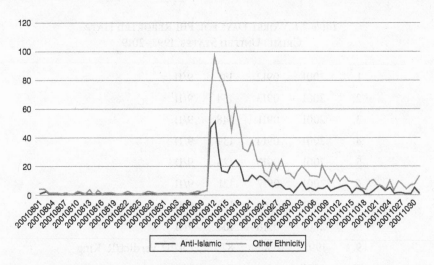

Chart 7.3 Anti-Islam and Anti–Other Ethnicity (non-Hispanic), August–October 2001
SOURCE: Center for the Study of Hate & Extremism

around these events and hate crime levels. An analysis of updated FBI hate crime data enumerated a wave of anti-Muslim hate crime following the September 11, 2001, terrorist attacks, which peaked primarily in the 2 weeks directly following the act (FBI: Hate Crime 1992–2019, 2020). After President Bush's statements of religious inclusion at the Islamic Center of Washington, DC, late on September 17, 2001, anti-Muslim hate crimes reversed course immediately and dropped dramatically across the country:

America counts millions of Muslims amongst our citizens, and Muslims make an incredibly valuable contribution to our country. Muslims are doctors, lawyers, law professors, members of the military, entrepreneurs, shopkeepers, moms, and dads. Moreover, they need to be treated with respect. In our anger and emotion, our fellow Americans must treat each other with respect. Women who cover their heads in this country must feel comfortable going outside their homes. Moms who wear cover must be not intimidated in America. That's not the America I know. That's not the America I value. . . . This is a great country. It's a great country because we share the same values of respect and dignity and human worth. And it is my honor to be meeting with leaders who feel just the same way I do. They're outraged, they're sad. They love America just as much as I do. I want to thank you all for giving me a chance to come by. And may God bless us all. (Bush, 2001)

For the 7 days commencing on 9/11 and ending on September 17, 2001, there were a total of 197 anti-Muslim hate crimes, compared to only 82 in the following week after the President's address (see Chart 7.4), ending on September 24 for a 58% decline (FBI: Hate Crime 1992–2019, 2020).

This decline in anti-Muslim hate crime extended through the following year of 2002, when the annual total dropped to 156, around the top end of a range until 2014 (FBI: Hate Crime 1992–2019, 2020). Following 2001, anti-Muslim hate crime levels saw various plateaus and spikes within that range. From 2002 to 2014, the range in anti-Muslim hate crimes occurred

	Jan	Feb	Mar	Apr	May	Jun	Jul	Aug	Sep	Oct	Nov	Dec	Total
1992	0	2	1	0	1	2	1	2	4	1	0	1	15
1993	0	0	1	2	1	0	0	2	2	2	1	2	13
1994	2	1	2	0	2	0	2	0	2	1	2	3	17
1995	3	2	1	10	0	2	0	6	1	2	1	1	29
1996	0	2	4	3	14	1	1	1	0	0	1	0	27
1997	0	1	5	6	1	4	2	1	2	4	0	2	28
1998	4	2	1	4	3	2	0	1	2	1	0	1	21
1999	4	6	1	0	2	2	1	5	4	3	1	3	32
2000	2	2	3	1	1	1	3	1	4	8	2	0	28
2001	1	1	2	2	5	2	4	3	314	93	25	29	481
2002	13	9	14	10	16	12	17	11	26	8	11	8	155
2003	12	7	23	21	16	12	8	14	19	6	7	5	150
2004	8	12	9	12	29	15	10	7	18	20	7	9	156
2005	10	3	9	12	13	14	15	11	13	7	13	8	128
2006	7	6	13	14	11	11	18	19	17	15	13	12	156
2007	12	13	7	16	12	7	11	6	13	10	2	6	115
2008	7	11	8	10	11	8	13	6	6	10	10	5	105
2009	9	9	6	6	8	4	12	14	9	9	14	7	107
2010	9	10	14	14	17	11	12	14	18	21	10 ·	10	160
2011	10	6	11	18	14	14	13	21	19	8	13	10	157
2012	17	8	10	7	12	18	10	15	20	6	17	8	148
2013	3	8	12	17	18	4	15	15	16	9	9	10	136
2014	6	7	14	13	6	12	14	16	28	18	13	7	154
2015	17	16	12	18	21	18	16	8	13	20	30	69	258
2016	23	14	30	23	20	32	28	25	19	25	40	29	308
2017	27	30	28	25	22	19	28	17	15	22	29	13	275
2018	14	17	22	22	17	19	14	13	13	18	7	14	190

Data for the graph obtained from the FBI Uniform Crime Reports: Hate Crime in the United States 1992–2018.
Bolded cells indicate five worst months and years for anti-Muslim hate crimes.
Color distribution of cells conditioned on the Tenth, Fiftieth, and Ninetieth percentiles.

Chart 7.4 Anti-Muslim Bias Motivated Incidents 1992–2018

in a channel between 105 and 160 annually, bisected by extended distinct plateaus (FBI: Hate Crime 1992–2019, 2020).

AFTERMATH: A DECADE OF LOWER PLATEAUS OFF RECORD PEAK

In the first 5 years following 2001, however, annual anti-Muslim hate crime totals were relatively stable, only deviating out of the 150s once, in 2005 (FBI: Hate Crime 1992–2019, 2020). From 2002 to 2005, there were 5 months of over twenty hate crimes against Muslims, including the time of the first anniversary of the 9/11 attacks in 2002, the Iraq War in 2003, and the execution of an American hostage in Iraq in 2004 (The Iraq War, 2020). From 2005 through 2009, annual totals never dipped below 100, and there was only one year, 2006, that exceeded 135 (FBI: Hate Crime 1992–2019, 2020). Still, there were no months during that period where anti-Muslim hate crimes rose out of the teens. Similarly, anti-Muslim assaults also hit a post-2001 peak of 54 in 2006, a level not exceeded until 2010's total of 63, at the start of yet another subsequent extended multiyear plateau of both elevated anti-Muslim hate crime and assaults (FBI: Hate Crime 1992–2019, 2020).

While overall anti-Muslim hate crime levels were relatively stable in those years immediately after 9/11, there was nonetheless a decoupling from these overall hate crime trends when it came to attitudes toward Muslims. For instance, a series of post–2001 ABC/Washington Post polls found unfavorable views of Islam steadily increased to hit 46% in 2006, a number higher even than 2001's 39% level. The survey further found that in 2006 "[N]early six in 10 Americans think the religion is prone to violent extremism, nearly half regard it unfavorably and a remarkable one in four admit to prejudicial feelings against Muslims and Arabs alike." By 2006, despite the absence of a single successful post 9/11 mass fatality domestic event by any religiously motivated extremists, negative attitudes about Muslims doubled those of 2002 levels. Smaller-scale domestic terror events and thwarted plots, as well as overseas military conflict in Iraq and terror attacks overseas, did, however, receive significant media attention (Washington Post-ABC News Poll, 2006).

THE 2010S: HATE CRIMES RISE AFTER TERROR STEREOTYPING YIELDS POLITICAL NORMALIZATION

That next decade began with a moderately elevated 5-year plateau for anti-Muslim hate crimes where no annual total dipped below 135, a key level rarely reached during the previous lower plateau (FBI: Hate Crime 1992–2018, 2018). Before 2010, in the previous 3 years, anti-Muslim hate never exceeded 115. From 2010 to 2014, there were 4 months with over 20 anti-Muslim hate crimes (FBI: Hate Crime 1992–2019, 2020).

As anti-Muslim hate crime remained elevated, hate crime totals overall experienced multiple declines during the first years of the decade. However, 2010 had the highest to date post 9/11 annual total, after stigmatizing discourse around the Fort Hood massacre late in the previous year, an increase in high-profile federal terror prosecutions, and the reemergence of organized and conspiracist opposition to mosque construction in lower Manhattan and elsewhere, that was amplified by increasingly mainstreamed anti-Muslim groups and in social media (Rempfer, 2019). Interestingly, just as anti-Muslim hate crime commenced a period of overall increases that sharply accelerated mid-decade, anti-Latino hate crimes hit a peak in 2010 before a multiyear decline, as both unemployment and undocumented border crossings started to fall from elevated levels—two items popular in negative stereotyping (FBI: Hate Crime 1992–2019, 2020).

A 2010 Gallup poll of Americans found "43% admit to feeling at least "a little" prejudice toward Muslims—more than twice the number who say the same about Christians (18%), Jews (15%), and Buddhists (14%)." The poll further found that 9% of respondents reported "a great deal" of prejudice toward Muslims ("In U.S., Religious Prejudice Stronger Against Muslims," 2010).

Similarly, a 2010 ABC News/Washington Post poll found the highest%age of negative views on Islam since 2001, with 49% of Americans self-reporting a negative perception of the faith, as opposed to 37% of respondents with favorable ones (Cohen & Dropp, 2010).

After an elevated plateau in the first several years, a mid-decade spike occurred in 2015 as anti-Muslim hate crime cases rose 67% to the highest level since 9/11(FBI: Hate Crime 1992–2019, 2020). The rise peaked the following year in a "head and shoulders" top in 2016, when both a fatal terror attack and extensive coverage of it, as well as a sustained period of intensifying stigmatization, occurred. The three worst months for anti-Muslim hate crime since 2001 were tightly clustered within a politically volatile 12-month period: December 2015, the month of a terror attack and the Muslim ban; June 2016, the Pulse attack and launch of major presidential campaigns; and election month November 2016 (FBI: Hate Crime 1992–2019, 2020).

WORDS MATTER: IMPACT OF ELECTION SEASON TERROR STIGMA ON INCIDENCES OF HATE CRIME

During the presidential primary campaign in 2015 and 2016, Muslims were the target of intense political invective and stereotyping amid calls for differential treatment based on their faith. During the presidential primary campaign in 2015, Muslims were the target of political stereotyping amid calls for differential treatment based on their faith. Curtailing immigration and anti-Muslim rhetoric were central themes of Mr. Trump's campaign, including discussions of creating broad surveillance databases on Muslims, strict immigration and refugee bans, and mosque closures (Diamond, 2016; "When Islamophobia turns violent," 2016).

After a nationally covered evening town hall in Keene, New Hampshire, at the end of September 2015, with only candidate Donald Trump, anti-Muslim hate crime doubled, from three the week before to seven in the week after this period. During the event, Mr. Trump, who by then was leading the Republican field, promoted the contention that ISIS had possible plans to invade the United States through refugee admissions. He also misstated the numbers, genders, and ages of Syrian refugees while exclaiming: "This could be one of the great tactical ploys of all time. A 200,000-man army, maybe. Or if they sent 50,000 or 80,000 or 100,000 . . . That could be possible." Anti-Muslim hate crimes rose each month of the last quarter of 2015 (Narea, 2019).

Following the November 13, 2015, Paris terror attack, there was another spike in anti-Muslim hate crime. There were five anti-Muslim hate crimes in the week prior, November 6 to 12, and 16 in the week of and following the attack. On the fourth day after the attack, Monday November 16, Mr. Trump discussed on television the tactic of shutting down mosques in the morning before a lengthier televised speech that evening in Knoxville, Tennessee, before an estimated crowd of 10,000. In that address, Mr. Trump received the most applause when he promised to "bomb the s--t out of" ISIS and vigorously demanded the nation return and not tolerate any Syrian refugees ("Trump re-enacts Carson's alleged stabbing, says he'll 'bomb the s**t out of' ISIS," 2015).

In late 2015, a CBS survey found that Americans with negative views about Islam outnumbered those with favorable ones and that those with "very" negative or positive views were unchanged from 2002. A November 2015 Brookings Institution poll found the split tilted more favorable, but with a sizeable minority of 46% holding a negative view (Religion, 2015).

By December 2015, Donald Trump had further solidified his position as the leading Republican frontrunner in the presidential race. On December 2, 2015, the most fatal terrorist attack since 9/11 struck San Bernardino, California, killing 14 Americans and wounding 22 more (Nagourney et al., 2015). Candidate Trump first proposed his "Muslim ban" ("Trump border policy: Who's affected?," 2017) on the Internet and later at an evening rally on December 7, 2015, 5 days after the San Bernardino terror attack (Nagourney et al., 2015), and almost a month after another one struck Paris ("Paris attacks: What happened on the night," 2015).

DONALD J. TRUMP STATEMENT ON PREVENTING MUSLIM IMMIGRATION (New York, NY) December 7, 2015,—Donald J. Trump is calling for a total and complete shutdown of Muslims entering the United States until our country's representatives can figure out what is going on. According to Pew Research, among others, there is great hatred towards Americans by large segments of the Muslim population . . . .

Mr. Trump stated, "Without looking at the various polling data, it is obvious to anybody the hatred is beyond comprehension. Where this hatred comes from and why we will have to determine. Until we are able to determine and understand this problem and the dangerous threat it poses, our country cannot be the victims of horrendous attacks by people that believe only in Jihad, and have no sense of reason or respect for human life. If I win the election for President, we are going to Make America Great Again."—Donald J. Trump (Johnson, 2015)

Before FBI data became available late in the following year, the Center for the Study of Hate and Extremism (CSHE) found a spike in anti-Muslim hate crime. For the 5 days from December 2 through December 6, there were 8 anti-Muslim hate crimes, with none on December 2. For the 5 days from December 7 through December 11, 15 anti-Muslim hate crimes occurred, with those occurring on December 7 taking place after the announcement. These crimes included multiple assaults and two fire bombings, including one in the overnight hours immediately following Mr. Trump's announcement. The study applied FBI data collection criteria, but with sourcing mostly from unofficial incident reports taken from media and NGOs (Levin & Grisham, 2017).

When official FBI data were released a year later, it confirmed the spike in anti-Muslim hate crime, first reported by the CSHE (FBI: Hate Crime 1992–2019, 2020). In the 5 days after the December 2 San Bernardino attack, the FBI's daily anti-Muslim hate average spiked by 318%, going from.67 hate crimes per day to 2.80 hate crimes per day (FBI: Hate Crime 1992–2019, 2020). In the 11 days following the December 7 Muslim ban announcement, hate crimes against Muslims rose to 3.5 per day or 415% above the January–December 1st daily average (FBI: Hate Crime 1992–2019, 2020). That additional rise right after the ban announcement was a 23% increase over the elevated levels found over the five previous days, whose rise commenced the day of the San Bernardino terrorist attack. (See Charts 7.5 and 7.6.) The five worst days for anti-Muslim hate crime in 2015, all tied at five, occurred during the 2 weeks following the Muslim ban announcement (FBI: Hate Crime 1992–2019, 2020).

Calendar year 2015 was the worst year for anti-Muslim hate crime since 2001 (Chart 7.4). Overall, hate crime declines in December of that year came amid a sharp increase in anti-Muslim and anti-Arab victimizations. December 2015 was the third-worst month for hate crime against Muslims ever (FBI: Hate Crime 1992–2019, 2020). For overall hate crime, December 2015 did not even register in the top handful of months for the year, and the month was slightly down from the previous one. In contrast, anti-Muslim hate crime rose 130%, from 30 to 69, over the previous month, for a total not seen since 2001 (FBI: Hate Crime 1992–2019, 2020).

The 6,121 hate crime incidents overall total tracked by the FBI in 2016 marked the first time since 2012, another presidential election year, when totals exceeded 6,000, then to 6,573. While overall hate crimes have increased in every presidential election year since national FBI recordkeeping began in the early 1990s, 2016 was different (FBI: Hate Crime 1992–2019, 2020). It marked the first time since 2004, yet another election year when the nation experienced a consecutive annual hate crime increase—although the 2016 total was still 20% less than that year's total of 7,649 (FBI: Hate Crime 1992–2019, 2020).

In 2016, the number of anti-Muslim hate crimes rose to yet another post-2001 record of 308, for the second-worst year on record and a near doubling of 2014 levels (FBI: Hate Crime 1992–2019, 2020). The proportion of anti-Muslim hate crimes relative to overall hate crime hit a record of 5%, while the number of assaults also hit outright records, exceeding those of 2001. In 2016 the 127 anti-Muslim annual assaults exceeded 2001's total of 93 by 36%, while the 39 aggravated assaults registered an 87% rise over that year (FBI: Hate Crime 1992–2019, 2020). A 2016 PEW survey of

2015: Anti-Muslim and Anti-Arab Hate Crimes (Combined)

Time Period	Total Number of Incidents	Average incidents per day	Time Period Compared	% Change in Average Incidents Per Day
Jan. 1 – Dec. 1 (335 days)	224	0.67/per day	Jan. 1 – Dec. 1 and Dec. 2 – Dec. 6	+318%
Dec. 2 – Dec. 6 (5 days) San Bern. Terror Attack	14	2.8/per day	Dec. 2 – Dec. 6 and Dec. 7 – Dec. 17	+23.2%
Dec. 7 – Dec. 17 (11 days) "Muslim Ban"	38	3.5/per day	Jan. 1 – Dec. 1 and Dec. 7 – Dec. 17	+415%

2015: All Bias Type Hate Crimes

Time Period	Total Number of Incidents	Average incidents per day	Time Periods Compared	% Change in Average Incidents Per Day
Jan. 1 – Dec. 1 (335 days)	5,406	16.1/per day	Jan. 1 – Dec. 1 and Dec. 2 – Dec. 6	+15.2%
Dec. 2 – Dec. 6 (5 days)	93	18.6/per day	Dec. 2 – Dec. 6 and Dec. 7 – Dec. 17	-6.2%
Dec. 7 – Dec. 17 (11 days)	192	17.5/per day	Jan. 1 – Dec. 1 and Dec. 7 – Dec. 17	+8.2%

Chart 7.5 Comparing Anti-Muslim/Anti-Arab Hate Crimes with Overall Hate Crimes in 2015

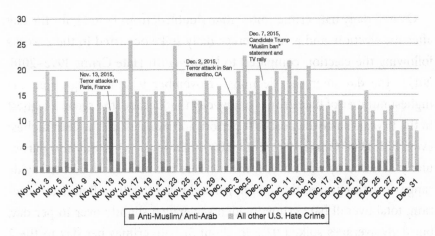

Chart 7.6 FBI: Anti-Muslim/Anti-Arab Compared to All Other U.S Hate Crime
November and December 2015
SOURCE: Center for the Study of Hate & Extremism

Americans showed that year's Pulse massacre was second only to marriage equality, as the most noteworthy event of the decade, while the 9/11
attack was the most significant event of their lifetime (Deane et al., 2016).
PEW also found high levels of anti-Muslim prejudice with almost half of
Americans, 49%, doubting their patriotism with a position that "at least
some are anti-American" (Pew, 2016).

The year 2016 had a record 10 months where anti-Muslim hate crime
exceeded 20 or more and three that exceeded 30 or more, including
June, the month of the Pulse massacre—the fourth worst month for anti-
Muslim hate crime since 1992 (FBI: Hate Crime 1992–2019, 2020). In contrast, 2015 saw 4 months exceed 20 or more, while 2014 only had a single
month above that threshold, and 2013 had none (FBI: Hate Crime 1992–
2019, 2020).

However, the worst month of the year for both hate crime and anti-
Muslim hate crime was November 2016, when the U.S. presidential
elections occurred. The 758 FBI enumerated hate crimes that month was
the highest number since the first anniversary of 9/11 (Levin, 2019). A similar hate crime pattern emerged earlier in the year in the United Kingdom,
as hate crime there hit a multiyear high around the summer's Brexit vote
(Hate Crime: England and Wales, 2018/19).

Overall daily hate crimes more than doubled, from 17 to 51, for the day after the election, and a 72% average daily spike occurred in the 2 weeks following the election compared to before (FBI: Hate Crime 1992–2018, 2019). The day after the elections—November 9, 2016—registered the highest number of hate crimes of any day that decade, the second highest in the 15 years since the post-9/11 period, and was tied for the 28th highest ever (FBI: Hate Crime 1992–2019, 2020). However, what was also particularly noteworthy was not just the increase but its breadth across a wide range of victim groups that do not generally rise together. Before the election, total overall hate crime incidents averaged slightly over 16 per day, but daily averages spiked 92% to about 31 hate crimes per day in the 2 weeks after the election.

Disaggregating total hate crimes by group revealed that anti-Hispanic/Latino hate crimes comprised the largest percentage increase, rising 176% after the election, from an average of 0.88 to 2.43 hate crimes per day. November 2016 was the worst month in over 5 years for anti-Latino hate crime (FBI: Hate Crime 1992–2019, 2020). The second-highest percentage increase in hate crimes were those committed against Muslims and Arabs, which spiked 78%, going from 0.92 hate crimes before the election to 1.64 hate crimes per day in the 2 weeks after the election. The day after the elections was also when a thwarted plot to bomb a predominantly Somali-Muslim apartment complex was to occur (FBI: Hate Crime 1992–2019, 2020; Hauslohner, 2018).

The Southern Poverty Law Center found that anti-Muslim "hate groups" rose 197% from 34 to 101 in 2016 (Potok, 2017). The Council on American-Islamic Relations (CAIR), a Muslim advocacy organization reported 2,213 anti-Muslim "hate incidents," which enumerated both crimes as well as noncriminal harassment and discrimination; in 2016, a 57% increase over the prior year total of 1,409. In 2015, CAIR's hate incident total rose 5%. CAIR also found a 44% increase in anti-Muslim hate crimes from 180 to 260 in 2016 ("Civil Rights Report 2017: The Empowerment of Hate," 2017). Later, anti-Muslim hate crime tracked by CAIR also exhibited a head and shoulders top, similar to that of the FBI data, but peaking a year later at 300 in 2017 ("2018 Civil Rights Report: Targeted," 2018).

PREJUDICE CONTINUES EVEN AS SPOTLIGHT SHIFTS

While FBI enumerated hate crimes against Muslims declined in 2017, the combined total of anti-Muslim and anti-Arab rose from 364 to 378, hitting a decade peak in 2017, doubling anti-Arab hate crimes from 56 to 103 (FBI: Hate Crime 1992–2019, 2020). In 2017 the FBI found a decline to 275 anti-Muslim hate crimes, and there were 8 months that year where totals exceeded 20 or more. For the second year in a row and despite a year over year decline in anti-Muslim hate crime, assaults against Muslims again exceeded the totals for 2001. Overall anti-religion hate crimes bottomed in 2014 and then reversed to hit its highest level in 2017 since 2001, as anti-Semitic, anti-Christian, anti-Sikh, and anti-Hindu hate crimes experienced multiyear highs that offset the declines in anti-Muslim ones (FBI: Hate Crime 1992–2019, 2020).

In CAIR's 2017 data, physical violence constituted 107 of the hate crimes tracked, more than one third of all, with slightly more vandalism and property destruction, at 113 ("2018 Civil Rights Report: Targeted," 2018). CAIR also documented 144 anti-Mosque incidents in the United States in 2017, with hate crimes accounting for 57 incidents, intimidation for 42 incidents, and harassment for 24 incidents ("2018 Civil Rights Report: Targeted," 2018).

In 2018, yet another rotation appeared to take place in victim targeting. Anti-Latino hate crime rose 13%, while anti-Muslim ones declined 31% to 190, as fearful stereotyping switched focus to "caravans of immigrants" from "foreign terrorists." There was only 1 month the whole year where hate crimes targeting Muslims exceeded 20 (FBI: Hate Crime 1992–2019, 2020). By 2019, even with three consecutive years of declines, levels were still higher than any of the dozen years following 2001 (FBI: Hate Crime 1992–2019, 2020). Spikes against other groups, including Latinos and Sikhs, occurred amid the late decade decline in anti-Muslim hate crime. In 2018 hate crimes against Latinos hit their highest level since 2008, with July's total of 72 making it the worst month in 11 years. The following August 2019 was the worst lethal hate crime event for Latinos ever (FBI: Hate Crime 1992–2019, 2020) (Associated Press, 2020). However, a report by the Center for the Study of Hate and Extremism analyzing police data across 10 major cities released before the FBI findings found a decline in anti-Muslim hate crime of 28% (Levin & Nakashima, 2019).

CAIR also found a similar decline in their 2018 totals as anti-Muslim hate crime incidents decreased 55%, to 134 in 2018, following a previous 15% increase between 2016 and 2017. CAIR's 2017 numbers roughly aligned with FBI totals, according to the organization's 2018 Civil Rights Report. In 2016, CAIR enumerated a 44% increase, from 180 to 260 ("Civil Rights Report 2018," 2018). Incidents involving physical violence constituted 32 of the hate crimes tracked in 2018, while 40 incidents involved vandalism and property destruction. In May 2019, a Muslim-oriented domestic policy NGO, the Institute for Social Policy and Understanding (ISPU)'s National American Islamophobia Index, which tracks perceptions of five bigoted tropes among the public, rose from 24 to 28 out of 100 (Mogahed & Mahmood, 2019). Another University of Chicago national survey found negative attitudes toward Muslims in about one third of those with a preference (General Social Survey, 2018). (See Figure 7.1.)

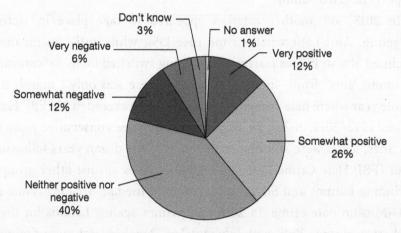

Figure 7.1 GSS/NORC: Americans' Attitudes Toward Muslims, 2018
Source: General Social Survey, 2018

CONCLUSION

The recent declines in anti-Muslim hate crimes off multiyear increases are noteworthy, but concerns remain. While catalytic drivers like highly publicized terror attacks and American involvement in overseas conflicts have briefly waned, the underlying anti-Muslim attitudes that label adherents as targets for aggression remain vibrant. In addition, overall religious-based hate crimes hit its second highest point in a decade in 2019, as hate crimes become more violent. Moreover, a horrifying global extremism overlay occurred over the last decade as a string of White supremacist terrorist lone mass killers around the world committed mass attacks against non-Whites and religious minorities, including Muslims at mosques. They frequently used the event to promote online bigoted extremist statements about demographic change, and these massacres generally were not in immediate retaliation for violence by extremist Muslims. Key to the emergent violent nationalist folklore of these xenophobic terrorists is combatting the demographic "replacement" of those with European ancestry through targeted violent attacks against various minorities, including Muslims, who were the original target of the doctrine ("New Hate and Old: The Changing Face of American White Supremacy," 2018). Unfortunately, a pandemic, economic stress, online bigotry, tribalism, and global shifts provide a backdrop where a rotating set of derided scapegoats, including Muslims, face periods of spikes, followed by extended but temporary declines. The winds of hatred often shift to traverse a path of least resistance to whichever group prejudice is widely felt and most prominently exploited in the normalized sociopolitical fears of the day.

REFERENCES

2018 Civil Rights Report: Targeted. (2018). Retrieved from http://www.islamophobia. org/reports/224-2018-civil-rights-report-targeted.html

ACT for America. (n.d.). *Intelligence Project: Extremist Files*. Southern Poverty Law Center. Retrieved from https://www.splcenter.org/fighting-hate/extremist-files/group/ act-america

Associated Press. (2020, June 24). Walmart mass shooting suspect will face new charges. Retrieved from https://apnews.com/article/el-paso-texas-mass-shooting-shootings-us-news-patrick-crusius-crime-76e907a3a8a57a4e348009ec455b2ccb

Bergen, P., Ford, A., Sims, A., & Sterman, D. (2020). Part I. Terrorism cases: 2001–Today. Retrieved from https://www.newamerica.org/in-depth/terrorism-in-america/part-i-overview-terrorism-cases-2001-today/

Bush, G. (2001). "Islam is peace" says president. Retrieved from https://georgewbush-whitehouse.archives.gov/news/releases/2001/09/20010917-11.html

Cai, W., & Landon, S. (2019, April 3). Attacks by white extremists are growing. So are their connections. *New York Times*. Retrieved from https://www.nytimes.com/interactive/2019/04/03/world/white-extremist-terrorism-christchurch.html

Camus, R. (2019). *Grand replacement: Introduction au remplacisme global.* Touchstone.

Civil Rights Report 2017: The Empowerment of Hate. (2017). Retrieved from https://ca.cair.com/sfba/wp-content/uploads/sites/10/2018/04/2017-Empowerment-of-Hate-Final.pdf

Civil Rights Report 2018. (2018). Retrieved from https://ca.cair.com/sfba/publications/2018-cair-national-civil-rights-report/

Cohen, J., & Dropp, K. (2010). Most Americans object to planned Islamic center near Ground Zero, poll finds. Retrieved from https://www.washingtonpost.com/wp-dyn/content/article/2010/09/08/AR2010090806231.html?tid=a_inl_manual

Cook, S., Danin, R., & Gordon, P. (2020). Israeli-Palestinian conflict—Global Conflict Tracker. Retrieved from https://www.cfr.org/global-conflict-tracker/conflict/israeli-palestinian-conflict

Deane, C., Duggan, M., & Morin, R. (2016). Americans name the top historic events of their lifetimes. Retrieved from https://www.pewresearch.org/politics/2016/12/15/americans-name-the-top-historic-events-of-their-lifetimes/

Diamond, J. (2016). Trump doubles down on mosque surveillance. Retrieved from https://www.cnn.com/2016/06/15/politics/donald-trump-muslims-mosque-surveillance/index.html

Dunne, D. (1995). O.J. Simpson: Life after the murder trial. Retrieved from https://www.vanityfair.com/magazine/1995/12/dunne199512

General Social Survey, University of Chicago. (2018). What is your personal attitude towards members of the following religious groups? Muslims. Retrieved from https://gssdataexplorer.norc.org/variables/7287/vshow

Halpern, T., & Levin, B. (1996). *The limits of dissent: The constitutional status of armed civilian militias.* Aletheia Press.

Hate Crime, England and Wales, 2018/19. (2019). Retrieved from https://assets.publishing.service.gov.uk/government/uploads/system/uploads/attachment_data/file/839172/hate-crime-1819-hosb2419.pdf

Hate Crime Data and Reports. (2017). Home: CSUSB. Retrieved from https://www.csusb.edu/hate-and-extremism-center/data-reports/hate-crime-data-and-reports

Hauslohner, A. (2018, April 18). Three Kansas militiamen who plotted to bomb Muslims are found guilty on terrorism charges. *Washington Post*. Retrieved from https://www.

washingtonpost.com/news/post-nation/wp/2018/04/18/three-kansas-militiamen-who-plotted-to-bomb-muslims-are-found-guilty-on-terrorism-charges/

Historic campaign ad: Wolves (Bush-Cheney '04). YouTube video, May 2, 2006. Retrieved from https://www.youtube.com/watch?v=MU4t9O_yFsY

Huntington, S. P. (1996). *The clash of civilizations and remaking of world order.* Touchstone.

In U.S., religious prejudice stronger against Muslims. (2010). Retrieved from https://news.gallup.com/poll/125312/religious-prejudice-stronger-against-muslims.aspx

The Iraq War. (2020). Retrieved from https://www.cfr.org/timeline/iraq-war

Kiely, E. (2015). Fact check: Donald Trump gets refugee numbers wrong. Retrieved from https://www.usatoday.com/story/news/politics/elections/2015/10/05/fact-check-donald-trump-syrian-refugees-obama/73384668/

Johnson, J. (2015, December 7). Trump calls for "total and complete shutdown of Muslims entering the United States." *Washington Post*. Retrieved from https://www.washingtonpost.com/news/post-politics/wp/2015/12/07/donald-trump-calls-for-total-and-complete-shutdown-of-muslims-entering-the-united-states/

Levin, B. (2019). Why White supremacist attacks are on the rise, even in surprising places. Retrieved from https://time.com/5555396/white-supremacist-attacks-rise-new-zealand/

Levin, B., & Grisham, K. (2016). Special status report: Hate crime in the United States. Retrieved from https://www.csusb.edu/sites/default/files/SPECIAL%20STATUS%20REPORT%20Final%20Draft.pdf

Levin, B., & Grisham, K. (2017). United States Department of Justice Hate Crime Summit: Hate crimes rise in major American localities in 2016. Retrieved from https://www.csusb.edu/sites/default/files/Levin%20DOJ%20Summit%202_0.pdf

Levin, B., & Nakashima, K. (2019). Report to the Nation 2019. Retrieved from https://www.csusb.edu/sites/default/files/CSHE%202019%20Report%20to%20the%20Nation%20FINAL%207.29.19%2011%20PM_0_0.pdf

Lipka, M. (2020, December 8). *Muslims and Islam: Key findings in the U.S. and around the world.* Pew Research Center. Retrieved from https://www.pewresearch.org/fact-tank/2017/08/09/muslims-and-islam-key-findings-in-the-u-s-and-around-the-world/

Nagourney, A., Lovett, I., & Perez-Pena, R. (2015). San Bernardino shooting kills at least 14; Two suspects are dead. Retrieved from https://www.nytimes.com/2015/12/03/us/san-bernardino-shooting.html

Narea, N. (2019). America is stepping down as a global leader on refugees. Retrieved from https://www.vox.com/policy-and-politics/2019/10/1/20886919/america-trump-refugee-cap-global-leader

National Crime Victimization Survey. (2019). Office of Justice Programs, Bureau of Justice Statistics.

New hate and old: The changing face of American white supremacy. (2018). Retrieved from https://www.adl.org/new-hate-and-old

Newport, F. (2020). What we learned from the people in the 2016 election. Retrieved from https://news.gallup.com/opinion/polling-matters/315890/learned-people-2016-election.aspx

Paris attacks: What happened on the night. (2015). Retrieved from https://www.bbc.com/news/world-europe-34818994

PEW Research. (2016). Half think at least some Muslims in U.S. are anti American. Retrieved http://www.pewforum.org/2016/02/03/republicans-prefer-blunt-talk-about-islamic-extremism-democrats-favor-caution/pf_2016-02-02_views-islam-politics-12/

Potok, M. (2017). The year in hate and extremism. Retrieved from https://www.splcenter.org/fighting-hate/intelligence-report/2017/year-hate-and-extremism

Religion. (2015). Retrieved from https://www.pollingreport.com/religion.htm

Rempfer, K. (2019). The mass shooting at Fort Hood was 10 years ago, on November 5, 2009. Retrieved from https://www.armytimes.com/news/your-army/2019/11/05/the-mass-shooting-at-fort-hood-was-10-years-ago-on-nov-5-2009/

Sastry, A., & Bates, K. (2017). NPR Choice page. Retrieved from https://www.npr.org/2017/04/26/524744989/when-la-erupted-in-anger-a-look-back-at-the-rodney-king-riots

Telhami, S. (2015). What Americans really think about Muslims and Islam. Retrieved from https://www.brookings.edu/blog/markaz/2015/12/09/what-americans-really-think-about-muslims-and-islam/

Trump border policy: Who's affected? (2017). Retrieved from https://www.bbc.com/news/world-us-canada-38781302

Trump re-enacts Carson's alleged stabbing, says he'll "bomb the s**t out of" ISIS. (2015). Retrieved from https://www.huffpost.com/entry/donald-trump-bomb-isis_n_56454ccee4b08cda348844bf

United States Department of Justice. (2015). Federal Bureau of Investigation. Uniform Crime Reporting Program. *Hate crime data collection and training manual.* Retrieved from https://www.fbi.gov/file-repository/ucr/ucr-hate-crime-data-collection-guidlines-training-manual-v2.pdf/view

United States Department of Justice. (2015). Federal Bureau of Investigation. Uniform Crime Reporting Program Data [United States]: Hate Crime Data, 1992–2018 [Record-Type Files]. Interuniversity Consortium for Political and Social Research [distributor]. Retrieved from https://doi.org/10.3886/ICPSR25107.v1

Washington Post-ABC News Poll. (2006). Retrieved from https://www.washingtonpost.com/wp-srv/politics/polls/postpoll_iraqwar_030606.htm

What we know about Orlando shooting. (2016). Retrieved from https://www.bbc.com/news/world-us-canada-36511778

When Islamophobia turns violent: The 2016 U.S. Presidential Elections. (2016, May 2). The Bridge Initiative. Georgetown University. Retrieved from http://bridge.georgetown.edu/when-islamophobia-turns-violent-the-2016-u-s-presidential-elections/

8

Conclusions

Veils Uncovered and Veils That Remain

CAROLYN TURPIN-PETROSINO■

INTRODUCTION

As of November 2020, the world population is estimated at 7.7 billion persons (U.S. Census). These 7 billion-plus inhabitants will continue to increase diversity within the human populace due to the inherent nature of social interaction and other tendencies. This trend toward an evolving diversity is likely also true for the 2 billion Muslim inhabitants on the planet (WorldPopulationReview.com). Furthermore, there are countless social identities that any individual can assume. Some are biologically based, such as race, ethnicity, and cisgender, while others may be more temporal in nature, such as religion, community group affiliation, or sports fan of a favorite local team. Social psychology informs us on the relevance of social identity; it is composed of group memberships that we choose for ourselves or that are placed upon us by others. With all the social identities that can be ascribed to, this concept has become far more complex, and this further problematizes how individuals come to make sense of the social identity of others. Of course, the added reality of intersectionality is part of the super complexity of social identity. For example, one could

Carolyn Turpin-Petrosino, *Conclusions* In: *Islamophobia and Acts of Violence*. Edited by: Carolyn Turpin-Petrosino, Oxford University Press. © Oxford University Press 2022. DOI: 10.1093/oso/9780190922313.003.0008 have concurring social identities that include gender and race or religion and age cohorts that could create intragroup social identities.

Since one's social identity is primarily self-determined, it is natural to think well of one's chosen social identity. However, preserving a positive outlook on one's social identity may also involve constructing a negative perception of social identities or social groups viewed as contradictory or somehow in opposition to one's social identity, for some. A negative perception, bias, or prejudice toward others may develop as a result (Nesdale, 1999). This may be an oversimplification of the social-psychological dynamics that undergird Islamophobia or bigoted notions held toward any social group constructed as the "Other." But when that prejudice becomes rooted, structural, and systemic, it results in a perpetuation of social injustice that is entrenched culturally and institutionally. It has, in effect, become an acculturation. The preceding chapters discuss various aspects of the diminution and devaluing of the social identities of Muslims and of Islam itself. As in any set of research studies, there are questions answered to some extent, questions that remain unresolved, and new questions that are recognized. It is with that understanding that this concluding chapter is offered.

This author chooses to use the terms "veils uncovered and veils that remain" to acknowledge the current state of scholarship underway toward lifting misperceptions of Islam and Muslim culture, while acknowledging the entrenched Orientalist perspectives that affect Western views. The title also serves to symbolize what is discovered or discerned in this collective work and what problems and issues remain somewhat hidden and unresolved. More explicitly, in this chapter I attempt to make theoretical or factual connections between some of the key observations made by the contributing authors—which are designated as veils uncovered. Following that, I identify the implications of conditions and issues yet unaddressed—and refer to them as veils that remain.

VEILS UNCOVERED

Arain and Barzegar offer a compelling and well-substantiated hypothesis in Chapter 2 that asserts that an American Islamophobia Network provides the care and nurturing of Islamophobia. They describe it as an effective network comprised of integral social processes and entities that package and present anti-Muslim perspectives as a sort of test for American patriotism. In other words, to be pro-Islam is to be anti-American, and vice versa. The strategies employed by the various participants in the Network may be thought of as far more strident than those used in opposition to the 1960s civil rights struggle for racial equality by Black and Brown citizens. Outside of blatant racial segregation, economic policies were frequently constructed to control minority communities. More subtle tools of obstruction were used to deny mortgage applications or employment opportunities and a range of oppressive economic conditions that rangeded from redlining in communities that were racially transitioning, displacement through gentrification, to the use of building infrastructures that literally cut off racial minority communities from potential economic opportunities that existed just beyond reach. However, the "Islamophobia Network" seeks to hinder the quality of life for Muslims—and it is not hidden or subtle in any way—because it posits that the very existence of Islam is a threat to all things American. Organizations that espouse the view that pro-Islam is anti-American connect with notable media outlets that willingly disseminate these views. The effectiveness of this Network is measured by the politicization of these views that are subsequently embedded in public policy. Just as structural racism is recognized by many socially conscious Americans, the existence of the American Islamophobia Network is also perceived and acknowledged, to some extent, by ordinary Americans.

The analysis of Nussbaum and Vitek points to a disturbing emerging trend in the targeting of the Muslim community. In addition to a noticeable increase in the rate of violent anti-Muslim hate crime, which Levin in Chapter 7 also underscores, the uptick in planned terrorist attacks against the community is also emphasized. These terrorism attacks distinguish themselves from hate crimes. They are rarer events characterized by a high degree of planned lethality, intended to produce mass casualties, and reflect some degree of serious organization and preparation. In contrast, hate crimes are often unplanned attacks that may or may not involve physical violence. Particularly unique in Nussbaum and Vitek's analysis is the inclusion of foiled attempts (in addition to successful ones) to cause deadly harm to the Muslim community. What is conspicuous is recognizing that of the 46 cases of planned terrorist attacks, the majority targeted mosques and cultural centers, targets that are very emblematic of Islam and the Muslim community. Another observation they make is that high-intensity planned attacks are not reactionary or in some way retaliatory against jihadist acts of violence. They occur in the absence of any actual precipitating incident of that nature. Nevertheless, the connection between the existence of mosques and the occurrence of jihadist violence—even if such acts occurred some years ago or in some other region of the world—is made by some perpetrators who link them regardless. Furthermore, most of these planned attacks occurred without any attribution or claims of responsibility. It may be that the desire to cause destruction and casualties is more motivating than pressuring authorities to change public policy or the need to be recognized as a group to be reckoned with. An Islamic target does not have to do anything to warrant targeting. Apparently, in the perpetrator's view, existing as a symbol of Islam or being a Muslim translates automatically as a threat warranting a "retaliatory" attack.

Nussbaum and Vitek underscore that Islamophobic sentiments do not usually stand alone as a single motivation but that there are multiple grievances at play in the thought processes of those targeting the Muslim community. There are several ideological currents within the extremist world, so multiple motivations are more commonly found than not. However, could many of these perspectives reflect a primary fear of being "replaced" by those who look, worship, and perhaps perceive the world differently from the White male heterosexual hegemonic prototype? In the extremist world of paranoia and irrational theories, it may be possible to collapse most grievances into a simpler equation.

Finally, Nussbaum and Vitek's discussion of the role of the Internet in the furtherance of anti-Muslim sentiment and its contribution as an operant of radicalization dynamics underscores the significance of the American Islamophobic Network. Arain and Barzegar meticulously describe the power of the Network but do not deeply extend their analysis

into the Network's connection to radicalization dynamics and subsequent violence aimed at the Muslim community. Still, what is apparent
is a semicoordinated network of Islamophobic entities that use a variety
of media platforms to disseminate their views. Noting that, Nussbaum
and Vitek, along with Levin, reiterate the advancement of anti-Muslim
violence, it is a reasonable inference to presume a possible connection
between the Network and the increase in radicalization and violence
targeting the Muslim community.

In Chapter 6, Al-Obaidi describes in detail where there are clear
misinterpretations of different passages in the Qur'an by non-Muslims as
well as those who claim to be followers of Islam. This is not unexpected.
I have attended engagements where an invited speaker argued for only
one meaning of *jihad*—that of justified violence against non-Muslims.
However, the primary point made by the Al-Obaidi is that extremists who
purport that they are adherents of Islam—not strangers to scriptures—
pervert the essential teachings in the Qur'an to justify their agenda of political violence. These are important unveilings that aid in making sense
of the confusion concerning Islamic teachings. However, a more sardonic
outcome regarding the perversion of Islam by radical Islamists is that they
are likely strengthening, with each act of terrorism that they commit, the
justification for the Islamophobia and anti-Muslim sentiment expressed
in the non-Muslim world. It would be a significant irony if Islamists
recognized that they were furthering the American Islamophobia Network.
This suspected dynamic underscores the importance of efforts to counter
misinterpretations or false teachings within the Muslim community itself
and the need to offer instruction on the correct interpretations of Islamic
precepts. There are fundamental and practical reasons for the Muslim
community to lead in addressing the errant perspectives of Muslim
extremists. First, the actions of extremists fuel the suspicion toward Islam
and impede its recognition as a religion that is on par with Judaism and
Christianity. Second, radicalized jihadists also target fellow Muslims who
then suffer enormously from death, serious injury, and other forms of de-
stabilization and destruction in their communities, particularly in Muslim
nations. Finally, if not directly targeted by Islamists, Muslims are too often

subjected to anti-Muslim hate crime by non-Muslims who hold this community in strong antipathy.

VEILS THAT REMAIN

Two perennial questions emanate from Randy Blazak's work and those of other scholars investigating the impacts of hate crime as described in Chapter 3. Now that there have been nearly 40 years of research on modern hate crime phenomena: (1) What prophylactic measures are most effective for preventing hate crime? The work of Ignaski (2001) and others on the occurrence of "waves of harm" emanating from a single hate crime incident across time and space is well recognized in the scientific literature. Multiple communities experience stress and anxiety concerning safety and security when a hate event occurs. For example, due to the recent surge in anti-Asian hate crime, 1 in 3 Asians fears being targeted and assaulted (Pew Research, 2021). This leads to the second question: (2) What community-level measures should be taken to meet the needs of those directly impacted by hate crime events and for those who are indirectly affected? These two questions that remain unsettled are particularly evident in Blazak's case study analysis concerning the aftermath of the 2017 Portland commuter train anti-Muslim inspired killings. His interview data measure the extent of posttraumatic stress symptoms across various community groups in the Portland area. Although the primary targets of the perpetrator were two young Black female Muslims, it was the three Caucasian men that intervened who were subsequently stabbed, seriously injured, or killed by the perpetrator. Several issues stand out in Blazak's work. First, the perpetrator was known to law enforcement as a violent White nationalist who had previously threatened minorities on the very same commuter train. Nevertheless, surveillance by police of a known dangerous figure was insufficient that day. Blazak also identified different degrees of impact experienced by interviewees. It followed that the most extensive psychological trauma described was expressed by the local Muslim community, with other affected communities reporting significant lingering effects from the stabbings that took place on the commuter train.

Much more research is needed to examine the capacity of local police departments to intervene and prevent hate crime attacks, especially when potential assailants are known to law enforcement. A related factor, discussed by Levin concerns the recognition of catalytic events which precipitate or trigger anti-Muslim hate crime. Since such patterns are discernible, in what ways could law enforcement make use of this information to become more effective in preventing hate crime incidents and perhaps save lives? The Muslim community would be better served and perhaps spared attacks if law enforcement became better adept in hate crime prevention.

Regarding the second question, even though scholarly literature on the impacts of hate crime victimization dates back 20 years, awareness of the importance of available community resources to support the mental health needs of those impacted is apparently lagging. However, with the recent announcement by the Centers for Disease Control and Prevention (CDC) that racism is now viewed as a public health issue on many different fronts, perhaps more resources for hate crime victims will become available for community-level mental health services (CDC, 2021).

The unflinching interrogation of the gendered perspective embedded in Islamophobic views is both revelatory and nuanced. Abdelkader takes us on an unsuspecting journey that examines the Savior complex within Orientalist perspectives that dominate Western views and uncovers existing Muslim stereotypes that are counterproductive to efforts to achieve equal protection and civil rights for women and others in the United States. She begins her examination referencing an award-winning fictional story that takes place in Afghanistan and uses the protagonist to animate the social conditions of her focus. The United States and its allies have had a presence in Afghanistan for 20 years, with the U.S. adhering to an August 31, 2021 withdrawal date set by the Biden administration. Part of the justification of the presence of the West in Afghanistan includes the reported brutal oppression of Afghan women by the Taliban. Under the Taliban regime, women are denied education and employment opportunities and are forced to contend with severe restrictions that significantly limit the opportunity for self-determination. If women violate Taliban codes of conduct, they may be subjected to corporal punishment or even execution. The presence of the West there included the protection of Afghan women as they seek fundamental rights, including education. However, irony is uncovered by Abdelkader, whose analysis exposes regulations in the United States, as well as in Western Europe, that discriminate against Muslim women. The author uses the elegant case examples involving Nashala Hearn and Samantha Elauf to explicate how regulations required by employers or public-school systems, such as prohibitions against wearing headgear like the hijab or other religious attire, or other garb that may be somehow construed as gang-related, or just not preferred in an employment setting, discriminates against practicing Muslim women who wear clothing items in accordance with religious custom. However, the case studies also highlight the self-efficacy utilized by the impacted individuals to confront the discriminatory treatment they received and effect change that would impact their lives and the lives of Muslim women in similar circumstances. Their agency contradicts the Savior narrative.

Fear of the Islamification of America or the failure to recognize Islam as a faith on equal footing as Judaism or Christianity may impede eradicating those industry regulations that have harmful impacts on U.S. Muslims. The question or challenge that presents is whether the United States can make more significant inroads into ensuring the equal rights of Muslims, in particular Muslim women, without compromising their religious and cultural traditions. Can enacting so-called neutral regulations and laws be accomplished without interjecting Orientalist or imperialist feminism thinking? Imperialist feminist thinking, in this case, involves Westernizing Muslim women by discouraging or disallowing the wearing of religious attire, as their continued observation of religious or cultural traditions may be viewed as subordinate or somehow inferior to Western culture and values.

CONCLUSION

It is undeniable that the United States currently sits at a sociopolitical crossroads and is having difficulty with deciding its own sociocultural identity as a nation. Tendrils of authoritarianism are attempting to challenge the profile of American democracy. Heeding "strongman" voices to scapegoat those perceived to be different and using legal processes to oppress them systemically are at the heart of authoritarianism, which is antithetical to the American ideal. What direction this country will go in will be determined by its citizens, and that decision will significantly impact the Muslim community, other marginalized communities and all other Americans. There are many countervailing actions committed by individuals and institutions that muddle the pathway toward the pursuit of equality. U.S. citizens have witnessed multiple displays of intolerance and inhumane treatment of those labeled "the Other." The Trump administration's "zero-tolerance" policy requiring the intentional separation of migrant children from family at the U.S. southwestern border from 2017 to 2018 was a means to impart cruelty and deter those seeking to escape egregious conditions in Central America. If these children were blond and blue-eyed, it is questionable whether the zero-tolerance policy would have been enacted. In El Paso, Texas, in August 2019, a White supremacist committed a mass shooting of Latino people, killing 20 individuals. The killer's rationalization was an ongoing invasion of Texas by Hispanics (NPR.org). The Mother Emanuel African Episcopal Church in Charleston, South Carolina, was another mass shooting site in June 2015. Motivated by White supremacist beliefs, the shooter killed nine African American parishioners after joining them in their weekly Bible study. Again, another community was targeted for violence with the August 2012 mass shooting at the Sikh temple in Oak Creek, Wisconsin. Six died that day at the hands of another White supremacist who reportedly believed he was killing Muslims (Intelligence Report, 2012). The Tree of Life Jewish Congregation in Pittsburgh, Pa. suffered the loss of eleven of its worshippers in October 2018. They were shot to death by an assailant wearing tactical gear and carrying multiple firearms who was motivated by his hatred of the Jewish people and immigrants. Most recently, in March 2021, mass shootings occurred at three spas in Atlanta, Georgia. Eight persons were killed, of which six were Asian women. Prosecutors are considering leveling hate crime charges as this country is witnessing a disturbing rise in anti-Asian violence. The group, "Stop A.A.P.I. Hate" reports that approximately 3,800 anti-Asian hate crimes have occurred since the beginning of the COVID-19 pandemic (PBS.org, 2021). The fact that these bias-motivated murders continue to happen, almost unabatedly, does not bode well for girding democratic freedoms. Nevertheless, there are encouraging developments.

The killing of George Floyd in May 2020 prompted a global reaction to the callous and cavalier way that his life was taken in broad daylight by law enforcement. Countless numbers of persons representing every demographic and nationality imaginable marched for weeks demanding racial justice. The Black Lives Matter movement, which galvanized the protests, saw supporters and marches that occurred transnationally, from Ireland to Poland to New Zealand and Syria (CNN.com, 2020). Are there any lessons that can be gleaned from these phenomena for the Muslim community?

Perhaps now is the time to consider the power of coalition building, developing alliances, working with other communities on issues of common interest, including justice and equality, and developing political capital. The desire of the Muslim community for fairness and equality is no different from that of the LatinX, LGBTQ, Asian, Native American, women, African American, and Jewish communities. Nevertheless, many marginalized groups are confronting aspects of division, self-hatred, colorism, classism, or sexism, which distracts and delays effective strategies and unity. Indeed, exposure to hundreds of years of Orientalism, White supremacy, and patriarchy has injected self-doubt, internal divisions, and self-hatred in minoritized persons and communities.

Erik Love (2009) offers an analysis of different models of civil rights activism and how they may be considered in the struggle against Islamophobia. He describes three models: (1) the use of civil disobedience and large-scale protests; (2) the establishment of a pan-ethnic identity-based coalition for increased political clout; and (3) using legal activism and lobbying capabilities. Upon initial consideration, it appears feasible that elements from any or all three approaches could benefit the Muslim community. Still, based on the messaging of Muslim advocacy organizations, it appears that the preferred strategy involves the use of legal remedies and the development and use of political levers. As described in Chapter 1, programs such as the CLEAR project located within the CUNY School of Law and the ACLU provide legal services to Muslims with discrimination allegations. Part of the described services involves educating Muslims on their civil rights. The Arab American Institute is a lobbying organization that also consults with community groups to encourage Muslims to pursue civil engagement. Similarly, the Council on American-Islamic Relations (CAIR) strongly advocates the franchise to affect public policy. Therefore, voting eligibility education is emphasized in the Muslim community. There is also evidence of the Muslim community forging alliances with others with similar goals for equality and fairness, such as the Muslim-Jewish Advisory Council.

As with other targeted communities, the crucible that Muslim Americans find themselves in has produced a stratagem that has successfully blunted some efforts to frustrate the visible expressions of Islam in the United States. Nevertheless, dismantling misunderstanding, bigoted notions, and suspicion toward Muslims and Islam is far more challenging. There is a high level of difficulty battling unexpressed ignorance. However, since Islamophobia is waged on multiple fronts, so, too, must the efforts to unravel it.

References

CDC. (2021). CDC director declares racism "serious" public health threat. Retrieved from https://www.aha.org/news/headline/2021-4-09

CNN.com. (2020). Thousands around the world protest George Floyd's death in global display of solidarity. Retrieved from https://www.cnn.com/2020/06/01/world/george-floyd-global-protests/

Intelligence Report. (2012). Sikh temple killer Wade Michael Page radicalized in army. Retrieved from https://www.splcenter.org/fighting-hate/intelligence-report/2012/

Love, E. (2009). A path forward? Confronting Islamophobia in the United States: Framing civil rights activism among Middle Eastern Americans. *Patterns* of Prejudice, *43*(3/4), 401–425.

Nesdale, D. (1999). Social identity and ethnic prejudice in children. *Psychology, Society, and Education.*

NPR.org. (2020). U.S. charges suspect in El Paso Walmart shootings with hate crimes. Retrieved from https://www.npr.org/2020/02/06/803503292/

PBS.org. (2021). What we know about the Atlanta Spa shooting that killed 8, including 6 Asian women. Retrieved from https://www.pbs.org/newshour/nation/

Pew Research. (2021). One-third of Asian Americans fear threats, physical attacks and most say violence against them is rising. Retrieved from https://www.pewresearch.org/fact-tank/2021/04/21/

U.S. and World Population Clock. Retrieved from https://www.census.gov/popclock/world

World Population Review.com. (2021). Muslim population by country. Retrieved from https://worldpopulationreview.com/county-rankings/muslim-population

For the benefit of digital users, indexed terms that span two pages (e.g., 52–53) may, on occasion, appear on only one of those pages.

Figures and tables are indicated by *f* and *t* following the page number.